HEAR AND BE WISE

HEAR AND BE WISE

BECOMING A PREACHER AND TEACHER OF WISDOM

ALYCE M. McKENZIE

Abingdon Press
Nashville

HEAR AND BE WISE
BECOMING A PREACHER AND TEACHER OF WISDOM

Copyright © 2004 by Abingdon Press

All rights reserved.

This book is printed on acid-free paper.

Library of Congress Cataloging-in-Publication Data

McKenzie, Alyce M., 1955-
  Hear and be wise : becoming a preacher and teacher of wisdom / Alyce M. McKenzie.
    p. cm.
  Includes bibliographical references.
  ISBN 0-687-05391-9 (book, printed/pbk. : alk. paper)
  1. Preaching. 2. Wisdom—Religious aspects—Christianity. I. Title.
  BV4211.3.M35 2004
  251—dc22

2004016171

04 05 06 07 08 09 10 11 12 13—10 9 8 7 6 5 4 3 2 1

MANUFACTURED IN THE UNITED STATES OF AMERICA

To my in-laws,

Paul and Doris McKenzie,

with many thanks

for your loving support

through all these years

Contents

ACKNOWLEDGMENTS

This book about the four qualities of wisdom, while it required much alone time, would not have been possible without all the together time I am privileged to spend with my immediate family, extended family, friends, colleagues, and students, all of whom not only teach me wisdom but also give me opportunities to exercise it!

I would like to thank the Lilly Foundation for choosing me as a Faculty Fellow for 2001–02 and funding the travel that was necessary to complete the interview portion of the book. Without their assistance, that vital contemporary connection would have been missing from the project.

I would also like to thank my editors, Bob Ratcliff and Terrie Livaudais, for the wise guidance they gave me when I was first conceptualizing this project, by suggesting ways to make it relevant for teachers and preachers. Thanks go to all the pastors who graciously granted me interview time, taking time from their busy lives to share their wisdom with me that can now be shared with readers. I appreciate the bibliographic leads given to me by my colleague Harold Recinos, professor of church and society at Perkins School of Theology. I also offer my thanks to two other Perkins colleagues, John Holbert, Lois Craddock Perkins Professor of Homiletics, and Charles Wood, Lehman Professor of Christian Doctrine, for their guidance and graciousness in reading portions of the manuscript. Kathy Black, Gerald H. Kennedy Professor of Homiletics and Liturgics, Claremont School of Theology, was helpful in advising me about grant writing and in supplying names of potential interview candidates in California. Carolyn Herring, my research assistant, offered invaluable help in tracking down bibliographical leads. Words are inadequate to express my appreciation for my husband, Murry, who went far more than the second mile in helping set up travel arrangements for my various interview trips around the country and caring for our children and the home front while I was away.

Hear instruction and be wise,
and do not neglect it. (Prov 8:33)

INTRODUCTION

When United Methodist Bishop Emeritus Leontine Kelly was eight years old and getting ready for school one morning in Cincinnati, Ohio, she heard a knock at the front door. She was coming down the stairs and could see a tall figure standing on the front porch. She opened the door and there stood a handsome black woman dressed all in black. Bishop Kelly says she stood there gawking at this imposing woman, who without any words of introduction or greeting, demanded, "Young lady, who do you plan to be? You must be somebody!"

"Well," says Bishop Kelly, "I was eight years old. My only plans for that day were to be a third grader! I went back to the kitchen where my mother was making breakfast and I said, 'Mama, there is *somebody* at the door!'"

That somebody was Dr. Mary McLeod Bethune, African American educator and political activist. Bethune was the fifteenth of seventeen children of a sharecropping family from South Carolina, the founder of Bethune-Cookman school for girls in Daytona Beach, Florida, and an advisor to the White House on African American educational issues. She had come to town to call on Mr. James Gamble, of Procter and Gamble, to raise money for her school. Bishop Kelly's father was the pastor of Calvary Methodist Episcopal Church, and she had come to call at the parsonage to get his help in her fundraising efforts.

"Young lady, who do you plan to be? You must be somebody!" Bishop Kelly says she never forgot the question. It was abrupt and direct and backed up by a woman of faith and accomplishment. This was a woman who, the more the girl got to know about her, the more of a role model she became for her.[1]

"Who do you plan to be?" This is the unspoken question people bring to church weekly. We all live with a vision of who that person is and a vague sense of falling short of that vision. Most of us want to live a life upheld by four qualities: living by loyalty to something or someone beyond ourselves, living alert and alive to each moment of experience, living with self-discipline in our speech and actions, and living with the moral courage that empowers us to speak and act in accordance with our loyalties.

These four qualities correspond to what I am calling the four pillars of biblical wisdom. The pillar metaphor is a helpful one to express insights, beliefs, or practices upon which a life can be built. Islam has five pillars; the Character Counts! movement that teaches the basics of moral character to school-age children and youth has six. Woman Wisdom in Prov 9 builds a fine house, hews seven pillars, and invites us in.[2] Simeon the Just, a rabbi of the Maccabean period, affirmed that there were three pillars of Judaism: Torah, temple service, and deeds of loving-kindness.[3]

What I have named the four pillars of wisdom are the four virtues of the wise person drawn from the Wisdom literature of the Hebrew Bible and the New Testament: the fear of the Lord, the listening heart, the cool spirit, and the subversive voice. The sages of the Hebrew Bible and New Testament taught their students to live lives upheld by these qualities and sought to live such lives themselves.

A Culture that Craves Sages

Many contemporary people across cultural, ethnic, and denominational lines have an appetite for spirituality, but a distaste for institutional religion.[4] One way this spiritual hunger expresses itself is as a craving for wisdom, sound advice on the conduct of daily life. What should be my priorities as I attempt to balance the various aspects of my life? How can I shake free from the anxiety that shadows me? What qualities of character should I aim for? What guidelines should I follow in conducting my relationships? How can I craft a life I can believe in and not just conform to the values around me?

Public appetites usually create flurries of publishing activity. Recently, there has been a population explosion of books descended from biblical wisdom genres: manuals of proverbs and admonitions, collections of reflections on various topics related to living daily life well, and memoirs galore. We can stop sweating the small stuff, slurp chicken soup for any kind of soul we happen to have, and access over twenty-one hundred Web sites that focus on how to write and publish our memoirs.

There is a public craving for sages to go with our wisdom manuals and memoirs. Many people navigate relationships, choose books, and choose sides on issues on the strength of the counsel of Judge Judy, Dr. Phil, Dr. Laura, Oprah, or Montel. New Age adherents attempt to govern their thoughts based on the teachings of popular, self-appointed gurus like Wayne Dyer, Deepak Chopra, Shakti Gawain, and Sylvia Browne.

We are reminded of Paul's dilemma at Corinth where the Corinthians were enamored of wisdom but were defining it in self-serving, divisive terms. It is in response to this situation that Paul reframes wisdom counterculturally: rooted in the primacy of God's action in the context of the cross, as a wisdom that leaves no room for human boasting.[5]

No Room for Preachers!

While our culture has carved out this role for the sage, it does not occur to many people to seek wisdom from the Christian preacher, the person in the life of a faith community who, by biblical and historical precedent, is called to be a wisdom teacher. When many people seek guidance for the ins and outs of daily life, the preacher and the sermon are not even a blip on their radar screens! While the culture turns up the heat on wisdom, many pulpits remain strangely cold. This is despite the interest biblical studies has taken in the wisdom literature in both testaments (Job, Ecclesiastes, Proverbs, and the aphorisms and parables of Jesus) for the past twenty or more years and the wealth of resources that now lie at the preacher's fingertips on the subject of wisdom.[6]

Maybe, just maybe, we preachers are being left out in the cold because we have not embraced a part of our own identity that is ours by reason of our scripture, tradition, calling, and training: our identity as wisdom teachers. In researching this book I traveled around the country and interviewed clergy from a variety of backgrounds and several Christian denominations in a variety of social settings regarding their understanding of the role of sage. When I made my initial phone contact with potential interviewees, I said pretty much the same thing. "This is Alyce McKenzie. I teach preaching at Perkins School of Theology in Dallas, Texas. I am on sabbatical this year working on a book about the preacher as wisdom teacher. I wondered if I might have an hour or so of your time in the next few months to interview you on this topic."

Surprisingly often, after my initial telephone pitch, there would be a long silence. It was the kind of silence I would have expected if I had just told them I was selling aluminum siding and would be in their neighborhood next week to give them a free estimate.

Then they would say something like, "You want to interview me about wisdom?"

"Yes."

Another awkward pause.

"I don't really know how much help I'll be."

To which I would have liked to have said, "Are you speaking out of false modesty or genuine low self-esteem?" or, "Are you calling me a bad judge of character?" or, "Would you like me to take you off my calling list?"

Resisting these temptations, I would simply pause for a little longer than was comfortable for them and then ask, "Would you be willing to meet with me?"

Then we would talk time and place. No one ever turned me down.

But the number of pastors who gave the "Why me?" response confirmed my suspicion that many of us preachers are out of touch with the concept of wisdom and the definition of a sage as we search the Scriptures and as we look in the mirror each morning. In my interviews with clergy, I discovered that while many of us think of ourselves as teachers, we do not view the substance of that teaching as wisdom. Laypeople I have spoken with in study groups on wisdom share the same hesitancy to claim their roles as sages and their goal as wisdom.

Why Are We Out in the Cold?

Preachers in workshops I have conducted over the past several years admit they very rarely preach on biblical wisdom texts (Proverbs, Ecclesiastes, Job, and Jesus' synoptic sayings), nor do they think of themselves as sages. A notable exception is the frequency with which a number of African American pastors said they use Proverbs for insights in sermons. They also said they frequently preach from the book of Job, regarding Job as someone with whom many of their people can identify. A pastor from Korea serving a large Presbyterian Korean church in Los Angeles affirmed that he preaches on Job because his people, like Job, are undergoing difficult and undeserved struggles.

Many of the preachers I interviewed were in their late forties and fifties. They reported that their seminaries had provided little instruction about the wisdom literature in their Old Testament survey courses and no mention of Jesus as a wisdom teacher in their New Testament courses. The African American and Japanese American pastors with whom I spoke had a view of Jesus as sage to a greater degree than the white pastors.

A white pastor from a suburban area near St. Louis commented, "The evangelical side of the church thinks of Jesus as savior. The liberal side thinks of Jesus as prophet. Both sides need to be taught what it means to think of Jesus as a sage."

If we Christian preachers do not think of our vocations as learning and teaching wisdom, is it any wonder that our laypeople have a blurry notion of what wisdom is and that it is learned through the disciplines and texts of our faith rather than through the pages of self-help manuals? We Christian preachers can continue to leave the business of wisdom to the self-help authors, political pundits, celebrity autobiographers, television judges, talk-show hosts, and New Age gurus, or we can embrace our role as sages, teachers of wisdom, and inspire our laypeople to do the same.

In chapter 1, "The Role and Message of the Sage," we shall explore the role and message of biblical wisdom teachers from Proverbs, Job, Ecclesiastes, and the synoptic Jesus.

Chapters 2, 4, 6, and 8 will be devoted to the four pillars of wisdom that uphold the character of the sage: the bended knee, the listening heart, the cool spirit, and the subversive voice. Chapters 3, 5, 7, and 9 deal with teaching and preaching strategies related to each pillar of wisdom. Each of these chapters ends with a meditation on its wisdom virtue.

Whether clergy or laypeople, we live as sages in the midst of faith communities. We are called to seek and to share wisdom's four virtues: reverence for God, alertness to the sacredness of the other and of daily life, self-discipline, and the courage to voice our convictions for the *shalom* of our communities. My hope is that this book will inspire and equip preachers to step up to our identity as sages and that it will help laypeople hone their gifts for their crucial teaching ministries.

CHAPTER ONE

THE ROLE AND MESSAGE OF THE SAGE

In lifting up the role of the preacher as sage, I join a chorus of other voices who call out suggestions to clergy as to who they should be. For the past several decades in the United States, social trends have shaped the advice pastors have received concerning who they should be. The 1960s told us to be prophets. The 1970s told us to be therapists. The 1980s told us to be church-growth consultants. The 1990s told us to be CEOs and player-coaches. I am convinced that this is the era of the sage. It is a model for ministry that integrates key aspects of all the others. It is a model that is deeply rooted in Scripture; it is one that is desperately needed by our culture; and it is an egalitarian model that honors the ministry of the laity on par with that of the clergy.

Appropriating the role of sage as a preacher or teacher does not primarily entail learning a new set of skills. To a large degree, it means naming what we are already doing in the several roles each of us fulfills in our daily lives.

In terms of social psychology, a role is the "organized set of behaviors that belongs to an identifiable position."[1] As every pastor knows, roles carry role expectations. Role expectations are the "rights and privileges, the duties and obligations, of any occupant of a social position (status) in relation to persons occupying other positions in the social structure."[2] Most positions or social functions entail an entire set of complementary roles. A few of the roles the pastor occupies are those of administrator, counselor, teacher, priest, mediator, preacher, community activist, and visionary leader. One or more roles may come to the foreground depending on the cultural context and specific situation of one's congregation.

Said an African American pastor from St. Louis:

> In the black tradition, the preacher is the sage. There is this riff in black preaching about Jesus: "Jesus is your lawyer. Jesus is your doctor. Jesus is the one you call on the telephone." Here I'm the sheriff; I create order. But I go beyond sheriff. I'm also a healer. I'm also a teacher and a sage. I'm also a facilitator—lots of hats!

A Puerto Rican Episcopal female pastor serving a mixed African American and Hispanic congregation in Los Angeles made this observation.

> In the Spanish culture, one turns to a religious figure for all kinds of problems. My English-speaking members have a sense that some things you use the pastor for, but some things you use a counselor or therapist. In Spanish-speaking homes, if somebody's arrested, I'm called before they call a lawyer. In the English-speaking homes I only find out weeks later if somebody's been arrested because they don't want to be embarrassed.

Reclaiming our identity as sages will help us offer wisdom in our particular context, making our preaching and our teaching more faithful to the witness of Scripture and the needs of our people.[3]

The Sage in the Hebrew Scriptures

An important initial question is, What is the nature of the wisdom the sage sought and taught? Sometimes this wisdom refers to concrete, practical, how-to skills in daily life. This meaning shows up in narrative texts of the Hebrew Bible. There, when the noun *wisdom* (*hokmah*) and the adjective *wise* (*hakam*) are used, they designate innate intelligence or shrewdness, artistic and administrative skill, or good judgment.[4]

Our interest is focused on the definition of wisdom as a way of approaching life, and lessons learned from that approach. This is the focus of the term as it appears in what is called the Wisdom literature of the Hebrew Bible (Proverbs, Ecclesiastes, and Job). These books feature far more occurrences of *hakam* (wise) and *hokmah* (wisdom) than do any other portion of the Hebrew Bible.[5] The term also occurs in two apocryphal Wisdom books: Ecclesiasticus (also known as the Wisdom of Jesus ben Sira) and the Wisdom of Solomon.

In the Hebrew Bible's Wisdom books, *wisdom* refers both to a way of thinking and to a body of teachings derived from that way of thinking.[6] Israel joins her ancient Near Eastern neighbors in understanding wisdom as skill in deciphering life. This understanding was accomplished by keen observation, discerning patterns of cause and effect in life, and drawing conclusions contrasting desirable and destructive behaviors.[7]

Proverbs' wisdom teachings are more optimistic about the possibilities for gaining wisdom and ordering one's existence in positive directions than those of Job and Ecclesiastes. In all three books, however, wisdom is gathered by the observation of life, and teachings are based on that observation.

Throughout Israel's history, sages observed and taught wisdom out of several contexts. In the premonarchic days, the sages' wisdom came out of their observation of village life revolving around home, farm, and town.[8] A number of proverbs make analogies between human behavior and the natural world, and seem to reflect an agricultural context.[9] The purpose of this early wisdom was individual and family harmony for the good of the village.

In the days of the monarchy, roughly the tenth through the sixth centuries B.C.E., the sages' wisdom focused on advice to kings and rulers, and the training of future scribes and courtiers. According to tradition and legend, King Solomon was a patron of wisdom and may well have commissioned sages to collect and coin proverbial wisdom. Both Proverbs and Ecclesiastes, literary works written after five hundred years had passed following his reign, are attributed to him.

In the days of Israel's kings, "scribes" referred to court officials whose job was to record the wisdom traditions that guided those who served at court (2 Sam 8:17; 1 Kgs 4:3). Those traditions encompassed various genres: legal, liturgical, political, and literary. Scribes transcribed documents that became the Law, Prophets, and Writings.[10] "The wise" came to signify a class of professional sages who were teachers of religion and ethics. Their subject matter included theoretical as well as practical knowledge. A number of sayings reflect this court background.[11]

After the death of Solomon, the Israelite people were split into two, the northern nation of Israel and the southern nation of Judah (930–586 B.C.E.). The Assyrians invaded Samaria in the northern kingdom in 722 B.C.E. and took over that nation. The Babylonians invaded Judah in

586 B.C.E., destroyed Jerusalem, and deported thousands of Judeans to Babylon.

During the period of the Babylonian exile, Israel's sages saw their role as being more important than ever, for their people desperately needed a faith that looked beyond temple, king, and land, and touched both those at home and those in exile. Wisdom provided such a faith. It was probably during this period that Israel's sages collated the proverbial sayings of centuries of wise observation and also began to reflect on the role of Wisdom as an expression of a Divine, community-stabilizing dynamic.

Their efforts are reflected in the first nine chapters of Proverbs and chapter 31, the final chapter. They portray Woman Wisdom as a personification of an aspect of the character of God, present at the creation and ordering of the world (1:20-33; 8; 9:1-6; 31:10-31). In Prov 8:22-36 Wisdom is personified as a woman. She knew God's plan from the beginning, functioned as a master artisan in Creation, and assisted in bringing all things into being. Woman Wisdom rejoices in all Creation, especially in human beings. She makes her home among us and instructs us in God's ways. The proverbial sayings of the intervening chapters (10–29), gathered from centuries of the sages' wisdom, are presented as the teachings of Woman Wisdom. They represent a tradition even older and more venerable than that of the Babylonians.

With the fall of the monarchy, the locus of wisdom became the home and hearth. The traditional female role as teacher of wisdom in the home was recognized as crucial. Frequent mentions in Proverbs to heeding the wisdom of the father and the mother reflect the importance of "home-schooling" in wisdom during the tumultuous postexilic period.[12] The loss of authority of traditional male figures like king and priest may have contributed to wisdom's being personified as a persuasive, proactive woman.[13] She became the spokesperson for the sages of postexilic Israel in advancing their urgent aim: to shape the character of their young students by habits of reverence for God (the fear of the Lord) and discipline in speech and action. Only by inculcating these attitudes and behaviors could the community attain social stability and preserve its identity over against foreign occupiers.

From 587 B.C.E. onward, the southern kingdom of Judah was under the control of the Babylonians, their educated elite deported, their traditional institutions of monarchy and temple destroyed. The Persians under Cyrus overcame the Babylonians and, in 538 B.C.E., Cyrus issued a decree allowing Judeans to return to their homeland and rebuild the temple at

Jerusalem.[14] The books of Job and Ecclesiastes may well date from the period of Persian rule. In different ways, each addresses the question of how the nation can continue to hope in a cycle of apparent futility and undeserved suffering. Alexander the Great took over Palestine around 333 B.C.E. The Roman general Pompey took over Palestine and made it a Roman province in 63 B.C.E.[15]

During the period of Greek rule, Israel's sages feared that the people of Israel would take on Greek customs and ideas and lose their own traditions and identity. Various literary works and movements arose in response to this fear. The apocryphal book of Ecclesiasticus (130 B.C.E.) responded to this concern by locating wisdom squarely in Torah, the Law of Moses. Wisdom comes to those who studied it and lived by its precepts. The one who devotes himself to the study of the law of the Most High will "show the wisdom of what he has learned, and will glory in the law of the Lord's covenant" (Sirach 39:8).[16] The term *scribe* began to refer to a person with special learning in Mosaic law.

During the second century B.C.E., various groups arose whose primary concern was preserving the uniqueness of the people's faith. The expression "the pious" (*hasidim*) described a group of interpreters who opposed lax interpretations of the Law that threatened the distinctiveness of Judaism.[17] They included scribes, priests, and Levites whose interpretations of the Law underscored ritual purity and separation from non-Jews to reestablish the people of Israel on the basis of their ancestral traditions (Ezra 7:6, 11; Neh 8:1).

The Pharisees were a group of nonpriestly interpreters of the Law who emerged from the Hasidic movements of the second century B.C.E. The Greek name "Pharisee" is probably from the Aramaic *Perisaye*, "separated ones." "They scrupulously observed dietary and purity laws, Sabbath and other feast days in order to preserve the unique character of their faith."[18] After the temple was destroyed in 70 C.E. by the Romans, the Pharisees became the leading teachers of Judaism. The priests and Levites were lost without the temple. The Essene separatist community at Qumram had been destroyed by the Roman army. The Romans permitted some Pharisees to establish a school for the study of the Law.[19] The Pharisees were the precursors of the rabbinic sages.

From the time of Ben Sira in the second century B.C.E., the figure of the sage was well known and played a central role in the life of the Jewish communities. The sages formed a distinct class during the first centuries of the Common Era, combining practical wisdom and common sense with the study of the Bible and Mishnah. They dominated the intellectual life of Judaism for centuries.[20] Whereas in the New Testament, *rabbi* occurs rarely and seems to be a general term of respect for a teacher, during the late-first century C.E., the term "rabbi" came to be used for a person who was a teacher and interpreter of the Law. Rabbinic traditions of torah interpretation came to be written down between 70 and 200 C.E. in a form we now call the Mishnah. *Pirke Avot, The Sayings of the Fathers*, one of the sixty-three tractates of the Mishnah, is a collection of rabbinic sayings. These memorable, often moving sayings stress the study of God's divinely given torah as the wellspring of reverence for God and compassion for others' suffering. They urge readers to accept the limits of human knowledge, realize that all actions have consequences, be attentive to the gifts of God in daily life, live by principles of justice, and perform acts of kindness.

The rabbis put particular emphasis on the difference between a discerning person who could call up wisdom when consulted on specific matters and the sage who was immersed in torah study accompanied by continual review for the good of the community. The rabbis gave special recognition to individuals who, because of their labors, preserved torah in difficult times. Among them are Shaphan, the scribe who read the newly discovered "scroll of the Teaching" to King Josiah that resulted in the King's sweeping reforms. Another was Ezra, also a scribe, who established the Torah as the constitution for the third generation of the restored community after the Babylonian exile. A third was Rabbi Akiba ben Joseph, one of the foremost early rabbinic sages and master of disciples, active during the critical period between the destruction of the temple in 70 C.E. and the Bar Kokhba revolt in 135. He is credited with having initiated the editorial compiling of the "oral torah."[21] The special status claimed for Shaphan, Ezra, and R. Akiba derives not from hereditary pedigree, but from their work of preserving Torah in their own times.

To be a sage, you had to work hard and work continuously. You had to be alert to your context and flexible and responsive in how you brought the wisdom traditions to bear on it. Your goals were peace in family and community, character building in habits of restraint and integrity capable of minimizing the chaos of life, survival in complex and dangerous political situations, and preservation of the community's religious identity in times of oppressive occupation.

However Israel's sages manifested their wisdom, its derivation, motivation, and goal were the same: staying in touch with Divine Wisdom so they could live wisely and teach others to do the same. Their aim was to embody and teach a piety founded on trust in God as the Giver of Wisdom. They lived by the motto "the fear of the LORD is the beginning of knowledge" (Prov 1:7).

Threefold Job Description of the Sage

Preservation of *Shalom*

The Hebrew sage's goal was to preserve the well-being, justice, and stability of the community, its *shalom*. The sages sought to help those they taught align their lives with Divine Wisdom and so help accomplish the purposes of the Creator. One of the sage's goals was to bring about a reconciliation between enemies and encourage them to be incorporated into this *shalom*. The sage had a certain "therapeutic power to mend broken relationships and to repair evidences of alienation and divisiveness in the body politic."[22]

A contemporary story that helps us envision this communal *shalom* goes like this: "A teacher tore a map of the world to shreds, and, thinking it an impossible task, gave it to a recalcitrant student to put back together. Within ten minutes the boy was back, the task completed. Astounded, the teacher asked him how he did it. The boy replied, 'When I turned the pieces over, I found a torn-up man. I put him together and when I looked at the other side the world was whole again.'"[23] The role of the sage in Proverbs was to promote *shalom*. Toward this goal, the sage evokes Yahweh's concern for justice (14:20-22, 31). The sage helps form future leaders of the community and reminds current leaders of their obligation to work toward *shalom*. The sage seeks to preserve peace amid the vagaries of human conflict.[24]

This communal emphasis is one we need continually to emphasize in our preaching and teaching, for we live in a society that has elevated individualism to our first and foremost virtue. We teach and preach in the context of a dominant cultural ethos that defines *freedom* as freedom from limiting obligations to others rather than freedom for building a just community together with others.

Fool Management

"I thought briefly about becoming a pastor," confided a friend of mine. "But then I realized that I don't suffer fools gladly enough!" Part of the job description of sages in Proverbs was to protect the community from the fools in its midst. Fools represent, to varying degrees, chaos in the community that is counter to the moral order created by God. Just as there are more than thirty-one flavors of Baskin-Robbins ice cream, there are at least eight different Hebrew words in Proverbs that represent various nuances on the theme of the fool.[25] Three are particularly striking. The first is the *pethi*, the shallow, gullible person. The *pethi* believes everything and anything (14:15). He lacks the wisdom that would stabilize his life and is therefore susceptible to evil companions. One of the aims of the wise teacher is to get to the *pethi* before it is too late and to help him gain prudence (1:4).

Another type of fool is the *lutz*, whose root means "to make mouths at." The *lutz* is a know-it-all, an unteachable type of person (9:7; 13:1). The word is often translated "scoffer" or "scorner." The *lutz* is haughty (21:24) and delights in mocking others, especially wisdom teachers (1:22). He delights in folly (1:22) and will not listen to wisdom (13:1; 15:12). His supercilious arrogance (21:24) sets the whole community on edge (22:10; 29:8). The old American proverb says, "It takes a carpenter to build a barn, but any jackass can kick one down." The *lutz* would rather tear down than build up. Heraclitus, a philosopher of the fifth century B.C.E., once said, with reference to his opponents, that the opposite of wisdom is not stupidity, but knowing it all. The *lutz* knows it all and has nothing to learn from God or other people.[26]

A third type of fool is the *nabal*, a churlish, brutal person who cannot control his anger and who enjoys the misery of others. The *nabal* says in his heart, "There is no God" (Ps 14:1). In his mouth sensible words are out of place (Prov 17:7). He is a source of grief to his parents (Prov 17:21). The existence, order, and character of God are threats to the *nabal* because they expose his destructiveness.[27]

In our teaching and preaching, it is important to acknowledge our own tendencies toward folly and the chaos it brings, but also to celebrate the progress we have made on the path of wisdom. In this way we humbly inspire others to seek the gift of God's Wisdom and to grow continuously in wisdom from day to day.

Character Building

The sages' goal, amid a society marred by temptation and corruption, was to instill in the young the qualities of character that make for harmony in both personal and public life: deference to God's guidance as the giver of wisdom, moderation and self-control, and compassion for the less fortunate. William P. Brown, in his book *Character in Crisis: A Fresh Approach to the Wisdom Literature of the Old Testament*, refers to Proverbs as an ancient "Book of Virtues," dedicated to the "Art of Community Maintenance."[28] For the sages, the function of character building was a communal process. It could not happen without conversation with others and managing conflict when differing views surfaced.[29]

By contrast with much contemporary self-help instruction, with its individualistic bent, the sages' goal was to integrate students into the life of the community. While looking after their own families, they were also to practice justice by looking out for the needs of the disenfranchised.[30] Woman Wisdom, who recent scholarship has determined is the focus of the final poem of Proverbs (31:10-31), embodies these qualities. Her sages imitate her, and instill her wisdom in their students.[31]

Throughout the 1990s there was a lot of talk about the recovery of virtue and character in American life. William Bennett's *The Book of Virtues* topped the best-seller list in the mid-1990s. A consortium of education and service organizations united and called themselves "Character Counts!" They developed a curriculum for teaching character in America's public schools. It featured posters depicting six color-coded "pillars of character" based on ancient Greek and Christian virtues. They are respect (yellow), caring (red), trustworthiness (blue), fairness (orange), responsibility (green), and citizenship (purple).[32]

Character is a term that has come to refer to certain basic qualities that distinguish one person from another. The traits that go together to form character have traditionally been called virtues or dispositions. From the feudal loyalty of medieval Europe, to the communal honor of many Eastern cultures, to the self-reliance of contemporary America, the understanding of what constitutes virtue has differed from culture to culture, both historically and today.[33]

We twenty-first-century Americans tend to define virtue in purely personal terms as sexual purity and abstinence from alcoholic beverages. The Greeks had a deeper view. For them, the virtues were persistent habits of the heart and mind that made for personal and social harmony. Abilities, like musical ability or athletic ability, while they can be honed with practice, are largely inborn. By contrast, virtues are largely acquired through education. They need to be deepened through daily practice until they become habits. The Greeks believed we develop character by exercising its virtues. They did not believe that the virtues necessarily led to material success. Rather, their reward is intrinsic.

The classical Greek notion of character articulated by Plato and Aristotle identified four virtues: prudence, justice, fortitude, and temperance. These are often designated as "cardinal virtues," a term used in traditional ethical discourse to refer to the most basic and highly valued virtues. *Temperance* is more far-reaching than just refraining from alcoholic beverages. It is the impulse-control necessary to attain any worthwhile goal. *Fortitude* is the stamina to keep pressing toward the mark despite setbacks and dangers. *Justice* is concern for fairness both for individuals and communities. *Prudence* is the practical wisdom *(phronesis)* that pulls together the other three virtues and decides right action in specific situations.[34]

Thomas Aquinas, writing in the thirteenth century C.E., sought a theological context for the formation of character. Not prudence, but charity (*caritas* [love]) took the lead with faith and hope close behind. "Charity is the mother and root of all virtues."[35]

Our biblical wisdom heritage offers us four cardinal wisdom virtues, four pillars of wisdom, and calls upon us both to model them and to teach them. Although they occupy some common ground with the Greek virtues, their purpose and focus are different. They are also different from the trinity of virtues that many Americans have been taught will lead to the good life: self-reliance, initiative, and hard work. It is central to our vocation as character builders that we distinguish between biblical virtues and seductive, competing versions of virtue.

The Message of the Sage in the Hebrew Bible

There Is an Order to Creation

For the sages of Proverbs, wisdom was three things at once: an expression of the creative power of God, a habit of canny observation that leads a person to discern divine order at work in daily life, and a body of teachings that articulate how to live in alignment with that order. As an expression of the creative power of God, Wisdom is the quality that was at work in creation, resulting in the order observable to sages within the world.[36]

> The LORD by wisdom founded the earth;
>   by understanding he established the heavens;
> by his knowledge the deeps broke open,
>   and the clouds drop down the dew. (Prov 3:19-20)

The sages, using their human reason, examined the data provided by observation and experience. They often expressed their wise observations in the form of analogies between the realms of nature and human conduct.[37]

> For as pressing milk produces curds,
> and pressing the nose produces blood
> so pressing anger produces strife. (Prov 30:33)
>
> Like clouds and wind without rain is one who boasts of a gift never given. (Prov 25:14)

From these analogies, they gleaned principles that formed the foundation for conduct. Generally, the diligent person becomes prosperous (Prov 10:4) and the foolish or wicked person will not prevail (Prov 10:30; 11:21; 13:25). The wise or virtuous person wins the day (Prov 10:2, 30; 13:25).

God Is Sovereign over Human Efforts to Order Experience

There are limits to human wisdom's discernment and control. We cannot name the events of the future and tame them in advance. We cannot fully know God. Wisdom is not an impersonal order by which God must abide or be called into question by us. Wisdom is an expression of the presence and guidance of God, and human construals of wisdom are subject to divine mystery and sovereignty.

A series of proverbs some scholars have called "the limit proverbs" (16:1, 2, 9; 19:21; 20:24; 21:30-31) reminds us of our limitations and calls us to humility before God and one another.[38]

The sage in both the Hebrew Bible and New Testament has a dual role: cooling the heated impulses of the young (Proverbs) and melting the frigid rigidity of the fossilized (Job, Qohelet, and Jesus). The sayings in Proverbs represent the traditional wisdom of the elders on how moderate, responsible living leads to prosperity and a good reputation. The sages responsible for the books of Job and Qohelet pointed to the exceptions to these rules, exposing traditional wisdom's overstatement of human control over life, its favoring of orderly inequities over untidy justice.

Jesus, in the tradition of his predecessors Job and Qohelet, taught a wisdom epitomized in his saying that whoever would find his life will lose it and whoever loses his life will find it. Paul calls this subversive wisdom the folly of God, and exhorts us to stake our lives upon it. Jesus did just that, and lives now as our Crucified, Resurrected Sage, present through the Holy Spirit. He is, it turns out, both teacher and message, Wisdom-in-Person.[39] His Presence emboldens us to live wisely, justly, and against the grain. He summons us to step up to our role as sages.

Sages in Ministry Today

When I look back on almost twenty-five years as a parent, pastor, and teacher, a collage of images greets me. I see myself pushing an AV cart loaded with bibles and confirmation workbooks down a long hall. It is a Sunday afternoon in October, and the golden light of a fall afternoon crisscrosses the carpet. The sounds of young voices waft down the hall to greet me. I wonder how the lesson will go this week.

I remember a Monday morning, sitting in my office with a representative from the congregation and a staff member, my stomach clenched in a painful knot. I clear my throat and launch into the opening speech I had prepared for this incredibly awkward situation fraught with moral, legal, and emotional conflict.

I remember gathering with a group of church members in a senator's office in Washington, D.C., to advocate for the nutritional and health needs of children and youth.

I remember holding my then three-year-old son in my lap as we sit together in the big reading chair in the corner of his bedroom. He is wearing a green sleeper, the kind with the built-in footies. I am holding him on my lap while we read a story from *The Children's Bible*.

Not only do I remember specific scenes, but I also anticipate them. This Sunday morning I will teach a class of fifteen or so sixth graders. I can already see their smooth brows creased with anger and anxiety, and can hear their chorus of questions about the events that are taking place in their community and world this week.

In a month or so, I will stand before a group of eight hundred clergy and laity at a United Methodist Annual Conference. I will preach the sermon during the service of ordination.

One of the questions I asked pastors when I interviewed them was, "What are a couple of lessons you have learned from life?" Their answers were often in the form of newly coined proverbs that sounded strangely familiar. Some examples are, "If you think it's all you in your ministry, you'll quickly do something that lets you know you're right—it is all you!" "Actions have consequences that we still have to face, even though we have been forgiven by God." "You can't teach someone to swim by standing beside the pool."

Clergy have no corner on the wisdom market, no exclusive claim to the role of sage.

Said a male inner-city African American pastor I interviewed in St. Louis:

> I see wisdom in my laity. I have learned perseverance through the struggle of black female church members to survive. They are the low person on the totem pole, beneath white males and black males. They are present in more numbers than black men, though they don't have as much influence. It's still a sexist environment. I have learned how to preach from them, how to be faithful to God in who I am. We have our "Aunt Janes." I'll be preaching a funeral and they'll be out there saying things like, "OK, now, Preacher. Hold your horses. Make it plain. Amen. Go on, preach it! You didn't do it today, Rev."

Ministry through a Wisdom Lens

When we look at our ministry through the lens of wisdom, we find that everything we do has the same origin, motivation, and goal: the Wisdom of God. What if we believed that, in all our mundane activities, we were acting in the role of sage? What if, in scrubbing dead bugs off whitewall tires at the youth carwash, in summoning energy to listen attentively to a troubled couple, and in focusing on a column of figures at a finance meeting, we were alert to the workings of Divine Wisdom in our hands, our ears, our eyes? For one thing, it would make us better teachers and preachers. Being constantly alert to the activity of God in the most minuscule of circumstances is a spiritual discipline that is absolutely crucial to communicating God's good news.

When we claim and name our identity as sages, we can speak more directly to our people's hunger for wise guidance for daily living from the pulpit and the podium. We can give the self-help authors and New Age gurus the competition they deserve. Following the rhetorical lead of the sages, we can use metaphor, saying, simile, and story to touch our people's emotions as well as their intellects. We can learn strategies of indirect confrontation that are the dynamic of proverbs and parables. These can empower us to preach and teach on topics we may have avoided in the past. Our words, in and beyond the pulpit, can be grounded in our biblical wisdom tradition.

Inviting People into the House of Wisdom

In claiming our own identity as sages, we empower the people of God to recognize their identities as seekers and teachers of wisdom for living. We invite others into the house of Wisdom.

A Mexican American pastor serving a church in South Texas told me:

> In Hispanic culture the wisdom comes from the grandparents and the parents. You are to honor the elderly. It is important to be a source of pride to your grandparents. We have a tradition of *dichos* (sayings). Many of them are from *Don Quixote* and Proverbs.

Said another Mexican American pastor:

> The mother is the center of the home. The grandmother has great authority. Mother's Day is a very important day in our church. I believe this is partly because of the Catholicism that lies in many of my Methodist Hispanic members' backgrounds. They were used to venerating Mary.

Another Mexican American pastor, serving a church in San Antonio, mentioned *dichos* or sayings, such as, "Tell me who you are with and I will tell you who you are. God does his part. You need to do your part."

A young female United Methodist pastor, originally from Mexico, serving a rural church in South Texas told me that she often feels like a "translator" between the younger people who don't always know their culture's language and traditions and the older people who still follow traditional cultural practices and speak Spanish as their primary language. She recalled:

> I remember the time I was sitting between some teenagers and some older people. The older people were sharing *dichos*. The younger people wanted to know, "What are they saying? What does that mean?"

African American Christian educators Anne E. Streaty Wimberly and Evelyn L. Parker identify black churches as "essential faith 'villages' that

14

generate . . . wisdom formation through giving gifts of time, information, insights, encouragement, and praise."[40] These Christian educators highlight the role of adults in mentoring youth, the effectiveness of small-group mentoring, and the importance of helping people get in touch with their African, black American, and Christian roots in our violent, uncertain times.[41] Wisdom comes through in the spirituals "Didn't My Lord Deliver Daniel?" It comes through in an elderly sage of the community, Mom Parker, hugging a young woman suffering the pain of infertility and assuring her that 'there is a Balm in Gilead to make the wounded whole.'" Wisdom comes through African stories and proverbs. For example, "To be rich, begin poor."[42]

Every faith community, with its own particularities of race and culture, is called upon to learn and convey its interpretation of biblical wisdom from one generation to another. The older teach the younger the lessons of experience. The younger criticize and energize their elders, pointing out the injustice of so-called wisdom that reinforces an inequitable status quo and expressing wisdom in fresh forms.

Upheld by the Four Pillars of Wisdom

Each pillar is crucial to holding up this house of wisdom. If one is missing, the roof is liable to cave in. Without the fear of the Lord, the other three virtues deteriorate into a vague pity for others, self-discipline for superficial ends, and social cynicism.

What is faith, discipline, and courage without compassion, the listening heart?

We have seen too often what happens when a religious leader has faith, compassion, a sense of justice, but no self-restraint.

And what happens if someone has trust in God, compassion, and self-discipline, but can never quite summon the courage to rock the boat? Not much.

Keeping in mind that all four pillars of wisdom are necessary to hold up our house, each of the chapters that follow will focus on a separate virtue, interweaving insights from biblical, historical, and contemporary sages.

CHAPTER TWO

THE FIRST PILLAR OF WISDOM: THE BENDED KNEE

"The fear of the LORD is the beginning of knowledge." (Prov 1:7)

The Lead Sled Dog Virtue: The Fear of the Lord

The lead sled dog virtue for the Hebrew sages was the fear of the Lord. "The fear of the LORD is the beginning of knowledge; fools despise wisdom and instruction" (Prov 1:7).[1] The fundamental proverb that the sages put forward as the basis of their teaching is this: "The fear of the LORD is the beginning (*reshit*) of knowledge" (1:7), the "first step" (*tehilla*) toward wisdom (9:10), or "instruction (*musar*) in wisdom" (15:33).[2] Injunctions to fear the Lord pepper the Proverbs collection (1:7; 9:10; 15:33; 31:30). This is because the fear of the Lord is the presupposition of wisdom, its essential condition. Old Testament scholar Gerhard von Rad correctly claims that the statement, "The fear of the LORD is the beginning of knowledge" (Prov 1:7), "contains in a nutshell the whole Israelite theory of knowledge."[3]

The Fear of the Lord: A Three-Stranded Braid

The fear of the Lord has different nuances that braid together in the Hebrew Bible: awe before the holy (Isa 6), covenant loyalty (Deut 10:20), and moral obedience (Prov 1:7). Each of these human postures is in response to the prior gracious initiative of God.

The Fear of the Lord as Awe before the Holy: Isaiah 6

Wisdom scholar Ellen Davis points out that the virtue of the fear of the Lord contains an element of "ordinary fright." We sense a tremor of terror in Isaiah's response to a close and unexpected encounter with the divine (Isa 6:5). Says Davis,

> To experience the full measure of God's power and *not* to feel some stirring of fear would indicate a profound state of spiritual numbness. . . . A sickly lack of fear in the face of God's power is exactly the condition described in the book of Exodus as Pharaoh's "hardheartedness" (see Exod 8:15, 32; 9:7, and elsewhere). . . . Moses diagnoses the spiritual condition that ultimately brings ruin on the whole land of Egypt: "But as for you and your officials, I know that you do not yet fear the LORD God" (Exod 9:30).[4]

Fear, in its most literal and basic sense, is a natural response to overwhelming force. The Israelites are said to have experienced fear (or terror) in the face of the thunder and lightning of their earthshaking encounter with the Lord at Sinai. Such fear is not altogether misplaced. But along with the terror, there is an attraction or fascination.[5]

To know God ought to be to fear God. This fear is not a cringing before the expectation of imminent punishment. It is, rather, an "awe and regard, a kind of wariness, probably the sort that would mean watching your step in his presence."[6]

A Presbyterian pastor from a suburban church near Harrisburg, Pennsylvania, made this observation:

> One of the churches downtown had on the bulletin board in front, "The fear of the Lord is the beginning of wisdom." And my first thought was, "What does that mean to most people, except be afraid of God?" And for the unchurched it doesn't have much more meaning than "Be afraid because God's gonna get you."

Clearly, we have some educating to do on this virtue of the fear of the Lord. At the same time that it brings trembling, the virtue of the fear of the Lord brings a peace and a security to the one who exercises it. It is a fear to end all other fears. To fear the Lord is to experience blessedness

(Prov 28:14) and security (Prov 19:23). When we embrace this virtue, we can relinquish lesser fears. "The fear of others lays a snare, but one who trusts in the LORD is secure" (Prov 29:25).

A United Methodist pastor in his early fifties serving a church in a north Texas town felt that clergy lack the fear of the Lord in the sense of confidence in our calling and courage in our proclamation.

> We have no confidence in our calling. We have the worst self-esteem of all the professions. We are so dependent on people's opinions of us. We have such a high need for others' approval. We feel we should only have strengths and no weaknesses. Early in my ministry I felt obligated to have answers. I am getting better at sharing with people my questions and my fears.

The Fear of the Lord as Covenant Loyalty: Deuteronomy

While it has similarities with "ordinary fright," the fear of the Lord is something more than a visceral response to God's power. It has volitional and cognitive aspects. Deuteronomy describes the covenant loyalty we need to cultivate in relationship to God. "You shall fear the LORD your God; him alone you shall worship; to him you shall hold fast, and by his name you shall swear" (10:20). To fear the Lord is to live out of a humble loyalty that begins in the heart. For the Hebrews, the heart was not just the seat of the emotions but also of understanding and will.

> So now, O Israel, what does the LORD your God require of you? Only to fear the LORD your God, to walk in all his ways, to love him, to serve the LORD your God with all your heart and with all your soul, and to keep the commandments of the LORD your God and his decrees that I am commanding you today, for your own well-being (Deut 10:12-13).

The same north Texas pastor I mentioned above tied the single-mindedness of our covenant loyalty to the quality of our witness in the community.

> Pastors are not always respected in the community. We must be willing to live out what we say and motivate our congregation to do so as well. People would look up to us if there were a seamless fabric between what we say on Sunday and do on Monday in our personal lives and in the church's life.

Based on Trust

An African American female pastor serving a black Baptist church in Washington, D.C., made this connection between the habit of fearing the Lord and the ability to trust in a sense of inward guidance.

> You know in the black church you're always hearing someone say, "The Lord told me..." or "the Lord dropped in my spirit" or "I had a vision." Well, I never had a vision. The Lord never dropped anything in my spirit. But there is a sense of being able to trust my relationship with God and to trust my connection with God so that as time goes on I can trust me. I can trust what I'm doing. I can trust what I'm saying. And if I make a mistake, it's all right.

A twentysomething white United Methodist chaplain from a college town in New Mexico had this to say about trusting God and trusting our own instincts.

> A preacher needs a combination of humility and confidence, not in his own abilities, but in what God has done and can do in his life and the lives of others. For example, I know from experience that God provides healing in times of emotional wounding. I know from experience that God can lead people beyond temptation into better ways of thought and life.

John Wesley, who often expressed his thought in aphorisms, stated his trust in God's care when he said, "God's time is always the best time" and "Whatever God calls us to He will fit us for."[7]

Open to Ongoing Transformation

The same female pastor from Washington, D.C., I just quoted had this to say about the fear of the Lord and our ongoing transformation.

> Recently I've been preaching this whole piece on being transformed and God being with you. It's not a destination, it's a journey during which we continue to find ourselves transformed by the Spirit of Christ. We have to stay open to being touched by the Spirit of Christ. We have to stay open to forgiving ourselves, to understanding that we also are being transformed.

The Fear of the Lord as Moral Obedience: Proverbs

In Proverbs, fear of the Lord consists of acknowledging that our human wisdom is limited and that God is the source of all wisdom. The fear of the Lord acknowledges that God is sovereign and inscrutable and that we are human with limited powers of perception (1:7; 9:10; 15:33). Since God is the source of all moral insights that guide the community, the wise person adopts a posture of obedience to God in all the particulars of daily life.

The fear of the Lord, then, connotes awe, loyalty, or obedience. Put in a more memorable, alliterative form, we could see that it consists in trembling, trust, and transformation (from folly to wisdom) through obedience. In all three aspects, both emotion and cognition come into play.[8]

The Fear of the Lord: A Relational Virtue

God's Contribution to the Relationship: A Divine Gift

Wisdom (*hokmah*) is multifaceted in the Hebrew Scriptures, but all the facets point to Wisdom as a gift from God. Proverbs 2:1-5 describes the relationship between wisdom and the fear of the Lord. After an increasingly determined and single-minded search in verses 2-4, the seeker finds not wisdom but the fear of the Lord (2:5-6). "From this somewhat unexpected conclusion the writer intends the reader to understand that wisdom cannot be acquired by human effort alone."[9] Wisdom is a gift. "For the LORD gives wisdom; from his mouth come knowledge and understanding" (Prov 2:6).

The sages responsible for the book of Job define the fear of the Lord as the acknowledgement of the limitations of human wisdom. Beyond human reach, wisdom is to be found nowhere in our world (28:12-22). Only God understands wisdom because God established wisdom when he created the orderliness of the universe (28:23-27).[10] God's wisdom is the total knowledge that the Creator has of the creation. Human wisdom, in the book of Job, is the fear of the Lord (28:28).[11]

The sages of Ecclesiastes command their students to "fear God" rather than cultivate the fear of the Lord (5:7). Visualizing an aloof, transcendent God, these sages remind wisdom students to acknowledge the limitations of their knowledge and the width of the gulf between the divine and the human. To "fear God" is to know one's place.

Implications for our Role as Sage

Channels of the Divine Gift

Some religious traditions emphasize an understanding of clergy as channels of a divine gift in their ministries. A Roman Catholic priest from Dallas expressed his tradition's perspective on his role in this way:

> In the Catholic imagination, the religious figure is huge. People want a connection with the divine. They don't want to call me by my first name, even if I tell them to. They'll say, "Oh, no, it has to be 'Father _____.'" When I address prayers to God for intercession, I am the intercessor, the human. When I offer the eucharistic prayer, "This is my body," well, that's a shift. Children see me and nudge their parents and say "There's Jesus!" The parents laugh, but there is truth to how the children see me.

A Puerto Rican female Episcopal priest from Los Angeles expressed her understanding of her role in this way:

> I love being a priest because the term priest, as opposed to pastor or minister or other titles, connotes for me the image of a shaman who brings wisdom to the people. I am like the connector of two realms, the one who points the way or guides the way to this other realm, a facilitator to the spiritual realm, a connection to their own wisdom, to he God who lives within them, to the wisdom of the ages. Wisdom for me is sacramental—it's a sense of an encounter with the divine that I facilitate, but I facilitate it by virtue of a gift that has nothing to do with me.

Entrusting Ourselves to God's Hands

A white male pastor in his early fifties from north Texas told this story from his own life.

> I have never been sick much at all in my life, which is a good thing, since I really like being in control of all aspects of my life and destiny.

But one night last year I became violently ill at home and had to be rushed to the hospital with what was eventually diagnosed as infected bile ducts. Visiting in hospitals is one thing. Not being not in control, lying in bed looking at the ceiling, not knowing what's wrong with you is another. The doctor ordered a series of tests to figure out what my problem was. A nurse came in to draw blood. "I'm sorry I have to do this and will have to do it pretty often for the next few days," she said. I answered her, "I am in your hands. Do what you need to do."

The fear of the Lord is to say to God, "I am in your hands. Do through me what you need to do."

Taking God Seriously, but Not Ourselves

An African American pastor in his midfifties serving a large black Baptist church in Washington, D.C., in reflecting on the qualities of wisdom in daily life, made these observations.

One of my great heroes is Abraham Lincoln. When I was a boy I thought he was a living saint and then, during the 1960s and 1970s I thought he was a racist who was, by necessity, doing what he did. Now I realize the truth is always more in the middle than at either extreme. He became lifelong friends with Frederick Douglass and you could make the argument that that's what got him killed by John Wilkes Booth. He made this speech about how the nation would have to rethink race relations, would have to find ways to incorporate people into all levels of society. You say that, and you can't live. I don't think any of our presidents, George Washington, Lyndon Johnson, and Jack Kennedy included, had more intense pressure on him than did Lincoln. But he had this marvelous way of sort of just stepping back and doing this self-deprecating thing. He was a man who suffered from terrible depression, but he had an ability to step back and laugh at himself and get others to laugh at his own foibles. I think he maintained his sanity and the nation's sanity at the same time.

Our Contribution to the Relationship: Humility

While "the fear of the LORD" is a divine gift, at the same time the sages speak of this virtue as something one chooses (Prov 1:29). Living by the fear of the Lord involves developing the habit of making choices that do not merely reflect our own self-interest or priorities. It means putting

God's preferences before our own. Says Old Testament scholar Ellen Davis, "Such a reversal of our natural priorities is what the Bible calls 'humility,' which is linked in several proverbs with fear of the Lord" (15:33; 22:4).[12]

One of the Desert Fathers—mystics who lived in the Egyptian desert during the fourth and fifth centuries C.E.—Abba Anthony, describes the power of humility:

> I saw all the snares that the enemy spreads out over the world and I said groaning, What can get through from such snares? Then I heard a voice saying to me, "Humility."[13]

St. Augustine describes Jesus' Incarnation in terms of his radical humility, his reverence for God.

> Humble I am come, I am come to teach humility, I am come the master of humility . . . he who cleaves to me will be humble.[14]

When one is humble, when one fears the Lord, one maintains openness to wisdom from unexpected sources, with unexpected implications. One does not become "wise in [one's] own eyes" (Prov 3:7). The fear of the Lord, a profound respect for the Godness of God, keeps human construals of wisdom open to their own subversion and reformation from generation to generation.[15]

Two Examples of Humility from World Religions

A version of the fear of the Lord is seen clearly in another of the three Abrahamic religions: Islam. The word *Islam* derives from *salam*, which means "peace" but in a secondary sense "surrender." Its full connotation, therefore, is the peace that comes from surrendering one's life to God.[16] The dominant theme of the Koran, the holy book of Muslims, is the unity, omnipotence, omniscience, and mercy of God. As a correlative, it also proclaims the total dependence of human life upon God.[17]

Humility is a particular emphasis in Chinese Taoism. Its great symbol of humility is water, which runs to the lowest ground, yet in that place remains nearest to Tao, the ultimate power, the unconditioned, the ground of being.

The highest excellence is like (that of) water. The excellence of water appears in its benefiting all things, and in its occupying, without striving (to the contrary), the low place which all men dislike. Hence (its way) is near to (that of) the Tao.[18]

The Fear of the Lord: Wellspring for the Other Three Virtues

From the fear of the Lord flow a host of virtues that make up the character both of the sage and of the students he or she seeks to shape. These are outlined in the first several verses that introduce the purpose of the book of Proverbs (1:1-7). They correspond to the four pillars of wisdom.

From the fear of the Lord issue habits of attention, focus, imagination, discernment, and judgment.[19] These have much to do with the listening heart.

"Wise dealing" (1:3a) and "prudence" (1:4b) flow from the fear of the Lord. These virtues have much to do with the "cool spirit," for they are instrumental virtues, those that promote the successful pursuit of desired objectives. Proverbs 1:4 states that a goal of the sage is to teach prudence to the young, a quality they often lack. "Wise dealing" (*musar haskel* [1:3a]) entails heeding admonition (15:5), caution, and the absence of gullibility (14:15). It is the ability to control one's temper (12:16) and the good sense to avoid danger (22:3; 27:12). It is an instrumental virtue founded on caution and discretion.[20]

From the fear of the Lord flow a trio of moral virtues that affect the community's life together: righteousness, justice, and equity (Prov 1:3b). These have much to do with the subversive voice; they describe the standards by which God judges the nation and to which wise leaders and prophets call them to adhere.

It is clear why the fear of the Lord, as distinguished from all other fears in life, is one to be cultivated. It is a posture of grateful attentiveness to God. Such an attitude is the wellspring of faithful teaching and preaching and the holy living it seeks to inspire. As Jesus ben Sira, a Hellenistic Jewish sage and author of Ecclesiasticus puts it, "the fear of the Lord delights the heart, and gives gladness and joy" (Sir 1:12).

A sermon by the seventeenth-century poet John Donne contains a moving meditation on "the fear of the LORD," which Donne calls "the art of arts, the root, fruit, of all true wisdom" (*Sermons*, 6:96). By his reading of Scriptures, this fear is paradoxically "the most noble, the most courageous, the most magnanimous, not affection (mere feeling), but virtue, in the world" (6:95). This is so because it drives out all lesser fears, which diminish rather than build up our character. "He that loves the Lord, loves him with all his love; he that fears the Lord, loves him with all his fear too; God takes no half affections" (6:109).[21]

A Joyful Spirit

African American mystic and educator Howard Thurman, in his book *Deep Is the Hunger: Meditations for Apostles of Sensitiveness*, writes these words:

> What is the source of your joy? There are some who are dependent upon the mood of others for their happiness. . . . There are some whose joy is dependent upon circumstances. . . . There are some whose joy is a matter of disposition and temperament. . . . There are still others who find their joy deep in the heart of their religious experience. . . . There is a strange quality of awe in their joy, that is but a reflection of the deep calm water of the spirit out of which it comes. It is primarily a discovery of the soul, when God makes known His presence, where there are no words, no outward song, only the Divine Movement. This is the joy that the world cannot give. This is the joy that keeps watch against all the emissaries of sadness of mind and weariness of soul. This is the joy that comforts and is the companion, as we walk even through the valley of the shadow of death.[22]

The Fear of the Lord for Jesus the Sage: "Do Not Be Afraid!"

Fear of Threats to Security and the Challenges of Life

Lots of people in the Gospels were filled with a fear that is very different from the fear of the Lord. Herod fears the new baby (Matt 2:7-12). Joseph is afraid to return to Judea because of a wicked ruler (Matt 2:22). The disciples fear the winds and the waves (Matt 8:26; Mark 4:40; Luke 8:24). The slave who buries his pound cites his fear of his master as an excuse for wrapping his pound in a piece of cloth rather than multiplying it (Luke 19:21). Peter "notices the strong wind" and begins to sink from fear of it (Matt 14:30-33). Lots of people in the Gospels fear the challenges of life and threats to their security and position.

Fear in the Face of Encounter with the Divine

The Gospels also depict lots of people filled with fear and trembling because God has initiated a close encounter with them in the midst of their daily activities without making a prior appointment. Scripture recounts a variety of human responses to these unexpected encounters with the divine. Some people beg for the divine to withdraw, as in Simon Peter's initial response to Jesus (Luke 5:8) or the villagers after they saw the former demoniac clothed and in his right mind (Matt 8:34; Mark 5:15-17; Luke 8:37).

Some people, when they encounter the divine, are felled on the spot, barely able to speak, as the disciples in the boat seeing a ghostly figure walking toward them on the water (Matt 14:26) or Zechariah, or the shepherds at the appearance of angels (Luke 1:12; 2:9). Mary is described as being "much perplexed" by the angel's visit (Luke 1:29). Both Matthew and Luke's versions of the Transfiguration emphasize the fear of Peter, James, and John at the sight of a strange cloud and the sound of the divine voice (Matt 17:5-6; Luke 9:34-35). People coming to Jesus for healing show signs of fear and trembling (Mark 5:34, 36). In John's Gospel, Jesus' disciples show fear at the prospect of the withdrawal of the divine presence (John 14:26-27). The Resurrection appearances in both Matthew (28:4) and Mark (16:8) highlight the fear of the witnesses.

"Be Not Afraid, Take Heart"

The words "Be not afraid" accompany these close encounters between the divine and the human. Uttered by Jesus himself or by angelic emissaries, they are a bridge between fright and faith.

The command to take heart occurs several times in the Gospels (Matt 9:2; 9:22; 14:27; Mark 10:35) as a companion to the injunction not to fear. "Take heart" means to be of good courage, to be of good cheer, to be confident. Fear is to be replaced by confidence, not in ourselves, but in what God is doing through Jesus' presence.[23] The angel tells Zechariah not to be afraid because his prayer has been heard. Mary has no need to fear because "she has found favor with God." The shepherds need not cower in fright because, says the angel, "I am bringing you good news of great joy that shall be to all people."

There seems to be a cumulative message in all these injunctions to "be not afraid." It is that in Jesus, the divine has drawn intimately close to the human world. The primary purpose of this approach is not to inspire fear in the sense of trembling in the knowledge of our human frailty and shortcomings before the divine. It is to foster faith, to create confidence, and to inspire peace. This is the peace that comes from a close encounter with the One who bears the character of God and who therefore yearns for reconciliation with human beings. To fear God does *not* mean to allow dread of punishment, a sense of unworthiness, or a fit of nerves to paralyze our response to Jesus, God with us. To fear God *does* mean to give allegiance to Jesus and to follow Jesus, allowing his teachings and presence to guide our thoughts, actions, and interactions. We are to share the good news in the same spirit as the two Marys running from the empty tomb. They go and tell the disciples "with fear and great joy" (Matt 28:8).

The Desired Response to Encounter with the Divine: Faith and Following

In all four Gospels, the desired response to a close encounter with the divine in Jesus is faith and following. This is the result of the Gerasene exorcism (Mark 5:18-20; Luke 8:38-39), the stilling of the storm (Matt 8:27; Mark 4:41; Luke 8:25), Jesus' healing of a paralytic (Matt 9:8), the Transfiguration (Matt 17:1-13; Luke 9:28-36), and the miraculous catch of fish (Luke 5:1-11).

A mountaintop experience of the divine is not meant to hold us up on the heights. Nor is it created for us to cower, covering our faces forever. We are not, like Isaiah, to hide behind the altar, our hands over our mouths, as the burning coal of forgiveness wings its way toward us (Isa 6:4-7). Nor are we, like Simon Peter, to curl up in the fetal position in the boat, overcome by the combined stench of fish and our own sins. We are to get out of the boat and become catchers of people (Luke 5:8-11).

Jesus, the Quintessential Sage: The Fear of the Lord Exemplified by His Life

"The fear of the LORD is the beginning of knowledge" (Prov 1:7)

For the sages of Proverbs the fear of the Lord meant the recognition that God is the source of all moral guidance for personal and communal life. It is this understanding of the fear of the Lord that is implicit in the life and teachings of Jesus the sage.

Proverbs 3:5-10 is the Hebrew sages' inspiring description of what a life guided by the fear of the Lord, understood as moral guidance, looks like. It describes the life they sought both to model and teach. The life shaped by the fear of the Lord encompasses the total person, heart (3:5), will (3:7, 9), and body (3:8). Written centuries before Jesus' lifetime to describe the life of the seeker and teacher of wisdom, these verses comprise a glowing cameo of the life Jesus, the quintessential sage, lived. It illumines the path that living by his teachings paves beneath our feet.

> 5 Trust in the LORD with all your heart,
>   and do not rely on your own insight.

> 6 In all your ways acknowledge him,
>   and he will make straight your paths.

> 7 Do not be wise in your own eyes;
>   fear the LORD, and turn away from evil.

> 8 It will be a healing for your flesh
>   and a refreshment for your body.

> 9 Honor the LORD with your substance
>   and with the first fruits of all your produce;

> 10 then your barns will be filled with plenty,
>   and your vats will be bursting with wine. (Prov 3:5-10)

Jesus trusted God and, step-by-step, walked the path of wisdom, guided by its primary virtue, the fear of the Lord. His life and his death were offerings of obedience from every aspect of his being: body, mind, will, and heart. Jesus' fear of the Lord caused him to question human construals of wisdom. His challenging teachings, couched in traditional wisdom forms of short sayings and parables, displayed a dynamic we have defined as the faithful genius of biblical wisdom; its subversive kernel. He sacrificed what conventional wisdom defined as the rewards of living wisely: a life conducive to longevity, a good reputation, satisfying intimate relationships, a large family, and a degree of material prosperity. These were the first fruits Jesus offered to God (Prov 3:9). He chose to embrace a life of loneliness, fear, physical discomfort, and disgrace. He chose to persist in teachings that challenged the status quo and angered its guardians. He chose to endure an excruciating and humiliating death.

He refused to allow his fear of others to rule his actions, and thereby his life, death, and ongoing life stand as a testimony to Prov 29:25: "The fear of others lays a snare, but one who trusts in the LORD is secure."[24]

Jesus, the quintessential sage, demonstrates the fear of the Lord in his own encounter with Satan in the narrative of the Temptation. Jesus' temptation epitomizes his life as he repeatedly minds his motives, refusing to test his God-given gifts in ungodly ways or to pay homage to anyone or anything other than God.

Jesus, the quintessential sage, demonstrates the fear of the Lord in a dark garden as he bows, his head in his hands. He does so again, in his honest, anguished cry from the cross, when breath is failing, "My God, my God, why have you forsaken me?" (Matt 27:46; Mark 15:34). This cry becomes, by the influx of the wisdom and power of God, the serene, yet strenuous promise, "I am with you always, to the end of the age" (Matt 28:20*b*).

Jesus, the Quintessential Sage: The Fear of the Lord in His Teachings

Jesus staked his life on the certainty that "the fear of the LORD is the beginning of knowledge" (Prov 1:7), but he is not recorded as ever having said so. Nor does he suggest that wisdom is foresight or that wisdom provides rewards that cannot be taken away, although the Greeks and Romans did. He never promises, as do the sages of Proverbs, that the cultivation of wisdom will help one make sense of life.[25] Yet, the spirit of the fear of the Lord undergirds his teachings. His teachings attest to his conviction that God, not the dictates of traditional religion, is the source of guidance for this life, in our thoughts, first, then in our actions. Implied in his teachings and made explicit by his early followers is this conviction: Jesus himself is God's authoritative representative, both a teacher of wisdom and Wisdom in person. From now on to fear the Lord means to follow Jesus.

In Proverbs, the fear of the Lord is the one fear in life that we are to cultivate, a radical trust in God to guide our footsteps when the future stretches out before us, shrouded in mist. The fear of the Lord banishes all lesser fears and, paradoxically, brings peace and spiritual security. "Do not be afraid, little flock, for it is your Father's good pleasure to give you the kingdom" (Luke 12:32). Jesus sounds the theme of freedom from fear and anxiety in Matt 6:34 (Luke 12:22) based on God's watchful care over those who trust in him. After enjoining us to cast aside obsessive worries about daily necessities, Jesus says

> Therefore do not worry, saying, "What will we eat?" or "What will we drink?" or "What will we wear?" For it is the Gentiles who strive for all these things; and indeed your heavenly Father knows that you need all these things. But strive first for the kingdom of God and his righteousness, and all these things will be given to you as well. So do not worry about tomorrow, for tomorrow will bring worries of its own. Today's trouble is enough for today. (Matt 6:31-34; see also Luke 12:29-32)

Jesus teaches that a degree of fear is entirely appropriate in an eschatological context. In the last days, "people will faint from fear and forboding" (Luke 21:26). He also points out that we should fear God who has the power over both body and soul (Matt 10:28), but who, at the same time, keeps a watchful eye over his children, whose every hair is counted (Matt 10:30).

In Matthew's Gospel, Jesus is identified with Wisdom. His radical teachings are presented as the authoritative interpretation of Torah for the conduct of daily life. To fear the Lord, to be a disciple means to hear those teachings, but also to obey them by following Jesus.

In Mark's Gospel, Jesus' wisdom is discerned only by those who are willing to trust the paradoxical wisdom of a crucified Lord. To fear the Lord is now to learn by faith to follow Jesus on the way of the cross.

In Luke's Gospel, Jesus' wisdom is depicted as coming from the Holy Spirit. To fear the Lord is, then, to pray for and accept the gift of the Holy Spirit.

In John's Gospel, Jesus is the Incarnate Word and Wisdom of God. Wisdom's qualities and fruits are expressed by means of the same images used to describe wisdom in Proverbs: life, food, fountain of water, way, and light.[26] One's eternal future hangs on whether one accepts or rejects this Wisdom, whether or not one fears the Lord.[27]

The theme of the fear of the Lord, while never explicit, runs through Matthew's Sermon on the Mount like an underground stream. It is pronounced in the Beatitudes, with which Matthew's Gospel begins. Jesus did not invent the beatitude. It is a wisdom form long used by Israel's sages, a statement of blessedness or happiness to one who engages in certain types of actions. It is sometimes called a macarism. In the Hebrew Scriptures beatitudes occur almost exclusively in the Psalms and the Wisdom literature. A beatitude is a declaration of well-being to those who engage in life-enhancing behavior: studying and obeying Torah (Ps 1; Prov 29:18), caring for the poor (Ps 41:2; Prov 14:21), trusting in God (Pss 112:1; 128:1; Prov 16:20), fearing God (Prov 28:14), finding wisdom (Prov 3:13), and listening to wisdom (Prov 8:33).[28]

Old Testament beatitudes, statements of blessedness, promise the sages a life-enhancing sphere in which they are surrounded by well-being. The sages did not endorse a strict theory of retribution, but they did believe that behavior led to consequences both for the actors and the context in which they operated. Desirable consequences were a large family, a long life, a degree of material comfort, and a good reputation in the community. Living by fear of the Lord did not guarantee these positive outcomes, but made them more likely.

Jesus' Beatitudes, by contrast, enjoin followers to risk those very things. The Beatitudes (Matt 5:1-11) call those happy who recognize their need for God and rely on God totally (the "poor in spirit" [5:3]). As a result, such people are filled with humility ("the meek" [5:5]), show mercy (5:7), and work for justice in their communities ("peacemakers" [5:9]), even in hostile situations, even against the world's better judgment. The one who fears God will be persecuted and reviled, and yet will rejoice (5:10, 11).

Jesus understands that wisdom is, at its heart, a matter of right motivation. When one fears the Lord, one guards one's intentions, maintaining a posture of radical dependence and trust in God in the inward person. Murder begins with anger. Adultery begins with lustful imaginings. Retaliation and revenge begin with hatred of one's enemy. Pompous public displays of religiosity begin with an inward craving for the good opinion of others. An obsession with the accumulation of wealth begins with an eye that looks upon outward treasures rather than inward ones. We can allow our thoughts and then our actions to be governed by our insecurities and our fear of others, or we can allow them to be governed by the fear of the Lord. We are freed from our compulsion to judge others when we leave the judging to the One who has all knowledge (Matt 7:1-5). We don't have to be consumed by a fear of an uncertain future when we fear the Lord (Matt 6:25-34).

I spoke with a Hispanic pastor who serves a large church in downtown San Antonio. He described the phenomenon of men staying at home and sending their wives to church.

Many men rely on their wives for a religious connection. They reason that women are more emotional and so naturally more religious.

These men, in a culture of machismo, feel they always have to prove themselves. It often takes a crisis in their lives, a close scrape with death or illness, for them to receive Christ. Then they say, "I need Jesus, and he has been here all along."

My little niece, when she saw me, used to say, "Here comes Jesus!" When she was older, I asked her, "Who is Jesus?" She answered, "You can depend on him. Ask anytime day or night and he is listening."

Fear of the Lord in Early Christian Reflection: Obedience to Jesus' Teachings and Belief in His Identity as "Wisdom in Person"

Both Matthew and Luke portray Jesus as epitomizing in his teaching and conduct the fear of the Lord, radical reliance on the Wisdom of God. Luke depicts Jesus primarily as teacher and envoy of Wisdom. Matthew's Gospel attributes to Jesus words that, formerly in the tradition, have been on the lips of Wisdom herself.[29]

This identification of Jesus as Wisdom came to Matthew largely through the Q document, an early collection of Jesus' wisdom teachings that connected him closely with Wisdom herself. This work attributed the exclusive revelation of Sophia to the Son, who is identified with Jesus.[30]

Developments in reflection on Wisdom during the intertestamental period paved the way for Matthew's depiction of Jesus as Wisdom. These developments are threefold. *The Wisdom of Jesus ben Sirach (Ecclesiasticus)*, an early second-century B.C.E. apocryphal work, identifies Wisdom (Sophia) with Torah. Sophia has come to reside in the Torah through whose instruction she now finds expression (24:23-34).[31]

The *Wisdom of Solomon*, a mid-first century B.C.E. wisdom work aimed at making Judaism appealing to Greeks, depicts Wisdom as the savior of God's people throughout Israel's history (9:18; 10:1–19:12). It affirms that God sends Wisdom from on high (9:17-18), and it identifies her with God's holy Spirit. She can be spoken of in the same breath with God's word (*logos*) (9:1-2), as the means by which God fashioned humankind.[32]

The books of *1 Enoch* (first century A.D.) and *4 Ezra* (also known as *2 Esdras*) portray Sophia as the sender of prophets and spokespersons throughout Israel's history.[33] We are told that she has been so regularly rejected on earth that she finally returns to heaven (*1 Enoch* 42:1-2; *4 Ezra* 5:10) awaiting an auspicious time to return.[34] This theme shows up in Matthew's claim that true prophets, sages, and scribes are rejected because Wisdom is rejected and they are Wisdom's envoys.[35]

The connections between Jesus and Sophia or Wisdom are explicitly drawn in the prologue to the Gospel of John, written near the end of the first century C.E. Jesus' preexistence and salvific role are expressed in concepts familiar to us from Wisdom reflection in Proverbs and the wisdom and apocalyptic reflection of the later intertestamental period. However, the assignation "wisdom" or "Sophia" is never used. Instead, Jesus is described in terms of the Son's relationship to the Father. The grammatically masculine metaphor *Logos* (Word) dominates the prologue.[36]

The rest of the Gospel characterizes Jesus very much as an expression of Sophia-Wisdom. Like her, he speaks in revelatory "I am" style and with the symbolism of bread, wine, and living water, inviting people to eat and drink. Like Sophia, Jesus proclaims a saving message aloud in public places. Like her, he is the light and life of the world. Like her, he promises to those who seek and find him that they will avoid the path to death and find life. The implied narrative message is that Jesus is Wisdom Incarnate. The dominance of the masculine metaphor in the prologue and the absence of the term *Sophia* as a description for Jesus in the narrative of the Gospel have a lasting effect on subsequent traditions. Jesus as the *Logos*, rather than expressing Sophia's function and qualities, replaces her.[37]

New Testament scholar Elisabeth Schüssler Fiorenza concludes, "Early Christian reflection "either absorbed those 'female' elements derived from Wisdom theology through the grammatical masculine term 'Logos,' or it has transferred them to Mary the mother of Jesus."[38] Clearly, Sophia largely vanished from early canonical Christian reflection on the identity of Jesus. However, she continued to be important, with varied nuances, in the theological reflection of some early Christian theologians, among them Marius Victorinus, Augustine, Theophilus of Antioch, Irenaeus, and Athanasius.[39] Later developments in Trinitarian theology resulted in Sophia's gradual disappearance from language and reflection on God's modes of self-revelation.

Mentions of Divine Sophia are almost completely lost in the self-understanding of the Western churches. Two Russian Orthodox theologians of the twentieth century, Vladimir Solov'ev and Sergei Bulgakov, gave Wisdom a central and integrative role in their theological reflections. Their work was and remains controversial in Eastern Orthodox theological circles.[40] Each viewed Sophia as the essence of God that pervades and unifies all three persons of the Trinity. Bulgakov coined the term *sophiology* to express the central dimension of Wisdom that "runs like a scarlet thread from his understanding of the doctrines of the Trinity and of creation, through the doctrines of Christ and the Church, to his eschatology."[41]

Bulgakov writes:

> In contemplating culture which has succumbed to secularization and paganism, which has lost its inspiration and has no answer to give to the tragedy of history, which seems in fact to have lost all meaning—we realize that we can find a spring of living water only by a renewal of our faith in the sophianic . . . meaning of the historical process. As the dome of St. Sophia in Constantinople with prophetic symbolism portrays heaven bending to earth, so the Wisdom of God itself is spread like a canopy over our sinful though still hallowed world.[42]

Trust in Christ: The Christian's Version of Fear of the Lord

For Christians, the wisdom virtue of the fear of the Lord manifests itself as trust in Christ. The one who fears the Lord now trusts Jesus to guide and empower priorities and choices. Jesus' trust in God, his fear of the Lord, was epitomized by his walk toward Jerusalem and his crucifixion. Our interpretation of that action on Jesus' part is therefore crucial to the way we live out the fear of the Lord. Three traditional understandings of the significance of Jesus' death have been scrutinized by various contemporary theologians. The first is the image of Jesus as *Christus Victor*, an early Christology in which the Crucifixion symbolized conflict and the Resurrection symbolized victory over the powers of death; Jesus rises victorious over the forces of sin and death to rule the world.[43]

The second understanding is of Jesus as the satisfaction for human sin against God. The satisfaction theory of the Atonement formulated by Anselm in the eleventh century emphasized the absolute necessity of the Atonement for the redemption of humankind. Anselm finds the necessity for the atoning sacrifice of Jesus Christ in the honor of God. Based on Roman laws that demanded that violations be either punished or sat-isfied, Jesus/Christ, fully human and fully divine, enters the scene as the perfect solution, a required and worthy sacrificial offering. He accom-plishes the two tasks of satisfaction: that humankind renders to God the willing obedience that they owed him and that they make amends for the insult to God's honor by paying something over and above the actual debt. Anselm looks upon satisfaction as a gift rather than a punishment. A gift surpassing all that is not God can only be God. God only could make true reparation, and his mercy prompted him to make it through the gift of his Son.[44] God had to become human and had to die volun-tarily to pay off the debt to "himself."[45]

The third understanding is the modernist understanding of Jesus as per-sonal Savior, Lord over an inward sanctum of individualized, psychologi-cal salvation. This understanding is a legacy of the Enlightenment's emphasis on the individual and twentieth-century therapeutic interpre-tations of religion.[46]

Over the past quarter century, male liberationist theologians as well as a growing number of feminist, womanist, Mujerista, Asian, and African women theologians from around the globe have raised three objections to these views. Their caution with regard to the *Christus Victor* understand-ing is that it can lead to an uncritical triumphalism, a literalizing of con-queror imagery that justifies the use of power-over strategies within the church. Their concern is that Christ can be identified with the powerful elites in social, political systems.[47]

Theologians have also been troubled by the view of Jesus as a satisfac-tion for human sin. Anselm himself resisted identifying the Atonement with divine punishment. However, his theory can easily be caricatured, and the implication drawn that a punitive God regards passive suffering as the highest virtue for Jesus and for us.

The trouble with personal, psychological interpretations of the Atonement is that they assume that genuine devotion to Christ is a pri-vatized affair, without implications for political, economic life.

A chorus of contemporary theological voices would warn that "fearing" Christ in traditional terms could come to mean enduring suffering with passivity, choosing a lifestyle that maintains the ecclesial, economic, and political status quo, or singing "I Come to the Garden Alone" as one's only hymn.

We need an understanding of Jesus' death that does justice to his life as a subversive sage. Such an understanding needs to acknowledge three aspects of Jesus' identity and role as teacher of wisdom: Jesus' suffering as a voluntary choice on his part; his identification with the expendables of his day in his teaching and his choice of companions; and the public, political challenge posed by his teachings.[48]

From varying cultural contexts and theological angles, the critics of traditional notions of the Atonement have made constructive proposals that honor these aspects of Jesus' identity. Male liberation theologians have emphasized Jesus' prophetic solidarity with the poor of his day as evidence of God's care for the least of these.[49] Feminist theologians interpret Jesus' death as a choice undertaken in solidarity with the suffering, marginalized people of his society. Mujerista/Latina theologians reject Anselm's theory of sacrificial suffering and turn their gaze to Mary the suffering Mother. She suffers as her children are being slaughtered and as the poor struggle for daily bread. She cares for the least of these.

Womanist theologian Delores Williams rejects the surrogate suffering Christ, refusing to see a redemptive role for the enforced surrogacy that has imprisoned black women for centuries as wet nurses and laborers for privileged women and men. She focuses on Mary, but on her role in the Incarnation rather than her role as sufferer. Mary is a life-giving symbol of the promise of life revealed through her woman's body. Jacqueline Grant views Jesus' death as an act of solidarity with suffering communities and a critique of hierarchy in all its forms. Kelly Brown Douglas views the Crucifixion as Christ's participation in the human condition, especially the condition of suffering.[50]

Asian women's experience of life occurs in contexts of extreme poverty and political oppression. Such suffering results in internalized resentment, and, often, self-loathing and passivity. This phenomenon is called *han* in Korean contexts. Jesus as an obedient sufferer is not empowering to women in this context. Christology here shifts to Jesus as priest of *han*, a suffering servant, but one who heals, comforts, and works against futility and resignation. Mary in her suffering for her crucified son mirrors his sorrow for humanity.[51]

A pastor from Bolivia who now serves a small Hispanic Methodist church in rural south Texas shared this:

> I took a course in popular religion among Catholics in Latin America a few years ago. For Protestant Christians, the empty cross represents the resurrected Christ and his victory. But Catholics are devoted to the crucifix. It represents the suffering of people for three hundred years under the conquistadors and then the social, economic struggle of the people

of Latin America. Christ on the cross represents Christ suffering with the poor. In Mexico, Peru, and Bolivia they have processions where someone depicting Jesus carries his cross through the city and people kneel along the way.

African women theologians operate in contexts characterized by desperate poverty. Their Christology involves honoring Christ for his honoring of women; notions of communal sacrifice to empower the community, rather than individualized female sacrifice in the private realm of the home in service of males. Remembering the ancestors, particularly strong mothers and sisters, is empowering and healing in this context.[52]

None of these constructive interpretations of Jesus' Atonement gives Wisdom a central role. I think there are several reasons for that. In Roman Catholic countries, a traditionally male clergy has not, until recently, encouraged laypeople to study the Bible where they would have encountered Woman Wisdom. The female aspects of God have come out in devotion to Mary the mother of Jesus. Feminist Catholic theologians focus on Mary as a female figure who can be associated with God and Jesus, not Sophia.

In Protestant congregations, people are not familiar with this Wisdom tradition for several reasons. One is because many preachers do not preach on Hebrew Bible wisdom texts. Another is that the female Woman Wisdom (Sophia) in the New Testament has been co-opted by male savior titles. A third factor that discourages Wisdom connections is the sexism inherent in the Hebrew Bible depiction of Wisdom. Said a white female pastor of a large United Methodist Church near Dallas, "I am ambivalent about the biblical wisdom literature because of its sexism. If anyone reads Proverbs 31 at my funeral, I've promised to haunt them!"

It is true that many of the strands of Hebrew Bible wisdom arose from the ranks of educated elites and, therefore, favored their interests. It is also true that Woman Wisdom speaks only to young men and personifies Folly as a Woman. She also utters a number of misogynist proverbs, a feature even more pronounced in The Wisdom of Jesus ben Sira than in Proverbs. For these reasons, some have judged Woman Wisdom to be an agent of those whose gender and income put them in power. They have judged her to be too connected with elitist interests to deserve to inform our understanding of who Jesus is in our preaching and teaching today.

I would argue that Woman Wisdom owes her subversive edge in large part to the outlook of Israel's critical sages through the ages. This debt forms a link between Jesus' challenging wisdom teachings in proverbs and parables and his death. Despite her shortcomings, Woman Wisdom has been a good influence on Jesus. His ministry and teaching is undeniably indebted to her in several respects. She is a strong, outspoken woman who shapes the young by the hearth but also leaves home to influence the public arena.[53] Her emergence as a theological symbol represented an honoring of postexilic Israelite women's roles and wisdom, an emergence that has the potential to honor those of contemporary women.[54]

While some of her sayings attribute poverty to laziness, several also adjure the wise to honor the poor or risk angering their Creator. (Prov 22:22-23; 23:10-11; 31:8, 9). She reminds us to acknowledge that true wisdom comes from God and begins with the fear of God, and that our human wisdom is limited and fallible. She reminds us to respect the mystery and sovereignty of God (Prov 3:5-10). In these insights, she offers the gift of a kernel of subversion, always ready to challenge conventional wisdom when it forgets where it is supposed to have come from and whose interests it is supposed to serve. Jesus the subversive sage is clearly indebted to Woman Wisdom.

When we move beyond the conventional wisdom of Proverbs to the subversive strands of Job and Qohelet, we continue to observe Jesus' debt to Hebrew Bible wisdom themes. He benefits from the book of Job's refusal to accept conventional wisdom's rationale for suffering and from the book of Ecclesiastes' disappointment with conventional wisdom's inadequacy to account for situations of injustice. We also appreciate wisdom's teaching form of choice: the proverbs. Jesus' subversive voice is his own, but his teaching method, in biting aphorisms and prickly parables, imitates a virtuoso teacher of wisdom, Wisdom herself!

Two contemporary feminist theologians do place Wisdom as a central dynamic in their understandings of the identity and role of Jesus.[55] One is Elisabeth Schüssler Fiorenza. She views Wisdom as a symbolic figure who is the theological impulse behind the Jesus movement. She emphasizes the apocalyptic dimension of Wisdom, its concern for social and political renewal. Wisdom was suppressed, she believes, in the early centuries C.E. because the church needed to placate, not alienate, the Roman Empire that had been challenged by Jesus' wisdom sayings and parables.

Elizabeth Johnson affirms Jesus' early identity as the "Sophia of God." This identification arose because it was familiar to the Jewish Scriptures and to secular culture. Sophia was "a female personification of God in outreach to the world."[56] Sophia as co-creator of the world, protector of the poor, and teacher of mystery, is an implicit paradigm for both Paul and

John. Paul calls Jesus the "wisdom of God" (1 Cor 1:24), while John models Jesus and his long discourses on Sophia in Proverbs. For Johnson, Wisdom offers the possibility for affirming the significance of Jesus Christ and for confessing his divinity in non-androcentric terms.[57]

Leo D. Lefebure, in his study of contemporary Wisdom Christology, says it well.

> While acknowledging and rejecting the patriarchal elements in the wisdom tradition and in the relationship of Jesus and Lady Wisdom, a contemporary Wisdom Christology can retrieve the figure of Lady Wisdom as an articulation of our experience of God and of the presence of God in Jesus Christ.[58]

There is a connection between Jesus' suffering and his indebtedness to Wisdom that theologians, for the most part, have not grasped, or at least, have not emphasized. In my view, Wisdom ought to figure more prominently in an understanding of the Atonement, for Jesus was killed because of what he taught, and what he taught was influenced by Hebrew Bible Wisdom.

Jesus owes a deep debt to the subversive strand of Hebrew Bible wisdom in Proverbs, Job, and Qohelet. Wisdom affirms the role of the earth as our sacred teacher. She is adamant about the importance of *shalom* for the whole community. She insists on honoring the mystery of God and the limitations of humankind. She knows they alone can keep human wisdom constructs from hardening into systems that favor powerful elites in each new generation.[59]

New Testament scholar Ben Witherington has referred to the earthly Jesus the sage as Wisdom in Person.[60] His teachings and his affiliations were expressions of the Wisdom of God. He took the risk of empathizing with the suffering, of uttering strategic verbal offensives against the status quo with his subversive aphorisms and parables. He had to know, from the beginning, that his teachings were a risk, that, not surprisingly, culminated in his death.

Says Brazilian Franciscan theologian Leonardo Boff, in his *Jesus Christ Liberator: A Critical Christology for Our Time*:

> [Christ] never simply took the religious norms and social conventions of the day to be his point of departure. He suffered the contradictions, risks, and temptations that the adventure of faith implies. . . . Death was not a catastrophe that came abruptly into the life of Christ. His mes-

sage, life, and death form a radical unity. . . . He [knew] that whoever tries to change the human situation for the better and free people for God, for others, and for themselves must pay with death.[61]

Jesus said it himself, "Whoever tries to save his life will lose it and whoever loses his life will save it" (see Matt 16:25; Mark 8:35; Luke 9:24). For the Christian, the willingness repeatedly to take that risk is the fear of the Lord that is the beginning of wisdom. The task of teaching, preaching, and living out this challenging depiction of Jesus is the high calling of the sage. We now explore insights for teaching and preaching with the fear of the Lord.

CHAPTER THREE

TEACHING AND PREACHING ON BENDED KNEE

The Purpose of Teaching and Preaching with the Fear of the Lord: To Refocus Attention from Human Fears to Divine Faithfulness

The overarching purpose of teaching and preaching the fear of the Lord is to replace anxiety, what we generally mean by fear, with what the Bible means by fear of the Lord (faith). I asked a Unitarian pastor of a large church in Dallas, "What is the purpose of preaching in the Unitarian tradition?"

She replied,

It is summed up in the words of the first Unitarian preacher to come to Dallas in 1899. "The people of Dallas are lost at sea without a chart or a compass for their spiritual nature." I believe that the purpose of preaching in our tradition is to give people a chart and a compass for their spiritual nature.

Preaching provides a compass that points us away from fear of human conditions and harms and toward the fear of the Lord, faith.

Rabbi Shimon in "The Sayings of the Fathers" observes,

Do not make prayer mechanical.
Let it be a cry for grace and mercy,

43

that love replace fear
In the place in which you stand.[1]

In excerpts from her book *Amazing Grace: A Vocabulary of Faith*, contemporary Christian author Kathleen Norris contrasts the fear of Herod with the faith of the season of Epiphany.

> Everything he [Herod] does, he does out of fear. Fear can be a useful defense mechanism, but when a person is always on the defensive, like Herod, it becomes debilitating and self-defeating. To me, Herod symbolizes the terrible destruction that fearful people can leave in their wake if their fear is unacknowledged, if they have power but can only use it in furtive, pathetic, and futile attempts at self-preservation. . . . [2]

> Herod's fear is the epitome of what Jung calls the shadow. Herod demonstrates where such fear can lead when it does not come to light but remains in the dark depths of the unconscious. Ironically, Herod appears in the Christian liturgical year when the gospel is read on the Epiphany, a feast of light.[3]

Norris tells of preaching on Herod on Epiphany Sunday in a small country church in a poor area of the Hawaiian island of Oahu. It was an area of the island tourists were warned to stay away from, an area where those who served the tourist industry as maids and tour bus drivers could afford to live. The church had much to fear: alcoholism, rising property costs, drug addiction, crime. The residents came to church for hope.

In her sermon Norris pointed out that the sages who traveled so far to find Jesus were drawn by him as a sign of hope. This church, Norris told her congregation, is a sign of hope in this community. Its programs, its thrift store, have become important community centers, signs of hope. The church represented, said Norris, "a lessening of fear's shadowy powers, an increase in the available light."[4] She continued to say that that's what Christ's Epiphany celebrates: his light shed abroad into our lives. She ended her sermon by encouraging the congregation to, like the ancient wise men, not return to Herod but find another way. She encouraged them to "leave Herod in his palace, surrounded by flatterers, all alone with his fear."[5]

When we teach and preach on bended knee, we open our hearts and minds to the fear of the Lord. When we open our doors, even just a crack, to allow the fear of the Lord to enter in, we have taken the first step in a lifelong process of exchanging Herod's fear for Mary's faith. Preaching and teaching the fear of the Lord replace fear with faith by teaching the delight the Creator God takes in us as part of the divine creation. They replace fear with faith by magnifying, not trivializing, the mystery of God.

Our instincts are correct. We are right to tremble when a transcendent God draws near, for we do not know what to expect, and we will not remain unchanged. Our self-loathing, self-imposed limitations, prejudices, idolatry, and false sense of security all come into question.

When we teach and preach on bended knee, we place a new frame around the agonizing question "Why?" That frame is the tough, not tidy assurance that a caring God is with us, of all places, in the valley of the shadow of death, illness, and tragedy. The fear of the Lord is the beginning of our being able to say "into thy hands I commit my spirit," even in times of our undeserved and profound suffering. The fear of the Lord is the impulse that shuts our self-righteous lips when we look upon the suffering of others. It impels us, rather, to extend comforting, capable hands.

Teaching and preaching on bended knee does not have as its goal offering all the answers. It derives its authenticity from facing into the reality of what we don't know, offering the good news we do know, that we are accompanied by a God who never abandons us. We both model and teach the abandonment of lesser fears so that we can rest in the fear of the Lord, source of our profoundest security.

Preaching and Teaching on Bended Knee Acknowledges Human Fears

Preaching and teaching on bended knee first faces into the insecurities and fears that accompany us through life.

Said a United Methodist pastor from a large church in a north Texas town,

> We do people a great disservice when we preach to them that everything is going to be all right. It's taking Jesus' "Consider the lilies of the field . . . God will care for you" too literally. The Bible also says the God knows when a sparrow falls. So they do fall. Life sometimes seems like one dead bird after another!

Preaching and teaching the fear of the Lord address not only the fear of tragic events in life but also the deep sense of unworthiness so many people lug around as daily baggage. They address the denial by which we seek to avoid the facts of life: that life is unpredictable and laden with loss and that we are limited in knowledge. This denial often presents itself as a hale and sometimes hostile certainty, the willingness to declare "Thus sayeth the Lord!" in the gray areas of life.

Honoring people's legitimate fears is especially important when teaching and preaching in times of crisis. It is often best in such situations to plan the sermon along inductive lines, moving from the particulars of the congregation's experience to the general truth that comes near or at the end. The speaker begins by, as one journalist put it, "speaking the truth that is in the room."[6]

In a town I lived in years ago a young woman who worked for a local computer company was brutally raped and killed in her hotel room on a business trip to a midwestern town. Her coworkers were shell-shocked. Her boss, a member of the church I was serving, asked if I would come to their workplace and, over the lunch hour, hold a memorial service in a conference room to help her coworkers deal with their grief. As I looked around at about fifty mostly young, drawn faces I realized that my plan to begin by acknowledging their shock and pain was a good one.

Our role as wisdom teachers is to acknowledge the harsh facts of life, while focusing listeners' attention on the faithfulness of our wise, creative, mysterious, transcendent, ever-present, unfailingly gracious God.

Preaching and Teaching on Bended Knee Focuses Our Attention on Our Transcendent, Ever-present God

Said one pastor,

> Life is a tangled web of relationships, pain, despair, goals. It will never make a bit of sense unless it is grounded and rooted in something beyond, above and beneath ourselves—God. God infuses meaning, value, and coherence into everything else that doesn't look like it has those things or any hope of ever having those things.

Homiletician Paul Scott Wilson calls contemporary preachers to recover a sense of the theological purpose of preaching. Preaching is not encouraging people to good attitudes and works; it is inviting listeners into an encounter with God.[7] The first thing many people do in times of crisis and bereavement is to question the motives and character of God. It is a natural response. Joseph Jeter, author of *Crisis Preaching: Personal and Public*, directs us to help prepare people for inevitable times of crisis by identifying the questions people have about God in times of crisis and preaching about them. How could God let this happen? If God loves me, why am I suffering? Harry Emerson Fosdick, an influential preacher of the twentieth century who believed that preaching is "pastoral counseling on a group basis," is reported to have said that, like trees in a storm, we think our concern is the high winds, when in fact, it is our rootage.[8]

The wisdom literature of both Testaments offers a deep rootage in times of temptation, crisis, and sorrow. Proverbs calls us to redirect our attention from our own bad choices to God's choice to offer us the gift of Wisdom who repeatedly calls to us to choose her path. Job directs our attention away from our own anguished questions toward God's unfailing presence. Qohelet shifts our focus from what we cannot change about life to what is precious, if precarious, in each moment. The Gospels depict a God whose Wisdom draws near, even incarnates in Jesus Christ with the message "be not afraid."

Preaching and Teaching Out of Fear of the Lord: Characteristics of Sermons and Lessons

When we allow the fear of the Lord to shape our preaching and teaching, they will have the following characteristics.

1. They honor the complexity and ambiguity in life.

A white pastor of a large suburban United Methodist church near St. Louis told me this:

> Life teaches me all the time that there is an incredible ambiguity about everything. . . . I am often offended by people who lack this appreciation.

Said a pastor serving a large church north of Dallas,

> I think people's capacity to understand and appreciate the gray areas of life is greater than we give them credit for. The number one failure of preaching is that we don't give people enough credit. They want straightforward answers, but not simplistic ones. Jesus' teaching was simple, but not simplistic. Conventional wisdom is simplistic and doesn't take life seriously. It's like the Rio Grande, six inches deep and a mile wide. Vince Lombardi was a great football coach, but you can't live by his principles.

A pastor serving a church in a rural Texas town told me this:

> The average male, especially in the South, wants concrete answers. In the South we want God to be in control. We want to believe that what is meant to be is meant to be. To consider that God may not be in control is a hard pill for people to swallow. I think I'll preach a sermon series called, "Meant to be, my butt!"

Sermons and lessons from bended knee honor the ambiguity of life by going against our expectations. We expect them to offer answers, but they do so only in the context of abiding questions. Many of the sayings in Proverbs embody the ambiguity of life in their identity as partial generalizations, true for some moments, not for others. The reader must work to set them in the complex context of his or her own life and times. Many of Jesus' sayings tie our tidy worldview in knots, complicate our perceptions of what is wise and what is foolish. They force us to struggle with the ambiguity in our certainties as an intermediate step toward an eventual reversal of our values.

A Unitarian pastor of a large church in Dallas told me the following story.

> I chose to come here fifteen years ago, choosing to come here rather than a church in San Francisco that was closer to some of my family. I assumed that God would bless my ministry here. After I had been here nine months, I went in for a routine surgical procedure and they put an injection of anesthetic too close to my spine and I became paralyzed from the waist down. The doctors made no assurances that it would be only temporary. I had crutches and a walker and a parsonage with seventeen steps. My mother and dad came to help me. My mother fell and broke her hip. My dad became mentally confused. They went home to care for themselves in their own home environment. My son came home for the summer and was diagnosed with TB. I found out the man I loved was an alcoholic. He kicked his alcohol habit, but he left me.
>
> The church tried to support me, but they were more suffocating than helpful. They would say things like, "You'll be a better minister for having this experience." Or, "God doesn't give us more than we can handle."
>
> It did make me a better minister. But I realized I had made a deal with God and God had not come through. Now, I never give easy answers, and sometimes I don't give any answers at all.

A concrete way we honor the ambiguity of life is to build pauses and questions into our sermons and lessons. A pastor of a Presbyterian church in Atlanta offered a helpful rationale into the biblical, theological reasons to build pauses and questions into our teaching and preaching. In her words,

> Wisdom is gentle. Wisdom is confident yet modest. When you hear it, you know it. And you suck in your breath. Wisdom is a pause worth stopping time. So I often pause when I preach, to give people time to process God's word.
>
> I often end my sermons with a question. I am more comfortable with ambiguity now. Mystery and ambiguity are important places of human possibility. When I was younger I had to tie everything up, but not anymore. Being in control seemed to be a good way to live, but it can be a fearful way to live. I'm older now and don't need to be in control of the church, of my family. I've learned the value of weakness and failure. Graceful experiences can happen then. Trying to be in control of everything blocks grace. When I am exhausted I sometimes experience God as an accepting, loving presence who knows and values me. This presence is available to me far more often than I take advantage of it.

It is no coincidence that Wisdom literature's genres of choice are proverbs and parables. Proverbs and parables are vivid, concrete genres for teaching and preaching that invite listener participation. They are humble genres that do not aspire to express universal truths, but claim only to offer a modest glimpse of wisdom.

2. They expect the unexpected.

The Unitarian pastor from Dallas I mentioned earlier had a pithy response to my question "What are some lessons you have learned from life?"

She said, "Suit up and show up. And never presume what God will do next or what people will do."

Christian Educator Charles F. Melchert explores the implications of biblical wisdom for educational ministry in his book *Wise Teaching: Biblical Wisdom and Educational Ministry*. He makes this observation with regard to teaching in the spirit of the fear of the Lord.

To learn anything requires a basic attitude of being or becoming open to what is unknown or not known. To learn, one must respect "what is there" even when it is not yet fully comprehended. This entails a certain degree of risk, for what is there is not yet known, even as it claims our attention. If a fundamental attitude of attention and reverence for what is there underlies all educational activity, then both teachers and learners must continually expect the unexpected, or not be too surprised at being surprised. Too often teaching and learning are experienced as thoroughly predictable. This undermines both curiosity and a genuine sense of participating in a journey (a path) where neither the destination nor the route is completely known ahead of time. Thus this journey on a path is a faith journey, for trust and anticipation (hope) are both intrinsically necessary.[9]

3. They acknowledge the limitations of the speaker.

It is sometimes when we are most anxious and insecure about ourselves and our lives that we become desperate for certainty, or even superiority, tempted to speak as if we had the final word on every gray area of life. To teach and preach on bended knee is to speak out of humility, the inward wellspring of our lives.

Said a white male pastor from a suburban United Methodist church near St. Louis,

> I got in touch with my limitations when I did CPE [Clinical Pastoral Education] in seminary. There was an elderly woman in the coronary care unit. I was assigned to follow her post-op progress. I was so unnerved by all the equipment she was hooked up to that I forgot about her for the weekend. I repressed her existence. She died. That blasted my assumption that if you had good intentions you would do the right thing. I have humility now. I am less ready than many other preachers to thunder "Thus Sayeth the Lord!" with regard to hot-button social issues. . . . I have a clergy friend who, when preaching on controversial issues, makes a conscious effort to personalize the issue and approach it confessionally. He tells stories. This is not usually my approach, though I see its merits in that case.

A female Episcopal priest from Los Angeles expressed herself in this way:

> We need to be real with ourselves, to know what's going on in our own spiritual life, because it makes us more compassionate teachers and

preachers if we know our own faults. We need to remember we are not God, that we have nothing to give these people except sharing with them what God has taught us. It's a very mutual thing. They are going to teach us what God has taught them. Some people are all about "I'm in charge. Let me fix your life. I don't have problems like everybody else." We need to be conscious of ourselves and of our office so those two things don't get confused.

Say the sages of *Pirke Avot*,

> Sages do not speak before those
> Whose wisdom and experience exceed their own;
> Do not interrupt another's words;
> Are not in a hurry to reply;
> Ask relevant questions, give relevant answers;
> Speak without deception;
> Feel free to say, "I don't know"
> When the matter is unfamiliar;
> Acknowledge the Truth and admit error.[10]

4. They honor the questions.

A female Episcopal priest serving a church in Georgetown, Washington, D.C., told me this anecdote.

> Right after the impeachment proceedings parents were calling me and asking me to talk to their children about Bill Clinton and Monica Lewinsky because they didn't know how to answer their questions about things. I was walking across the church parking lot on my way to my car, mulling this over when I heard this little boy calling me. "Pastor, Pastor, wait! I have a question, and you're the only who can answer it for me." His mother said, "Danny's been waiting to ask you this question." He looked up at me, an earnest expression on his freckled face, and he said, "Pastor, can you answer this question?"
>
> I said, taking a deep breath, "Well, I don't know Danny. Tell me what it is."
>
> "Do dinosaurs go to heaven?"
>
> And I said, "Oh, absolutely! They're the biggest of God's creatures. Of course they go to heaven!"
>
> I was so relieved! I shared that with the congregation the next Sunday, and I said, "If only all the questions were that easy!"

We don't always get such soft pitches in our encounters with others. More often the questions are "How can we trust the Bible?" "Why did this have to happen to us?" "How could God do this, or allow that?" Our job as teachers and preachers is not to smooth over all the rough edges.

5. They accept and respect diversity of interpretation.

When we look at the sayings of Proverbs, we find diverse views on several important topics: when to keep silent and when to speak, poverty's causes and wise responses to it, and how to handle fools. The sages weren't contradicting one another. They were preserving varying strategies in their proverbs, trusting their students to discern the appropriate applications.[11]

When we widen our canonical lens, diversity is even more apparent. Proverbs promises us if we seek Wisdom we will find guidelines for moderate, faithful, often prosperous living. Ecclesiastes reminds us of the inevitability of death, the unpredictability of life, and the inscrutability of God. The book of Job insists that we are not the center of creation, the designated judges of others' inward characters based on their outward circumstances. We cannot assume God has abandoned us because suffering has embraced us.

And then there is Jesus. Proverbs counsels diplomacy. Jesus embodies a fearless, passionate outspokenness. Ecclesiastes depicts a distant God and a resigned acceptance of life's injustices. Jesus teaches a God who draws near, empowering us to live lives that challenge those injustices.

This respect for diversity in the community's search for wisdom is a model for contemporary preaching on hot-button topics. The preacher is not always the answer giver, but the one who helps clarify the context and points to various options for action, calling upon the congregation to act as sages determining wise courses in their specific situations.

Preaching and Teaching about the Fear of the Lord: Ideas for a Teaching and Preaching Series on the Fear of the Lord

A three-part series could be taught or preached based on the metaphor of the fear of the Lord as a three-stranded braid consisting of awe before the holy, loyalty to God's covenant, and obedience to God's moral guidance.

The series could be entitled "Fear Is Good!" It could deal with the three benefits of the fear of the Lord mentioned in various passages from Proverbs.

Week One: "The Fear of the Lord Is a Fountain of Life." Proverbs 14:27 and 10:27 explicitly mention the metaphor "the fear of the Lord." They can be supported by Prov 1:7; 9:10; and 15:16 that states the fear of the Lord is the beginning of wisdom. Proverbs 15:33 states that "the fear of the Lord is instruction in wisdom." Throughout Proverbs wisdom and life are connected. Wisdom is "a tree of life to those who lay hold of her" (3:18). Wisdom is a gift that is a wellspring of life.

Sometimes life is expressed by the Hebrew word *hayim* and refers to long years, prosperity, and honor, conditions that often result from a life lived in pursuit of wisdom. (See Prov 3:22; 8:35; 10:27; 13:14; 21:21; 22:4.) Sometimes life is described by the word *nephesh*. Then it refers to the living being whose inward life resides in the breath and the blood. (See Prov 13:3; 16:17; 19:16; 29:10.) Proverbs indicate that God will guard this inward life from harm and that often one's outward life will be characterized by long years, prosperity, and honor (16:17).[12]

Week Two: "The Fear of the Lord Is an Antidote to Sin." Several verses in Proverbs mention that the virtue of the fear of the Lord causes a hatred of evil to arise in the one who pursues it. One turns from evil (3:7); one hates evil (8:13); one avoids evil (16:6).

Week Three: "The Fear of the Lord Banishes Other Fears." A recurring theme in Proverbs is that the fear of the Lord is our only true security. It is our strong confidence (14:26), "filled with it one rests secure and suffers no harm" (19:23). When we trust in the Lord we are secure (29:25).

In preaching such a series, one's insights could be enriched by the occurrences of the theme of the fear of the Lord in Psalms and Deuteronomy. In Deuteronomy it has much to do with covenant loyalty, and in the Psalms the connection between fearing God and praising God is strong. This suggests themes of active, ongoing commitment and radical gratitude. In Job and Qohelet, recognizing our human limitations is front and center.

We could do a series entitled "The Gifts of Fear."

- "A Life of Joy." Taking God seriously, but not ourselves.
- "A Life of Openness to Others' Views and New Experiences." We accept our own limitations with a sense of relief, not embarrassment or frustration.
- "A Life of Trust." We trust God to guide our future.

Again, themes and passages from other areas of Scripture could be called on to substantiate and illustrate these approaches.

When we turn to look at Scripture's account of Jesus' life and teachings, a number of themes present themselves.

I can envision a series entitled "The Great Exchange" that deals with various situations in Scripture in which people were afraid but received Jesus' response, "Do not be afraid."

In each instance, someone was being invited to exchange fear for faith: These fears include fear in the face of chronic illness as in the woman with the hemorrhage (Mark 5:25-34); fear at the prospect of being left alone (John 14:26-27); fear in the face of death, as in the case of Jairus (Luke 8:40-42); fear at the prospect of believing and spreading the news that is way too good to be true (Mark 16:8).

In several passages people cower at the prospects of a good but uncomfortably close manifestation of divine power. These include the angelic messages to Mary (Luke 1:29) and the shepherds (Luke 2:8-14), the miraculous harvest of fish (Luke 5:1-11), the Transfiguration (Matt 17:1-8; Luke 9:28-36), the exorcism of the Gerasene demoniac (Matt 8:28-34; Luke 8:32-39), Jesus' walking on the water in the midst of a storm (Matt 14:22-33), and the indications of Jesus' resurrection (Matt 28:1-10; Mark 16:1-8). All these passages speak of a divine power that draws near and addresses our very real fears and empowers us to exchange them for faith. They form the gospel context for the fears we live with in daily life.

Meditations on the Fear of the Lord

"Fear Is Good!"[13]

Scriptures: Proverbs 3:5-8; Matthew 26:36-46; Philippians 4:4-9

My friend Gary gave me permission to tell you this story. More than that, he said he would be honored if I did so. Gary is a computer analyst in his mid-forties, and he has been married and divorced twice, the most recent divorce occurring about three years ago. For about a year he has been dating a wonderful woman at our church named Gina, who is also divorced with an adorable seven-year-old daughter. Gary and Gina came to me in February and asked if I would marry them at the end of April. Our counseling and wedding planning were going along fine until, along about mid-March, Gary began to develop a case of very cold feet. When he shared this with Gina, she suggested he get away for a day to clear his head. Gary started driving with no particular destination. He ended up at a beautiful site near Lake Texoma, Texas.

He got out of his car and began to walk, to soothe his jangled nerves, to direct his thoughts to God. He came to a bench that looks out over the lake. He sat down and tried to breathe more deeply, to unravel the knots in his stomach.

As he stared out at the lake, some things suddenly became clear, as if he were looking into a soul-mirror. He realized that there were three knots in his stomach and each had a name. One of the knots was his fear was that he would just keep repeating the same relationship patterns. The second knot in his stomach was his fear of the challenge of blending two families. And the third knot in his stomach was maybe the hardest, knot-tiest fear of all: it was the fear that maybe he was just not worthy of another person's love and was destined to have to face his future alone.

Maybe the thing to do when we are starting out on a new venture or stuck in an old rut is to sit by ourselves somewhere and name the knots in our stomachs. What are your fears? It's a good thing to know their names, because what we fear controls our lives.

The book of Proverbs tells us that the fear of the Lord ought to control our lives.

"The fear of the LORD is the beginning of knowledge" (Prov 1:7).

Notice there are lots of fears the verse doesn't mention.

It doesn't assert that

- the fear of spiders is the beginning of wisdom.
- the fear of heights is the beginning of wisdom.
- the fear of everyone finding out what you are really like is the beginning of wisdom.
- the fear of change is the beginning of wisdom.
- the fear of the test results is the beginning of wisdom.
- the fear of getting old is the beginning of wisdom.

- the fear of failure is the beginning of wisdom.
- the fear of what other people will think is the beginning of wisdom.

Every other fear we fight to get rid of. The fear of the Lord we are to cultivate!

Why? Because "the fear of the LORD delights the heart, and gives gladness and joy" (Sir 1:12). "In the fear of the LORD one has strong confidence, and one's children will have a refuge" (Prov 14:26). "The fear of the LORD is a fountain of life, so that one may avoid the snares of death" (Prov 14:27). "The fear of others lays a snare, but one who trusts in the LORD rests secure" (Prov 29:25).

What is this strange fear that is a fountain of life, a refuge, a source of joy and security, and the beginning of wisdom?

Faithfulness to God

The fear of the Lord is first and foremost, faithfulness to God, loyalty to God. This is the notion of covenant loyalty from Deuteronomy. "You shall fear the LORD your God; him alone you shall worship; to him you shall hold fast, and by his name you shall swear" (10:20). When our heads swirl with human fears, we are allowing an idol to rule our lives. Fears rule our lives, raise our blood pressure, ruin our love lives, sour our moods. They are idols, something other than God we allow to control our lives. Throughout the biblical witness, injunctions to fear God become most fervent in times when communities are threatened by chaos and violence. It is then that they need the assurance that God's promises hold steady in shifting times.

Trembling before God

We come before our mysterious and transcendent God, not with dread of punishment, but with awe. So Isaiah trembled before the vision of God in the temple, a completely appropriate response when a human encounters the majesty, the otherness, of the divine. "Woe is me! . . . for I am a man of unclean lips . . . yet my eyes have seen the King, the LORD of hosts!" (Isa 6:5). I like the way one biblical scholar puts it. The fear of the Lord means a certain wariness appropriate to being confronted by a good but mysterious, uncontrollable Presence. We ought to be wary, because while God intends good for us, we do not know what form that good will take. We fear it will change us. Bringing hope where there is no reason for hope; light where we see only shadows.

Taking Directions from God

In Proverbs, the fear of the Lord means the realization that God is where we get directions for daily living. No one has ever accused me of having a great sense of direction. For someone who travels as much as I do, that can be a problem. That's why I was so excited when they started offering the option of satellite navigation systems in Hertz rental cars. You punch in where you are and where you want to go and this competent female voice directs you all over town: "Approaching highway exit in 1.4 miles." And then when you, for whatever reason, don't do what she said to, she says, with just a hint of annoyance in her voice, "Please proceed to the highlighted route." They call the navigation system "NeverLost." The fear of the Lord promises guidance in navigating the confusing variety of paths before us. Listening to it, we are guided to choose the way that leads to light and to life.

What is the fear of the Lord? It consists of faithfulness to God amid all the competing claims on our loyalty, awe in the presence of God who is good but mysterious and beyond our control, and directions for daily living for those who are attentive.

When, by faith, we allow human fears to give way to the fear of the Lord, I call that the "fear exchange." We get better at it by practicing. All three of our Scripture passages describe people practicing the fear exchange.

Proverbs 3:5-8

Read between the lines of the confident words of Prov 3:5-8. The sage is praying these words in solitude. He's worried about something. His path is taking a crooked bend. He is afraid he hasn't handled things on his own very well. He feels physically tired and run down.

> Trust in the LORD with all your heart, and do not rely on your own insight. [I've been relying on my own insight and I am standing on shaky ground.] In all your ways acknowledge [God], and [God] will make straight your paths. [I have not thought of God in weeks and my path is crooked and choked with thorns.] . . . Fear the LORD and turn

away from evil. [I've been turning toward evil.] It will be a healing for your flesh and a refreshment for your body. [My body is sick and tired and so is my spirit.] (Prov 3:5-8)

This is my friend Nancy's favorite passage of scripture. She sits in her chemo chair every three weeks with it open in her lap, her eyes closed, practicing the fear exchange.

We behold the fear exchange at work in Jesus' own approach to God in the face of suffering in the garden of Gethsemane.

By Jesus' resurrected power and presence, we can employ the fear exchange to do what Paul commends to us in Phil 4:4-7, to be filled with faith and peace rather than frantic panic.

Several years ago a friend of mine was just starting out in her ministry. Tina had been through seminary and done well. She was young, still in her twenties, but she felt confident in her counseling and administrative skills. The preaching was what had her scared: Getting up in front of people and having the high task of speaking on behalf of God to people twice her age. She was shaking in her shoes, so anxious that she could hardly function. Berating herself about her lack of faith didn't help matters. She had read about visualizing in prayer somewhere and so she got the idea to pray each day, visualizing herself standing up to preach, and Jesus standing right beside her with his hand on her shoulder. Day after day, week after week, she prayed and pictured this prayer. She would get up in front of everyone and look out at them, the elderly ladies who sat in the middle aisle halfway back, their stiff joints aching, but their backs straight, their smiles expectant; the teenagers on the second row, their arms crossed over their chests, as if to say, "I dare you to say something remotely related to my life!" And there in the front middle section was what she thought of as the "Crayola section." Here sat parents with their elementary-school–age children. The children had their bulletins open, crayons out, drawing to pass the tedious time. My friend would visualize her mental picture, take a deep breath and begin.

Things didn't immediately become easy, but gradually they got better. She still felt the tremor of nerves, but her confidence was growing and her anxiety no longer ruined her whole week.

In her church there was a girl about seven years old named Emily who sat with her mother in the Crayola section. Emily was too shy to talk to the preacher, but she would smile at her sometimes on her way out. One week she came up with her mother and tugged gently on Tina's sleeve. "Emily wants to show you something," said her mother. Tina got down on her knees. "Look, Pastor Tina, there's you! Emily said, pointing at her bulletin drawing. "And guess who that is?"

We left poor Gary sitting on a park bench, his stomach in three knots of fear:

1) That he would repeat his mistakes; 2) That the struggle to blend a new family would be too much for him; 3) That maybe he wasn't even worthy of someone else's love.

Gary says that as he sat there meditating, he felt rather than heard the words, "Let them go. You don't need them anymore. Let them go."

He opened his eyes, and as he gazed out at the calm waters, three geese toddled up to him, prodding his legs with their beaks. Then, seeing that he had no bread for them, one after the other, they took flight out over the water and into the distance. He sat and stared at them until they were specks on the horizon.

And then he got up and walked to his car filled with an entirely different kind of fear.

He knew they'd circle back, time and again, honking loudly, wings flapping. But he also knew that he would be more ready for them the next time.

CHAPTER FOUR

THE SECOND PILLAR OF WISDOM: THE LISTENING HEART

"Give your servant therefore an understanding mind to govern your people, able to discern between good and evil." (1 Kgs 3:9)

Solomon's "Right Answer"!

In the story of young King Solomon's dream at Gibeon, God invites him to make a request: "Ask what I should give you." Solomon prefaces his response by expressing gratitude to God for bringing him to the throne. At the same time, he expresses a sense of inadequacy at the prospect of being king over Israel. Suspecting that he would be called upon to offer wisdom in all kinds of complex, conflictual situations, the green young king gives a good answer to God's request: "Ask what I should give you" (3:5). "Give your servant . . . an understanding mind [lev shomea'] . . . able to discern between good and evil" (1 Kgs 3:9). Given the fact that the Hebrew mind did not place mind and heart in separate, hermetically sealed compartments, this phrase could also be rendered "listening heart."[1]

The word *heart (lev)* in Proverbs has many connotations. It indicates the seat of understanding and therefore the faculty whereby wisdom was apprehended. The heart is referred to as the seat of reflection in several proverbs (6:18; 15:28; 16:9; 19:21; 24:2) and is often translated in the

61

NRSV as "mind." Elsewhere, the heart is equated with memory (6:21; 7:3) and with wisdom (14:33; 18:15).

The heart is also regarded as the seat of emotions: joy (15:30), sorrow (14:10, 13), pride (16:5; 18:12; 21:4), obstinacy (17:20; 28:14), or evil (26:23). The heart is at times viewed as the seat of character, either bad or good (11:20; 12:8). The heart refers to the disposition (25:20) and the inner person (3:5).[2]

Solomon has asked for the quality that will enable him to be a good ruler, a "hearing mind" (*lev shomea'*) that "will enable him to 'judge' (*shaphat*) the people and to discern (*havin*) the difference between good and evil" (v. 9a). God, in granting the request, refers to it as a request for "discernment to hear justice" (*havin lishmoa' mishpat*, v. 11b), and gives Solomon a "wise and discerning mind" (*lev hakam wenavon*, v. 12).[3]

The idiom "to hear justice," indicates the hearing of testimony from parties in a dispute. It indicates an active attentiveness to the witness of others. "This ability actively to engage with the reality of what people say is illustrated by the story of Solomon's justice in the case of the two prostitutes (1 Kgs 3:16-28). The problem depends upon the fact that there were no witnesses (v. 18b), and both stories are equally plausible (vv. 22-23). . . . Solomon resolves the problem with a proposal which is successful precisely because it enables an expression of the character of the women which could not be discerned from the basic testimonies he had already been given. Solomon is able to make the women reveal what one could not, and the other would not, reveal."[4]

Solomon's "listening heart" or "understanding [hearing] mind" involves attending to God as well as to people. The Hebrew verb for "hear" (*shama*) is a prime word for depicting responsive obedience to God. Wisdom scholar R. W. L. Moberly points out that listening to or hearing God is not a different activity from attending to the people in dispute. Rather, if we are fully to attend to people we must first attend to the will of God as expressed in the judgments (*mishpatim*) of torah.[5]

This attentiveness, to both God and other people, is an active rather than a passive pursuit. Says Hebrew Bible scholar Gerhard von Rad,

> A wise and understanding mind, a "listening" mind—that was the content of Solomon's royal request (1 Kings 3:9). What he, the paradigm of the wise man, wished for himself was . . . an "understanding" reason, a feeling for the truth which emanates from the world and addresses man. He was totally receptive to that truth, but this was not passivity, but an

intense activity, the object of which was response, prudent articulation.[6]

To cultivate a listening heart is to commit to a lifetime of attentiveness to all of life, one's own experiences, those of others, and the created order. For they are all arenas of God's revelation.

One of the pastors I interviewed, a Lutheran pastor of a large church on the outskirts of San Diego, told me that he begins his staff meeting every week with Solomon's prayer for wisdom. "That way, we are more likely to have our priorities in line with God's priorities as we work on behalf of God's people."

"For lack of attention," writes the English mystic Evelyn Underhill, "a thousand forms of loveliness elude us every day."[7]

Prominent in the opening chapters of Proverbs are the calls to the disciple of wisdom for openness and attention: "Hear . . . turn . . . receive . . . be attentive . . . cry out for insight . . . seek . . . incline your ear . . . keep your heart with vigilance . . . let not your heart turn aside . . . listen!" So valuable is the quality of attention that it is thought of as a gift from the Creator's hand.

> The hearing ear and the seeing eye—
>   the LORD has made them both. (20:12)

Only from the attentive can enduring words be expected:

> A good listener will testify successfully. (21:28b)

Good deeds are the consequence of attention:

> The discerning person looks to wisdom, but the eyes of a fool to the ends of the earth. (17:24)

Nothing in God's creation is too small or obscure to warrant profound attention. The sage's attentiveness brings with it a profound sense of wonder.

> Three things are too wonderful for me;
>   four I do not understand:
> the way of an eagle in the sky,
>   the way of a snake on a rock,
> the way of a ship on the high seas,
>   and the way of a man with a girl. (30:18-19)

In Proverbs, the sage enters the world of the ant, the badger, the locust, and the lizard, attentive to the lessons they may hold (30:24-28).[8] Macrina Wiederkehr is a Catholic nun, a member of St. Scholastica Monastery in Fort Smith, Arkansas. In her book, *A Tree Full of Angels: Seeing the Holy in the Ordinary*, she uses the metaphor of harvesting crumbs for our spiritual lives. It expresses the habit of looking for the sacred in the ordinary that underlies teaching and preaching with a listening heart.

> There is a yearning deep in the human heart—so deep it is an ache within. An ache for God! . . . The ache in our heart needs to be fed. . . . Crumbs are those small things that the world would toss aside, seeing little value in them. However, to the one who lives under the eye of God they are far from valueless. . . . Everything . . . in life can be nourishing. . . . Everything can bless us, but we've got to be there for the blessing to occur. Being present with quality is a decision we are invited to make each day. . . . [9]

> Due to the reality of our terribly distracted, cluttered, and noisy existence, the decision for real presence is not easy. If we can make this decision and live it, it will be a kind of salvation for us. It can save us from many kinds of death: the death of apathy . . . selfishness . . . meaninglessness. There is nothing so healing in all the world as real presence. Our real presence can feed the ache for God in others.[10]

Macrina Wiederkehr invites her readers to see the holy in the ordinary, to harvest angels out of the crumbs. She believes we live in a world of theophanies.

> Holiness comes wrapped in the ordinary. There are burning bushes all around you. Every tree is full of angels. Hidden beauty is waiting in every crumb. Life wants to lead you from crumbs to angels, but this can happen only if you are willing to unwrap the ordinary by staying with it long enough to harvest its treasure.[11]

She says that it's time to harvest

- a spider web, wearing the morning's dew
- a mistake, reflected upon and learned from
- reconciliation after a quarrel
- an autumn tree letting go of her leaves
- a spring tree putting leaves on again
- a wound, embraced and understood.[12]

Frank Davis, a spiritual elder from the Pawnee tribe tells a story about his mother's expression of wisdom to him.

> My mother was a good woman. I thought she was the wisest person in the whole world. So one day—when I was just a little feller, maybe six or seven—I asked her how I could become wise like her. She just laughed and laughed and said I was awfully young to be asking such questions. But, she said, since I asked, she would tell me. "Life is like a path," she said, smiling down at me, "and we all have to walk the path. . . . As we walk down that path we'll find experiences like little scraps of paper in front of us along the way. We must pick up those pieces of scrap paper and put them in our pockets. Every single scrap of paper we come to should be put into that pocket. Then, one day, we will have enough scraps of papers to put together and see what they say. Maybe we'll have enough to make some sense. . . . Take them to heart and then put them back in your pocket and go on, because there will be more pieces to pick up. Keep walking and every now and then take them out and make some sense of them. That's how we become wise, or at least wiser than we were."[13]

The Listening Heart and the Fear of the Lord

The virtue of the listening heart flows from the chief wisdom virtue, the fear of the Lord. Fear of the Lord expresses itself as a reverent, humble attentiveness to all of life as the arena of God's revelation. If we fear the Lord, we will live life with a listening heart. Wisdom scholar Kathleen Farmer points out that "to be 'wise,' as the authors of Proverbs, Ecclesiastes, and Job use the term, means both to reflect on one's own observations and to pay attention to the observations of others, to sift through and weigh one's own experiences over against the testimonies of others."[14]

A Baptist pastor in his midforties from Maryland shared this experience with me in our interview,

> When I went through my divorce I thought that was the end of the world. I thought God was done with me. I was done professionally. I was done morally and relationshipwise. The congregation stepped in. They cared about me, and also, they were thinking of self-protection, which I understand and respect. They didn't want their pastor to do something in his time of need that would damage the church. They put together a

group of six people called the Pastor's Ministry Commission. We would meet every few weeks and they would just listen to me and ask, "What's going on?" And I would tell them. And they would say, "Watch this. It sounds like you're getting some bitterness here. I don't think that's where you want to go." I needed somebody to walk this part of the journey with me and they volunteered for the job and were sensitive and trustworthy listeners.

The moral evaluations of Israel's sages was based on their keen observation of human behavior in society and its consequences, with an occasional appeal to social life in the animal world—all the way from ants to lions.[15] Paying attention is key. That means listening to God. That also means listening to our own experience, both its contributions and its limitations. It also means listening to the experiences of others, especially when they are different from our own or have led another person to conclusions that are diametrically opposed to those we cherish.

"Be Attentive!" The Listening Heart in Proverbs

Repeatedly throughout Proverbs, the young are enjoined to listen and hear the wisdom that is continually being offered to them by both mother and father (1:5, 8).[16]

The parental teachings are compared to a "fair garland for your head, and pendants for your neck" (1:9). The wise youth will

> bind them upon [his] heart always; tie them around [his] neck. When [he walks], they will lead [him]; when [he lies] down, they will watch over [him]; and when [he awakes], they will talk with [him]. For the commandment is a lamp and the teaching a light, and the reproofs of discipline are the way of life. (6:21-23)

> Keep my teachings as the apple of your eye; bind them on your fingers, write them on the tablet of your heart. Say to wisdom, "You are my sister," and call insight your intimate friend. (7:2b-4)

If one does not listen to Wisdom, it is not because she has been inaccessible! The eloquent Wisdom discourses in 1:20-33 and in chapter 8 speak of Wisdom as here and now and available. We have a choice, of course. One can refuse to listen to Wisdom and come to ruin (5:13; 8:35-36). One can actively go against Wisdom's teachings, listen to the wrong lips, and become a malicious fool (Prov 7:24-27; 17:4). A better alternative is to hear Wisdom, live by her wisdom, and find life (1:33; 3:13-18).

Wise living is a process of noticing things, very small things, that add up to bigger conclusions.

General Observations[17]

When pride comes, then comes disgrace. (11:2a)

Where there is no guidance, a nation falls. (11:14a)

The timid become destitute, but the aggressive gain riches. (11:16b)

Those who are kind reward themselves, but the cruel do themselves harm. (11:17)

Some give freely, yet grow all the richer; others withhold what is due, and only suffer want. (11:24).

Observations on the Inward Life[18]

Anxiety weighs down the human heart, but a good word cheers it up. (12:25)

Hope deferred makes the heart sick, but a desire fulfilled is a tree of life. (13:12)

The heart knows its own bitterness, and no stranger shares its joy. (14:10)

Like a city breached, without walls, is one who lacks self-control. (25:28)

Like a dog that returns to its vomit is a fool who reverts to his folly. (26:11)

Observations on Human Relationships[19]

A soft answer turns away wrath, but a harsh word stirs up anger. (15:1)

One who forgives an affront fosters friendship, but one who dwells on disputes will alienate a friend. (17:9)

Let your foot be seldom in your neighbor's house, otherwise the neighbor will become weary of you and hate you. (25:17)

Like somebody who takes a passing dog by the ears is one who meddles in the quarrel of another. (26:17)

Better is open rebuke than hidden love. (27:5)

Observations about Wealth and Poverty[20]

A slack hand causes poverty, but the hand of the diligent makes rich. (10:4)

The poor are disliked even by their neighbors, but the rich have many friends. (14:20; see also 19:4, 7)

Those who oppress the poor insult their Maker, but those who are kind to the needy honor him. (14:31)

Do not rob the poor because they are poor, or crush the afflicted at the gate; for the LORD pleads their cause and despoils of life those who despoil them. (22:22-23)

A ruler who oppresses the poor is a beating rain that leaves no food. (28:3)

Observations about Relating to Rulers

When you sit down to eat with a ruler, observe carefully what is before you, and put a knife to your throat if you have a big appetite. (23:1-2)

Do not desire the ruler's delicacies, for they are deceptive food. (23:3)

Do not put yourself forward in the king's presence or stand in the place of the great; for it is better to be told, "Come up here," than to be put lower in the presence of a noble. (25:6-7)

The Listening Heart in Job

Proverbs' wisdom did acknowledge the limitation of human knowledge and the mystery of God, but these truths were not its major themes. To bring them to the forefront was the task of the sages responsible for the books of Job and Ecclesiastes.[21] They cultivated the wisdom virtue of the listening heart by acknowledging the limits of human wisdom and the gracious freedom of God. They realized that when we think we have everything figured out, we stop listening to any voice but our own. It may take an unexpected and undeserved misfortune to unstop our ears so we can hear the sounds of others' suffering. If we can meet such occasions with a listening heart, we just might meet God. Says Hebrew Bible Wisdom scholar John Collins, "No degree of mastery of the rules and maxims of wisdom can confer absolute certainty. Life retains a mysterious and incalculable element, and it is precisely in this incalculable area that Yahweh is encountered."[22]

Job and Ecclesiastes train their listening hearts on precisely those situations that did not fit traditional wisdom's rather optimistic mold. Job's attentiveness to his own inward responses to his sufferings led him to contest the traditional notion that suffering is a result of inward sin. His friends, by contrast, are so focused on defending that notion that they are stubbornly oblivious to the anguish of the friend before them on the ash heap.

What happens when we listen to what Collins has baptized the "incalculable area" of life? What happens when we alert ourselves to the situations in life that we cannot explain, to the people whose experience seems to defy our least-questioned assumptions and our most-cherished convictions? We become sensitive to the pain of another. We acknowledge the limitations of our own experience, that we have assumed is objective and universal. Our attentiveness calls us out of our cocoons into community. It dares us to challenge conventional wisdom and to speak out for justice for those people and situations it has discounted.

The pastors I interviewed agreed on the importance of facing into the sufferings and struggles of life rather than numbing ourselves to them. One pastor, a United Methodist in his early fifties, put it especially well,

> Life is the anvil on which we hammer out our new growth. We can choose to learn something and grow, or we can choose not to. I have seen people die young but take years to bury! To learn and to grow we must not ignore our own or others' pain. Experience continually moves us out of each stage and each comfort zone into the next.

The more experiences we open ourselves to, the more intensely we struggle. Job's friends did not want to open themselves to the emotional impact of his situation. They didn't want to have to struggle along with him. They didn't want to factor his pain into their theology, didn't want to widen their life-lens to take it in.

The sages responsible for the book of Job are attentive not only to human suffering but also to the suffering of earth. Job 12 as well as Job 38–41 testify to their attentiveness to nature and earth. Job 12 depicts Job accusing God of having treated the earth as capriciously as he has treated Job. We can see from Job 12 that Job's sufferings have plunged him into chaos. From his dunghill he is convinced that he understands earth and can even speak for her. In his view, his undeserved suffering is an example of God's lack of justice and predictability in relating both to him and to earth. He regards earth and her inhabitants as expert witnesses to divine injustice. So he seeks to speak on earth's behalf as well as his own. He will not rest until he can confront the God who exercises such harsh power to destroy the innocent and sustain the wicked.

Job 12 provides a compelling argument for valuing the earth and acknowledging our need of the earth and speaking and acting against her prevailing abuse and devaluation. Job has come to recognize the sufferings of earth through his own torment and suffering. She has become his teacher. Job as a wise man looks to the created world for wisdom and focuses on how he sees the transcendent interfering deity treating the earth.

However, the text does not sustain an image of God as a capricious intervening force. In 38–42, God speaks out of the whirlwind of Job's misunderstanding of what he has seen and heard. A shift occurs in the conclusions Job draws from his listening heart. He shifts from resentment to reverent obedience to a Creator God whose creation is full of forceful beauty and whose ways exceed our human knowledge.

When God speaks from the whirlwind (Job 38–42) we hear and see a creative and participant artist and artisan with an interconnected world whose vision embraces earth's inhabitants from the least to the greatest. Job, who relied on what he heard and listened to "with his ears," can now look at earth and say to God "my eye sees you."[23]

Not only does Job's listening heart sensitize him to the sufferings of earth, it also opens his eyes to the sufferings of the earth's poor. Job undergoes a second change of perspective. The Job described in the prologue was "blameless and upright" (1:1), a patrician figure, comfortable and safe in the confines of his estate, offering charity and prayers for the poor. His experience of suffering leaves him sick, naked, and vulnerable, feeling a kinship with those from whom he had formerly been able to distance himself. Liberation theologian Gustavo Gutierrez calls Job 24:1-12 "the most radical and cruel description of the wretchedness of the poor found in the Bible." Job portrays the condition of the very poor, lacking the necessities of physical life, exploited by their employers and subjected to capricious, repeated violence. Job cries out on their behalf. Gutierrez observes that here the language of Job more closely resembles the language of the prophets than any of the other Hebrew Bible wisdom writings.[24]

There is no clearer testimony to the power of poetic attentiveness than Job 38–41. The poet of Job has watched the dawn with wonder. He has noted how, when daylight grew from the east, lines and forms stood out in the distance, like clay responds to a seal (38:12-14). Light and dark, snow, hail, rain, lightning, ice, and constellations; he considers them all with deep reverence (38:16-38). He reflects on the wonders of animal life: the birth of the young, the free running of the wild ass, the strength of the wild ox, the migrations of the birds. To all these the poet-sage gives his attention. In return, they speak to him of the mystery of creation and the Creator. In them, his listening heart meets that mystery.[25]

Job, attentive to God's voice, learns of the two primordial beasts, Behemoth (40:15-24) and Leviathan (41). The existence and the subduing of these formidable creatures make clear to Job that God has concerns and struggles beyond his own and that God is the Lord of the mysterious order of a complex creation. There is evil and chaos in the complex web of creation: God's world. We can continue to dream our dreams of divine retribution or we can accept life as it is, with a measure of apparent randomness and very real injustice, and be about the work of noticing and comforting the sufferings of others.[26]

Both the blessings and the risks of attentiveness glimmer through these chapters of Job. For attentiveness is a risk. Attentiveness promises that, as we continually exercise it, we will continually encounter God—sometimes where we could never have imagined we would encounter God. And the God we encounter may have little resemblance to the God we have expected. In the sufferings of the poor, with whom we are compelled by our own sufferings to identify more fully, in the artistry of a sunrise, in a thousand other observations, we discover both an anguish and a glory we have, until now, allowed to escape our notice.

The Listening Heart in Qohelet

No one embodies the pleasure and the pain of attentiveness more poignantly than Qohelet, the author of Ecclesiastes. This name probably comes from the Hebrew verb *qahal*, which means "to gather." Qohelet's wisdom reflects his attentiveness to his particular time and place. It reflects the Persian period when utopian dreams had gone by the wayside and the prospects for freedom from social and political domination seemed remote. The challenge is to live faithfully in the present while maintaining a degree of openness to the future. This challenge is faced in a pointed way by people in communities struggling for dignity and justice. Oppressive systems then and now deny the dignity of life. Those who struggle can be paralyzed by the frustrating realities of daily life. Qohelet's message of reverence for the present and reorientation of life to God's time is a needed antidote.[27] In his own time, apocalyptic speculation was one antidote to hopelessness. But Qohelet eschews that avenue to hope, observing that "there is nothing new under the sun" (1:9). His goal is to realistically strive to deal with an extended present in which all is not as he thinks it should be. He does so by the scrupulous observation of life around him.

In his pursuit of wisdom, Qohelet experiments with self-indulgence in a much more attentive way than most of us do! Along the way, he notices that drinking, building elaborately landscaped custom homes, having many possessions (including people as well as gold bullion), and having sex with multiple partners does not pave a path to happiness (2:1-11).

He notices that everyone dies, the wise as well as the fool. He notices that one's hard-earned wealth, at one's death, sometimes goes to slacker relatives who did nothing to assist in its accumulation (2:21-23). He notices that, contrary to prevailing wisdom, wise actions do not always lead to good fortune, nor do evil ones necessarily lead to misfortune (8:14). He observes slaves riding on horseback and princes walking on foot (10:7).

He notices the cyclical quality of nature. "The sun rises and the sun goes down, and hurries to the place where it rises. The wind blows to the south, and goes around to the north; round and round goes the wind, and on its circuits the wind returns. All streams run to the sea, but the sea is not full" (1:5-7).

He notices that each stage of life has its joys and its sorrows, and that everything has its time (3:1-8). He notices that the rich oppress the poor. Coming from a middle-class, privileged social position, he did not feel motivated to do anything about it, but he had the good grace to shed some tears over it (4:1-3). He notices that envy motivates many human actions (4:4) and that wealth creates not contentment but a craving for more wealth (5:10). He observes that, in human relationships as well as nature, "a threefold cord is not quickly broken" (4:12).

He discerns the unpredictable quality of life, that "the race is not to the swift, nor the battle to the strong, nor bread to the wise, nor riches to the intelligent, nor favor to the skillful; but time and chance happen to them all" (9:11).

He faces the reality that "like fish taken in a cruel net, and like birds caught in a snare, so mortals are snared at a time of calamity, when it suddenly falls upon them" (9:12*b*).

He acknowledges that while a wise person can have a good influence (9:13-17), "one bungler destroys much good" (9:18*b*).

He notices that "dead flies make the perfumer's ointment give off a foul odor" and compares this to "a little folly outweighing wisdom and honor" (10:1).

He knows from observation and experience that "calmness will undo great offenses" (10:4*b*). He realizes that manual labor has its risks. Digging a pit puts one in danger of falling into it (10:8*a*). Breaking through a wall puts one at risk of being bitten by a hidden snake (10:8*b*). Blunt iron needs to be sharpened or it will take more strength to wield it (10:10). "When clouds are full, they empty rain on the earth," and "whether a tree falls to the south or to the north, in the place where the tree falls, there it will lie" (11:3). Just observing the wind and clouds is not the same as sowing and reaping (11:4).

He is alert to the dimmed vision, the trembling limbs, the bent back, the worn teeth, the deafness, the weakening sexual powers, and the white hair of the elderly (12:1-8).

He notices that "wisdom excels folly as light excels darkness" (2:13). He experiences the pleasures of toil, eating and drinking, and human relationships, and he deduces that these are gifts from God (2:24; 5:18-20; 7:14; 8:15; 9:7-10). He notices that, while we yearn to know God, God remains hidden, as do the mysteries of what lies beyond this life (3:9-11; 5:2*b*; 8:16, 17).

If Qohelet had only noticed the negatives in life we could dismiss him as a pessimist. But he was an equal opportunity listener—he gave the upside of life as much of a chance as he did the down. He believed that wisdom was a guide to life (2:14), that toil held inherent enjoyment

(2:22), and that wisdom was better than might (9:16). Yet each of his positive affirmations is paired with its pessimistic twin. Wisdom is a guide to life, but the wise die just like fools (2:14). Toil holds enjoyment but it is ultimately futile and injustice is rampant (8:14). Wisdom is better than might, yet the poor man's wisdom is never heeded (9:16).

Qohelet's trust in conventional notions of retribution had been undermined by his close observation of life and all the situations that give a lie to it. What stands out about his book for me is not its pessimism but its realistic grasp of the joy that can be ours in the midst of an often unjust and unpredictable world. I respect him for the way his wisdom honors the complexity of life. It promises no fairy-tale endings, no warm and fuzzy deity, no permanent bliss. God is distant, and yet gift-giving. Wisdom cannot free us from death, and yet is worth pursuing. Pleasure is fragile and fleeting, yet real and gratifying. Joy is only in the present but is thereby doubly precious.[28]

A contemporary pastor's experience echoes Qohelet's. Trying to balance his suburban congregation and a busy family life led this fortysomething Baptist pastor from Maryland to these insights.

> I've learned I should live more in the moment and try not to spend so much time with a divided mind. I still struggle with that. If I'm preparing a sermon, I should be visiting someone in a nursing home or at a meeting. If I'm home cooking dinner I should be playing with my two-year-old. If I'm with him, I should be helping my seven-year-old with his homework. I'm thinking about what I have to do tomorrow or brooding about what happened yesterday. The ability to stay connected with what's going on and to feel whatever's present in that moment, and to either feel the joy or the sadness without trying to eject or check out because of something beyond it—I've struggled with that my entire life. When I am able to stay connected to whatever is going on right there I find a closeness to the abundance of life I miss when I'm dreading tomorrow or brooding about yesterday.

> Ecclesiastes has beautiful insights relevant to this struggle. I love its earthiness about work and loving the work you do and the people around you, living in the moment because that's all we really have. I don't think it's depressing. I think it's encouraging, almost soothing to people. It tells them, "You don't have to always be dissatisfied. This is enough." I preach Ecclesiastes at weddings a lot. To live in the present and to enjoy your love for each other, that's good advice for married people.

The rabbis whose wisdom is collected in *Pirke Avot* (*Sayings of the Fathers*) emphasized attention. "Live without hesitation. Dwell not on outcome or reward. Act with full attention."[29]

Attentiveness is at the heart of the preaching life. The great English spiritual writer William Law (1686–1761) observed that, "All the world preaches to an attentive mind . . . and if you have but ears to hear, almost everything you meet teaches you some lesson of wisdom."[30]

Contemporary homileticians have names for this capacity, so crucial to seeing life in light of the gospel and the gospel in light of daily life. Barbara Brown Taylor in her book *The Preaching Life* calls on preachers to become "detectives of divinity," emphasizing "the extraordinary hidden in the ordinary."[31] Tom Troeger challenges preachers to train their eyes to trace the play of heaven's light upon earth's shadowed surface, and to tune their ears to hear the overtones of graces that sound in human speech. He observes that "it takes discipline to see and to hear the visions and voices of God in our life, discipline every bit as strenuous as exegesis."[32] Mystic theologian Howard Thurman insisted that Christians ought to be "apostles of sensitiveness."[33]

What goes for preaching applies also to teaching. Christian educator and Wisdom scholar Charles Melchert commends the use of proverbs as reflection as tools for congregational education precisely because they stimulate this virtue of attentiveness.

> By concentrating on ordinary life and by requiring of reader-learners active learning, these texts imply that the purpose of learning to read texts is to become able to read life more clearly, more truthfully, with a sense of solidarity, humility, and awe. The texts assume and intend that as one learns to read the ways of life, one learns to discern the ways of God.[34]

The Role of Attentiveness in World Religions

All the major religions commend three interrelated types of active listening to their followers. They are to be attentive to signs of the divine presence that is a pervasive force in the universe; they are to listen to their inward lives as at least one realm where the divine reality is present and communicative; and they are to listen to the sufferings of others as a prelude to a helping response. A few words of elaboration on each will help us set our Christian understanding of wisdom's habits in a broader cultural, religious perspective.

In the first place, all major religions concur that a divine force pervades the world beyond the human being as well as one's inward terrain. The Abrahamic religions (Judaism, Islam, and Christianity) posit a distinction between Creator and creatures, while Eastern religions generally affirm their essential oneness. Various spiritual disciplines are a means of remaining alert to that presence amid the demands of daily life.

In the second place, a variety of religions commend attentiveness to the inward life, based on an acknowledgment of its power to influence the actions of the individual as well as outward circumstances. The goal of this attentiveness is to overcome the ego's greedy grip on the life of the individual. The ego-driven life is characterized by materialism, destructive addictions, and spiritual tumult that prevent human life from being and becoming a full expression of divine life.

Hinduism has its psychophysical yogic disciplines. Buddhism has its emphasis on "right mindfulness," the seventh step in its "eightfold path." The term refers to a rigorous, continuous self-examination aimed at keeping the mind in control of the senses and impulses rather than allowing one to be driven by them.[35] Islam has its discipline of prayer fives times a day focusing on praise and gratitude due to the Creator by the creature.

The third habit of attentiveness commended by many religions focuses on the sufferings of human life, not just one's own, but also the lives of others. One's religious life is to be at least to some degree, directed toward the alleviation of human suffering. Islam's third pillar is charity, whereby the comfortable should share with the unfortunate.[36] Confucius considered benevolence to be the virtue of virtues and emphasized concern for one's parents and respect for the aged. Buddhism commends the four noble virtues of loving-kindness, compassion, equanimity, and joy in the happiness and well being of others.[37]

All the religions mentioned have in common the use of imagery, metaphors, legends, anecdotes, and pithy sayings to convey religious truths both in relation to the individual's meditative life and to his or her interactions with others. The use of these vivid vehicles is evidence of the sages' attentiveness to daily life around them.

Jesus' Listening Heart

Recent scholarship has pointed out that Jesus, in addition to being a prophet and healer, was also a sage, a wisdom teacher. The miracles and healings of Jesus, as depicted in all four Gospels, are meant to lead people to faith, repentance, and discipleship.[38] But the miracles and healings do not bring about these results by spontaneous combustion. Jesus' teachings are equally important. Those whose faith is inspired by miracles and healings are those who have been listening. For this reason, following the feeding of the four thousand, Jesus chastises his disciples in Mark's Gospel (8:14-21). They can give him precise statistics about how much bread was left over, but they have missed the event's spiritual significance. Jesus asks a rhetorical question, "Do you have eyes, and fail to see? Do you have ears, and fail to hear?"

A Detective of Divinity

The sages of Proverbs talked a good deal about proper speech. Jesus has more to say about the importance of listening. "Let anyone with ears listen!" (Matt 11:15; 13:9) said Jesus. To be disciples, we need to listen to his words and also observe his life.

Jesus' teachings reveal that he was a "detective of divinity," an "apostle of sensitiveness"—like the sages of Proverbs. Jesus observed and learned from the created world. His many analogies and similes between aspects of the kingdom of God and the everyday world make this clear. He heard the sound of seeds hitting the earth, heard a woman ransacking her home searching for a coin, saw a house sinking because it was built on sand, heard someone knocking on a friend's door late one night begging for bread. He noticed foxes crawling into their holes, birds settling in their nests, and trees barren of fruit. He noticed someone trying to get a speck out of his eye, reeds blowing in the wind, the beauty of lilies, and the behavior of vultures.

Many of Jesus' sayings sound like they could have come right out of the pages of the book of Proverbs. They convey conventional wisdom. "A city built on a hill cannot be hid" (Matt 5:14). "Today's trouble is enough for today"(Matt 6:34). "Where your treasure is, there your heart will be also"(Matt 6:21).[39]

His listening heart, that flowed from his radical trust in God (fear of the Lord), generated a number of unconventional wisdom sayings that he applied to the religious and social conventions of his day, thereby challenging traditional, status quo–preserving wisdom. For example, "It is not what goes into the mouth that defiles a person, but it is what comes out" (Matt. 15:11). "Whoever would save his life must lose it." We will explore this topic more fully in chapter 9 when we discuss Jesus' subversive voice.

Jesus' parables shine with attention to detail. While most rabbinic parables dealt with stock characters and situations, many of Jesus' parables dealt with circumstances and characters he observed in everyday life in his culture. Unlike rabbinic parables that most often confirmed conventional interpretations of torah, Jesus' parables contain a strange twist—someone doesn't act the way a reasonable person would act.[40] A vineyard owner pays those who worked the least hours as much as those who worked the most hours. Things turn out in parables the way they would not turn out in everyday life. At the last minute, the leading lights of the community renege on attending a banquet they have already agreed to attend. The host fills the banquet halls with the people from the alleys, the bus station, and the shelters. Our minds are teased into considering how the story is both like and unlike the way we usually behave. We are also teased into considering how the kingdom of God is different from conventional contemporary culture.[41]

An Apostle of Sensitiveness

Most of all, Jesus listened to people's pain, and heard their fears. Proverbs enjoin us constantly to "fear the Lord." We have seen how this did not refer to a fear of imminent punishment, but to a three-stranded braid composed of awe before the divine (Isa 6), covenant faithfulness that puts no other loyalty above God (Deut 10:20), and confidence in God for moral direction (Prov 3:3-5).

The words on Jesus' lips are more often, "Do not be afraid. It is I." The fear of the Lord, in the New Testament, takes the form of acknowledging Jesus' Sonship and authority. We have seen how, in one encounter after another in the Gospels, Jesus meets someone who is afraid and helps the person exchange fear for faith. He does so by exercising his listening heart, by being radically attentive to the nuances of others' body language and expressions. He cultivated his listening heart during periods of prayer.[42]

An Episcopal priest in Georgetown, Washington, D.C., shared her reflection on this topic with me:

> I remember making a phone call to a priest in California and his secretary said, "Oh, I'm sorry but Father's at prayer." And I thought, "How lovely. Why am I not at prayer?" I know people who say that if they don't have their prayer time their whole day is just not the same. The edges are a little bit more raw. Their behavior is not as centered.

A young African American pastor from Dallas spoke of the connection between trusting communion with God and action on behalf of God's people when he said,

> You have to have your eyes open to be a sage. I get up and pray every morning, sometimes half an hour, sometimes two hours. The longer into the day it gets, the more I think of the meeting tonight and this person sick and I hear my cell phone ringing in the other room . . . all this stuff pulling on me. I remember I have nothing to give unless I first receive.

Sustained by Prayer

When Solomon in 1 Kgs 3 asks for an understanding mind (or a listening heart), he is asking to be radically attentive to people in future encounters with them in which his wise judgments will be crucial. He is asking to be attentive to the will of God as expressed through the interactions he has with his people.[43] Jesus is periodically described as going off to solitary places to pray, to listen attentively to God (Mark 1:35; 6:31; 14:32; Luke 4:42; 5:16). He prays at the crucial moments in his life. Luke is particularly concerned to emphasize the role of prayer in Jesus' ministry. In Luke 3:21, Jesus is depicted as having prayed at his baptism, in Luke 6:12 to have prayed all night before the choice of his twelve disciples, in 9:18 to have been praying when he asked his disciples "Who do the crowds say that I am?" and "Who do you say that I am?" and in 9:28 to have been at prayer on a mountain at the time of his transfiguration. Luke also notes in 22:39 that when Jesus went to the Mount of Olives to pray it was "his custom" and indicates a particular place he habitually prayed (22:40) when he was in Jerusalem. Luke's account of Jesus in the Garden of Gethsemane (22:39-46) suggests the themes of withdrawal for prayer and intensity in prayer, for Jesus spends at least one night in prayer.[44] Jesus apparently prayed to regenerate and to prepare during his ministry of intense attentiveness to others. We do well to follow his example.

Jesus was uncannily perceptive in listening to hidden human motives: "Why do you raise such questions in your hearts?" (Mark 2:8); "he was grieved at their hardness of heart" (Mark 3:5); "Who do you say I am?" (Mark 8:29); "What were you arguing about on the way?" (Mark 9:33); "You lack one thing" (Mark 10:21); "Let her alone. . . . She has performed a good service for me" (Mark 14:6); "Where is your faith?" (Luke 8:25); "What is your name?" (Luke 8:30); "Who touched me?" (Luke 8:45).

Jesus listened to people's faith. He noticed the faith of the four friends lowering the paralytic through the roof (Mark 2:5). He commended the centurion for his faith with these words: "Not even in Israel have I found such faith" (Luke 7:9). He offered healing words of encouragement to the woman who had suffered for twelve years with a hemorrhage, "Daughter, your faith has made you well; go in peace" (Luke 8:48).

He also listened to people's fears. Telltale phrases express his attentiveness to the pain and fear of others: "Moved with pity" (Mark 1:41); "I have compassion for the crowd" (Mark 8:2); "Do not weep" (Luke 7:13).

Jesus listened to people's fears and countered them in both his teachings and in face-to-face encounters. "Do not fear those who kill the body but cannot kill the soul; rather fear him who can destroy both soul and body in hell. . . . Even the hairs on your head are all counted. So do not be afraid (Matt 10:28, 31; see also Luke 12:4-7). In Matt 14:26 Jesus walks toward the disciples on the water. When they cry out in fear, he says, "Take heart, it is I; do not be afraid" (v. 27). At the Transfiguration, when the disciples fell to the ground and were overcome by fear, Jesus came and touched them and said, "Get up and do not be afraid" (Matt. 17:7). To the disciples after his resurrection, he said, "Do not be afraid; go and tell my brothers to go to Galilee; there they will see me" (Matt 28:10).

Jesus comforts the leader of the synagogue whose daughter was believed dead with these words, "Do not fear; only believe" (Mark 5:36). He teaches his disciples, "Do not be afraid, little flock, for it is your Father's good pleasure to give you the kingdom" (Luke 12:32).

Jesus' spirit is reflected in the life and writings of Amy Carmichael (1867–1951), a missionary to India for over fifty years who wrote on the devotional life. She established the Dohnavur Fellowship, a mission dedicated to rescuing and rearing children at risk, including orphans and young girls given by their families as temple prostitutes. Her intense activism was matched by her intense prayer life. In *Candles in the Dark*, the best-known of her thirty-five books, she wrote:

> Keep close, keep close. If you are close, you will be keen. Your heart will be set on the things that abide. You will not be attracted by the world, but you will love the people in that world. You will live to share your joy. Nothing else will count for much.[45]

Keeping close to God and to others through the listening heart describes our ministry in a nutshell; when we keep close to God, we are attentive to others' pain and fear and invite them into wholeness and healing, to follow with us the path of devotion to our teacher, Wisdom in Person.

The life of the listening heart is not an easy path. Theologian and social prophet Georgia Harkness wrote these verses of a poem called "The Agony of God" during the height of suffering in World War II.

> I listen to the agony of God
> I who am fed,
> Who never yet went hungry for a day,
> I see the dead—
> The children starved for lack of bread
> I see, and try to pray.
>
> I listen to the agony of God—
> But know full well
> That not until I share their bitter cry—
> Earth's pain and hell—
> Can God within my spirit dwell
> To bring His Kingdom nigh.[46]

The life and meditations of Dom Helder Camara, Roman Catholic bishop and mystic from northeast Brazil (1909–99), exemplify the listening heart. Convinced that the church needs to be a servant rather than served, he lived austerely and was devoted to justice for his people. He would awaken at 2 A.M. and write meditations on his daily life in his journal. In one of them he wrote to God, "If you had not given me the grace during my nightly vigils to drink the stillness and to submerge myself in it, letting it pervade me through and through, how could I guard that inner stillness without which one can hear neither human beings nor you, O Lord?"[47] Camara's mysticism of liberation voices God's presence in the beaten down and defeated life. For him, "everything, really everything speaks to me of you, thanks to you. The milkman's cart, the poor beggar, the pregnant woman, the newspaper vendor, and the street cleaner, all speak of God, as does a piece of wood, a sugar cane, or an old car."[48]

In one of his poems he writes of seeing hungry childen with bloated stomachs and no one to care for them. He asserts that in them "it is Christ whom I meet."

Christianity's listening heart is characterized by four qualities. It is social, specific, sacrificial, and subversive. In the first place, it is social or communal. One exercises the listening heart on behalf of the community. It is a spiritual habit empowered and directed by the Holy Spirit, the ongoing Presence of the risen Christ with us in his physical absence, a personal and pervasive power in the church, the world, and the individual. Second, the listening heart is specific. We see in the ministry of Jesus that he was not just attentive to the needs of humanity in general, but he was attentive to the specific needs of particular people. Third, the listening heart in the Christian tradition is sacrificial. We are to listen to life and others on the way to losing our lives in order to find them again. Using our listening heart is a way of loving others as we do ourselves. We are called to risk encountering pain and suffering on behalf of others, not to escape from it on some individualized spiritual quest. Finally, the listening heart, in Christian context, is subversive. It is more than willing to use existing imagery, stories, and sayings to subvert unjust attitudes and behaviors in society and individuals. It is also ready to create fresh fodder to foster justice.

CHAPTER FIVE

TEACHING AND PREACHING WITH A LISTENING HEART

Purpose of Teaching and Preaching with a Listening Heart

Our goal in teaching and preaching with a listening heart is to help hearers replace habits of distraction and self-preoccupation with attentiveness to the revelatory glimmers of God's redemptive work in everyday life.

Teaching and Preaching with a Listening Heart Encourages Listeners to "Pay Attention!" to What God Is Doing

Many authors have given the general counsel that we harvest daily life for preachable, teachable insights. Wisdom's third pillar offers us directions for where to look and what to look for. Each wisdom book offers a slightly different variation on the theme "Pay attention!"

The book of Proverbs insists that, first and foremost, we pay attention to the faithfulness of God at the core of our lives, in our relationships, and in the world of nature that surrounds us.

Where are evidences of the positive results of self-restraint, hard work, honesty, forgiveness, generosity of spirit, honoring the poor, wise speech, a humble attitude, and seeking wisdom as one's life priority?

Attentiveness to our hearts, relationships, and nature in a given week might yield the following scenarios:

- At an airport you observe a restaurant owner serving a free meal to a homeless person at a back table and you note the glance of kindness and gratitude that flashes between them.
- At a social reception at a professional meeting, you see a colleague new to the group standing at the edge of the room, obviously feeling awkward. You approach her and engage her in conversation, and ease her discomfort at entering a new social situation. Later in your career, that person is asked to write a letter recommending you for a promotion.
- As for the animal world, perhaps your family already has a dog, but your child brings home a kitten too adorable to turn away. You observe how, gradually, the kitten and the dog make peace with each other and even nap together in the bed provided for the dog.

The sage also is called on to be on the lookout for signs of the negative consequences of overindulgence, anger, hardheartedness, disrespect for the poor, and prideful self-promotion. Again, a given week could yield a rich harvest of cautionary tales:

- A teenager loses her keys. Her mother chews her out about it, calling her irresponsible, and so forth. Later that day, the mother loses her own keys.
- A government official builds his career on "family values," condemning in political and religious terms all those whose lifestyles deviate from his views. He is discovered at an hourly rate motel with an underage girl.
- A pastor is visiting a local shelter for abused women and children. She observes an exhausted mother snap at her seven-year-old son, "One more word and I'm leaving you here and never coming back." The pastor, observing the combined rage and anguish on the young boy's face, realizes that she is seeing a future batterer in the making.
- You hear of the high incidence of cancer and the destruction to plant and animal life in a low-income area affected by nearby factories dumping chemicals into the river.

The listening heart in Proverbs encourages preachers and teachers to be attentive to the realms of the human heart, human interactions, and the world of nature. Why? Because it is there that clues to the distinction between wise and foolish behaviors are to be found.

In Qohelet the listening heart prods us to exchange melancholia for attentiveness and insecurity for enjoying the present blessings of faithful relationships, work, and food and drink. Perhaps you hear a story of a friend who goes along to the clinic with another friend to keep her company while she waits for serious medical test results. The two friends have lunch together in the hospital cafeteria and express how much each values their friendship, all the more poignantly in light of life's uncertainties.

Perhaps, despite the things you dislike about your job, including aspects of your boss's personality and the tedium of repetitive tasks, you have a day when you find joy in your work. A customer comes back to your station and expresses appreciation for your job well done.

Qohelet also insists that we look and listen for situations in which the poor, through no fault of their own, are oppressed and mistreated. We are to view them as reminders of the bankruptcy of conventional wisdom's assurance that wise choices will ensure personal, social, and financial success. For example, you encounter statistics on the high percentage of children in your county who have no health insurance; you read of a group of illegal immigrants who suffocated when left by their traffickers in a crowded truck in the desert heat; or your child comes home from elementary school and tells of a group making fun of a girl for living in the homeless hotel.

The listening heart in Job encourages us teachers and preachers to shift our attention from anger and attributing blame to the beauty and pain of a complex creation. I am reminded of a friend who was home under hospice care due to failing kidneys. One afternoon, he told me he was awakened by the tolling of his clock, looked out his window and saw the pink of a gorgeous sunset beginning to thread the sky and heard the sound of children laughing as they played in the street outside his home. "And, despite my anger and hurt, I couldn't help giving thanks that everything God made is good and that those sights and sounds will continue after my time is up."

My father died after a two-year struggle with liver cancer. I was to offer his funeral sermon at a United Methodist church in Harrisburg, Pennsylvania. The faculty at Perkins School of Theology, where I teach, was holding its annual faculty retreat in Dallas at the same time. When I got up to preach, I sensed a wave of calm wash over me, and I knew my colleagues were praying for me at that very moment and I gave thanks for their caring.

Job wants us to listen with our hearts to a mysterious, transcendent God who draws near in times of suffering to challenge our doubts about the Divine presence and care. Preachers and teachers are prodded to ask themselves, "What scenes come to mind that embody such an encounter?"

Jesus, as he is depicted in the Synoptic Gospels, urges us to exchange convention for compassion. He urges us to tear our attention away from exclusive preoccupation with guaranteeing a secure future for ourselves, and the accumulation of wealth, status, and power to train it on those who are suffering. For Jesus, such suffering is more than Qohelet's evidence that conventional wisdom is bankrupt. It is a sign of the dominion of the present era to the thrall of forces that oppose God. It is a sign of the imminent advent of the empire of God. It is a call to commit ourselves to a life of sacrificial compassion in action.

Jesus' teachings encourage contemporary teachers and preachers to lift up individuals and groups whom society does not consider worth listening to. Who are those who have fallen through the cracks of our national gospel of success that preaches the self-help slogan, "If you can conceive it and believe it, you can achieve it"? Who are those not listened to in our community, our nation, even the biblical text we are studying? What are their stories? How might their stories threaten our current perspective and way of life? How might their stories inspire listeners to exchange adherence to convention for active, sacrificial compassion?

Preaching and Teaching *Out of* a Listening Heart

Sermons and lessons from a listening heart bear the fruits of our attentive living. They incorporate the vivid images, stories, and insights we glean when we listen to God, Scripture, self, and others.

Listen to One's Inward Life through Prayer

The insights and scenarios gleaned by the listening heart in the fields of daily life are preserved and processed during times of daily prayer. One must listen for what God seeks to do in one's inward life.

A white male pastor of a multicultural church in Los Angeles told me this:

> The discipline that is most life-giving for me is journaling. Reflecting on the journey, reflecting on yesterday and last week and focusing on that, a half-second facial expression by somebody and what it did for me. I remember that the next morning when I journal. That is when wisdom really gets processed for me. That is the connection between experience and wisdom—the vehicle is journaling.

Three spiritual disciplines of most direct relevance to the wisdom virtue of the listening heart are the examination of consciousness, contemplation, and spiritual reading or biblical meditation. The examination of consciousness involves a nightly review of the day for moments when God's grace has been in evidence and a review of our responses to those moments. It is unparalleled as a means of exercising and strengthening the listening heart.[1] Contemplation is wordless resting in the presence of God, actively listening, having cleared away mental distractions through breathing, visual focus on some object of inspiration such as an icon, candle flame, or flower, or through the repetition of a brief mantra. Biblical meditation takes at least two forms, the meditative repetition of a word or phrase or prayerful entry into biblical narratives using methods devised by St. Ignatius of Loyola.[2]

The listening heart issues from our life of prayer. We become attentive to the particulars of both text and contemporary life. Our sermons and lessons brim over with snippets of overheard conversations, quirky billboards, redemptive encounters, places in daily life—however mundane—where we can see the good news going toe to toe with the six o'clock news. Many of the pastors I spoke with described their preaching and teaching ministries in terms of listening. Our habit of listening, through our sermons and teachings, is contagious. It motivates listeners to live daily life listening with their *hearts*.

Listen to Scripture

A Lutheran pastor of a large suburban church on the outskirts of San Diego told me this:

> In our Lutheran understanding of the pastor's role, the pastor is that person most knowledgeable in the church regarding Scripture. The pastor is the interpreter of Scripture.

This pastor strove to model in his study and preaching how to come to the Bible with an expectant spirit. Martin Luther himself would have approved!

Listen to the Wisdom People Have Gained from Family and Culture

A Roman Catholic priest from a suburb near Dallas, well known for his effective preaching, told me this:

> People often get conventional wisdom from their families. This is why Jesus said that to be his follower you had to turn your back on your family. We have to turn our backs on conventional wisdom to embrace his wisdom. People also get wisdom from the culture. If preaching can tap into that experience we've had from family and culture, it can speak to those places and it is magic. That's why people will often say to me, "How did you know that's what I was going through? Were you under my bed last night? Were you in the car on the way to church with us? How did you know?"

Listen to the Many Cultures that Make Up Our Congregation

A white Presbyterian pastor in a socially active multicultural congregation in Los Angeles said:

> In my nine years living in a Mexican squatters' community, I learned a great deal. I have a lot of formal education. I wouldn't expect to learn from somebody who has a second-grade education. I'm a wealthy person. I wouldn't expect to learn from somebody who's economically poor. Yet I've learned some of the most important lessons in life from people who are poor. I was there to teach them about the Bible and I do know more about the Bible than they did. But for me to teach them about community was a little absurd, because my experience of community is so shallow compared to their reality of struggling together to create a community. So I put my learning alongside theirs.
>
> From them I learned generosity. It is a concept for us, but for them it is a habit. Generosity is a journey from concept to habit. When we ran out of water, they would appear at the door with buckets full for us, even though I knew they were running low themselves. I saw that kind of

generosity happen over and over again. I have not yet integrated that kind of generosity into my spirit.

A pastor at a large Chinese Baptist church in Chinatown, Los Angeles, made this comment.

> We have four languages in our congregation: English, Chinese, Cantonese, and Mandarin. We emphasize the theme of "one family" in church. Even though they are all "yellow-skinned," the people are such a diverse culture.

The pastor of a large Korean Presbyterian church in Los Angeles told me,

> My congregation has many immigrants. There is a conflict between old-comers and newcomers. They come from different regions with different ways of thinking. The oldcomers have more Western ways of thinking. Newcomers have more Korean ways of thinking. I emphasize in my sermons that the newcomers are human beings to be accepted into the church. I encourage them and comfort them but also challenge them with their new mission in this land, which is to pray for their new country.

> The in-between generation, often called the 1.5 generation, is bilingual and bicultural because they came and are still coming from Korea while teenagers. They don't belong to the first or the second generation really, so there can be a problem of not fitting in.

> Korean people are hesitant to approach a pastor for counseling because in their culture "face-keeping" is very important and losing face is shameful. That would include anyone else finding out anything negative, such as alcohol problems, medical problems, domestic abuse, etc. So I often see preaching as collective counseling.

> Korean people take comfort in Psalms, they like Proverbs, and they very much relate to Job because their history is one of suffering. Ecclesiastes is more along the lines of Buddhist thought. They enjoy the parables because storytelling is part of their culture. They like the parables because they are open-ended and leave room for thought. Older people prefer to be told what to do at the end of the sermon, but younger people can respond to an open-ended finish. The congregation appreciates a prophetic challenge as well. I preach a kind of liberation

theology, that Jesus was oppressed and that he was like an immigrant, traveling to Egypt as a young boy and coming back to Nazareth. Korean people are influenced by Buddhism, Confucianism, and shamanism, in addition to Christianity.

A young female pastor from Mexico City serving a church near San Antonio said this,

> I try to preach to my congregation's needs. I know they often feel like life isn't going well and that maybe God has withdrawn. I know they often feel exhausted. I preach about Joseph. They like to remember that God was always with him, even when Joseph didn't think so. I preach about Peter fishing but not getting any fish. God has a good idea when he suggests Peter try again. I ask them to imagine this by saying, "Sometimes you feel so tired. Jesus says 'try over there.'"

A Mexican American pastor serving a church in a rural area of south Texas made this comment:

> Mexican Americans are more individualistic than Latin Americans, who are family oriented, collective, and community focused. Mexican Americans have as their goals more education, a higher salary. They have taken on the individualistic social mentality of American culture.

A United Methodist pastor originally from Mexico, now serving a church in San Antonio made this comment:

> Hispanics have borne a double burden with regard to both Mexican culture and Mexican American culture. They are outsiders in both camps with something to prove to each. Many Mexican Americans even changed their names to fit better into American culture.

Listen to Our Listeners During the Sermon Event

A black Baptist pastor from a historic downtown church in Washington, D.C., told me,

> Being in the black church you have the amens to assess how things are going. I've preached in a number of white churches and other cultures where they don't do that and you can still tell. You know whether they are engaged or whether they're not. The folks who have that little smile, the little old ladies with their heads bowed, you can see the kind of pensive look on the face. I watch faces.

Listen to the Wisdom of the People

A female pastor serving a large United Methodist church in a suburb near Dallas said,

> In every sermon I refer to something I have learned from someone. I ask the people what they'd like to hear sermons on. One request was for a sermon on science and religion. We had an award-winning chemistry teacher from a local high school come up and talk about the perfection of the water molecule. We did the sermon together. It had a credibility it wouldn't have had if it had been just me up there quoting her.

Listen to Events in One's Community

A female Episcopal priest at a historic church in Georgetown, Washington, D.C., said,

> On September 11 when I looked out at my congregation, I remember seeing congressmen sitting there, just stricken, and people from the Pentagon weeping. And I talked about forgiveness. I quoted that wonderful line from "The Merchant of Venice," about the quality of mercy and how it is not strained. And my associate said that he looked up and saw everybody's mouths moving. They all knew it. You can't ignore the city you live in. You can't ignore the truth. You preach the truth in your city.

Listen to Our Own Goodness

A Roman Catholic priest serving a large parish near Dallas told me,

> If one is not in touch with his own goodness, he cannot sense the goodness in the world. We must believe it and feel it. When we are filled with self-loathing we are not likely to notice and nurture the wisdom of others.

Listen to the Shame and Guilt of Others

This same priest went on,

> I listen to people's sins so much. I am struck by how much shame and guilt people carry around, sometimes just for being human. In the

sacrament of absolution we heal people of their shame and guilt. We need a more affirming style in our preaching. There are a lot of people with smiling faces who are carrying major burdens of shame and guilt for just being human. I've learned that people make heroic efforts to deal with their lives. I've learned how burdened people are. I want to be an agent of release for that burden, not add to it. I've learned the things people put up with, their persistence, the pain they carry.

One of the pastors I talked to, an Episcopal rector and spiritual director in Harrisburg, Pennsylvania, recounted a story about his mentor in preaching. He was Theodore Parker Ferris, a well-known preacher and pastor at Trinity Episcopal Church in Boston.

> One morning, Dr. Ferris's secretary came in and said, "Dr. Ferris, there is a man here who wants to see you."
> When the man was seated in Dr. Ferris's office, he leaned forward and said, "I'd like to thank you for saving my life." "But I've never seen you before!" Dr. Ferris answered. "A few months ago I was very depressed. I was on my way to the Charles River to jump in and end it on a Sunday night. I saw the lights on here and heard the music. For some reason I came in and sat in the gallery behind a pillar. What you said changed and saved my life. I came to thank you."
> "From that day on," said Dr. Ferris, "I always preach to the man behind the pillar."[3]

Listen to Our Own Inward Lives

A United Methodist pastor serving a large church an hour north of Dallas told me,

> One time in the Bible study I lead, I mentioned that at one time I went through a period when I hated God. A young man came up to me afterward and said, "I've felt that. I didn't know it was OK. Thank you!"

A young United Methodist college minister from New Mexico told me,

> I became more empathetic after my wife and I lost a baby while we were in seminary. I stood in the yard and shook my fist. Later we had a service called "Why?" We started with a skit in which a young couple lost a baby and an adoption fell through. This came out of my own experience.

Listen to Our Own Everyday Experiences

A Unitarian pastor from Dallas told of her experience of having a therapist, helping her work through a life transition, be very blunt with her. She reflected on how she later wove this uncomfortable experience into a sermon.

> A few weeks later I was preaching a sermon on Gabriel and Zechariah called "Struck Dumb!" I said, "Gabriel, if he had had therapeutic training, would have offered Zechariah his options, broken the news to him more gently, been a more empathetic listener. But Gabriel was not involved in an act of pastoral care. He had not just come from 'angelic therapy school.'"

Listen to Our Own Need for Healing

A white male Presbyterian pastor serving a multicultural church in Los Angeles said,

> I used to believe that seeking my own healing was something I sort of did on my own time, and was a part of my life journey over here, and then there is ministry and work over there. I think I'm seeing that my call is a call to be healed and to be a healer out of my own experience of getting healed. My contribution is going to be channeled toward the things that I need healing in, so that working on my own healing may be one of the most important things I do in this job.

A female African American pastor from a Baptist church in Washington, D.C., made this observation,

> I tend to think women share more of themselves in their preaching and teaching than men do, and I think that's been real helpful for the congregation to loosen up, to be able to be real. . . . I've used my own life experience in my preaching and teaching. Sometimes that has to do with being an incest survivor and being an adult child of an alcoholic. I think my sharing helps the congregation to open up and be real. They see that you can show your weaknesses and the sky won't fall. . . . I've learned to move forward, trusting God with whoever I am and that it's OK to do that with my weaknesses and my strengths.

Listen to the Wisdom of Both Young and Old

The same Washington pastor had this to say about age and wisdom.

> We need to recognize that everyone has something to offer. We're trying to teach the children about those persons in the congregation who are older, trying to give some reverence to them. When I was a guest preacher at a church in Bethesda, I began talking to a man in his eighties. And he said that he felt he still had so much to offer but that nobody had time to talk with him. They would smile and say "How are you doing?" and keep on going. We're trying to impress on people how important it is to pay attention—to the elders, to the younger ones. Everybody has something to say and everybody has something to offer.

A white fortysomething United Methodist pastor from central Texas told me,

> I learn from children. When my son, at that time a somewhat timid soul, was around five years old, he stood on the side of the pool, stuck out his chest and proclaimed, "Except for the swimming part, I am the lifeguard of this pool!"

The Shape of Sermons and Lessons on the Listening Heart: From Particular to General

The listening heart is a Wisdom virtue that empowered the sages to shape the proverbs, parables, reflection, and dialogue genres we find in Proverbs, Ecclesiastes, Job, and the Synoptic Gospels. Clearly, these genres are specific, concrete, memorable, and evocative. They are the products of acute attentiveness to the particulars of life, and they seek to foster such an attentiveness in readers. So when we preach on them, a wise choice would be to preach inductively, from particulars to general conclusions. Just as the listening heart challenges us to exchange preoccupation for attentiveness, so our preaching on Wisdom texts challenges us to exchange generalizations for concrete and vivid specifics. Following the lead of these texts of wisdom, we do well to use dialogue, imagery, metaphor, suspense, questions, plot, and characters.

The Shape of Sermons and Lessons on the Listening Heart: The Great Exchange!

We have seen how, with the virtue of the fear of the Lord, our purpose in preaching is to help listeners exchange fear for faith. So with the listening heart, we are to help them exchange attention to current preoccupations for attention to God working to repair the world. Proverbs challenges the young to exchange undisciplined behavior for self-discipline that benefits the whole community. Qohelet urges us to shift our focus from melancholy to thanksgiving. Job invites us to exchange a focus on the suffering self for a focus on God's complex universe in which we are not the center, but in which we are strongly assured of God's faithful presence. Jesus' teachings prod us to shift our attention from superficial religious ritual to sacrificial compassion out of love for the neighbor. A helpful sermonic form might be labeled "the great exchange." The preacher would begin with a description of our society's current preoccupations, offer the biblical wisdom text's challenge to them, and, finally, ask how our lives would look different if we exchanged preoccupation with self for attentiveness to the work of God.

Preaching and Teaching about the Listening Heart: Ideas for Series on the Listening Heart

A compelling teaching and preaching series on the listening heart could be called "The Great Exchange!"

"The Great Exchange"

Week One: We Exchange Luxuries for the Basic Necessity of Life

Paying attention is the way we learn wisdom. First, we exchange preoccupation with self-preservation and advancement for a focus on God's gift of Wisdom within us and around us. This is the fear of the Lord, and when we live listening to it we understand that wisdom is not a luxury but a necessity vital to our existence. We begin to crave wisdom, to require wisdom. And whenever our eyes encounter one of the other necessities of life, it reminds us of the one thing necessary: Wisdom herself.

Israel's sages compare wisdom to the necessities of life: food, water, and light. "The path of the righteous is like the light of dawn, which shines brighter and brighter until full day" (Prov 4:18). By contrast those who "forsake the paths of uprightness . . . walk in the ways of darkness" (Prov 2:13). Wisdom's teachings are a lamp (Prov 6:23). Wise words are "pleasant . . . like a honeycomb, sweetness to the soul and health to the body" (Prov 16:24). Wisdom is more honorable than a crown (14:18, 24; 16:31). Wisdom causes one to utter wise words that nourish like food (Prov 13:2; 15:14-15). One's mouth becomes a "fountain of life" (10:11; see also 18:4b). "The fear of the LORD is a fountain of life, so that one may avoid the snares of death" (Prov 14:27; see also 16:22).

Week Two: We Exchange Glitter for True Treasure

Over and over the sages look at the things that we value, that attract us in life. And they remind us that wisdom is more beautiful, valuable, and lasting than these things. The sages often compare wisdom to jewels and precious metals. "For wisdom is better than jewels, and all that you may desire cannot compare with her" (Prov 8:11). "My fruit is better than gold, even fine gold, and my yield than choice silver" (8:19; see also 16:16). "The tongue of the righteous is choice silver" (10:20a). Wisdom brings to the seeker wealth, and it fills his treasuries (8:21). (See also 2:4-5; 3:14-15; 10:20; 20:15.) "In the house of the righteous there is much treasure" (15:6). We can point our hearers to the material things that appeal to us most, describe their beauty, their appeal, their value and, at every turn, point listeners to Wisdom that exceeds them all.

Week Three: We Exchange Crooked for Straight

When we live with our hearts attuned to the fear of the Lord, radical trust in God to guide our steps, we are able to discern the difference between crooked and straight. "Trust in the LORD with all your heart, and do not rely on your own insight. In all your ways acknowledge him, and he will make straight your paths" (Prov 3:5-6).

The life of wisdom is often referred to as a path or way. We are told that God "[guards] the paths of justice and [preserves] the way of his faithful ones" (Prov 2:8). Fools are "those whose paths are crooked, and who are devious in their ways" (Prov 2:15). Their speech is crooked and devious (Prov 4:24). They are "crooked of mind" and "perverse of tongue" (Prov 17:20). Those who would be wise are advised to "walk in the way of the good, and keep to the paths of the just" (Prov 2:20). Of Woman Wisdom it is said that "her ways are ways of pleasantness, and all her paths are peace" (Prov 3:17). We are to avoid the path of folly (Prov 4:14) "which is like deep darkness" (Prov 4:19) in favor of "the path of the righteous [which] is like the light of dawn, which shines brighter and brighter until full day" (Prov 4:18). Fools are often lazy, and therefore their way is "overgrown with thorns, but the path of the upright is a level highway" (Prov 15:19). "The way of the guilty is crooked, but the conduct of the pure is right" (Prov 21:8). "Better to be poor and walk in integrity than to be crooked in one's ways even though rich" (Prov 28:6). "One who walks in integrity will be safe, but whoever follows crooked ways will fall into the Pit" (Prov 28:18).

Week Four: We Exchange Danger for Safety

When we live with a listening heart, we are able to discern the difference between those actions that bring short-term gain, but, in the long-term, endanger our relationship with God and others in our family and community.

When one follows the path of wisdom, the sages say, "you will walk on your way securely and your foot will not stumble" (Prov 3:23). One will have no need to fear or panic, "for the LORD will be your confidence and will keep your foot from being caught" (Prov 3:26). Repeatedly, the sages use the metaphor of a snare for the dangers of folly. "The evil are ensnared by the transgression of their lips, but the righteous escape from trouble" (Prov 12:13). "The mouths of fools are their ruin, and their lips a snare to themselves" (Prov 18:7). "The fear of others lays a snare, but one who trusts in the LORD is secure" (Prov 29:25). "In the transgression of the evil there is a snare, but the righteous sing and rejoice" (Prov 29:6). In addition to "snare," they use the metaphor of "ambush." "The words of the wicked are a deadly ambush, but the speech of the upright delivers them" (Prov 12:6).

By contrast, the way of wisdom offers profound though not always obvious security. "In the fear of the LORD one has strong confidence and one's children will have a refuge" (Prov 14:26). "[Wisdom] is a shield to those who walk blamelessly" (Prov 2:7). "No one finds security by wickedness, but the root of the righteous will never be moved" (Prov 12:3; see also 12:12b). "The righteous find a refuge in their integrity"

(Prov 14:32*b*). "The LORD tears down the house of the proud, but maintains the widow's boundaries" (Prov 15:25). "Pride goes before destruction, and a haughty spirit before a fall" (Prov 16:18).

Week Five: We Exchange Death for Life

The life of wisdom begins with an exchange of human anxieties for the fear of the Lord (faith). When we live life through the fear of the Lord, listening for God's guidance in interpreting life, we are able to exchange those attitudes and behaviors that lead to death for those that lead to life. For the sages, the fear of the Lord, understood as humble obedience to God's moral guidance in all of life, was the source of life itself. In part they understood *life* as one's physical well-being, longevity, and prosperity. Wise choices tended to nurture life understood in this way. But more deeply, *life* meant one's core connection with God that the most heinous misfortune cannot sever. That meant that poverty, loss of reputation, and suffering at the hands of the wicked could not separate the wise person from God and therefore could not destroy his or her life.

Conversely, one could have wealth and power and not have life, but rather, be marked as on the way to death. Choosing wisdom was a matter of life and death. "There is a way that seems right to a person, but its end is the way to death" (Prov 14:12). "The fear of the LORD is a fountain of life, so that one may avoid the snares of death" (Prov 14:27). "Do not be wise in your own eyes; fear the LORD, and turn away from evil. It will be a healing for your flesh and a refreshment for your body" (Prov 3:7-8). "The highway of the upright avoids evil; those who guard their way preserve their lives" (Prov 16:17). "The name of the LORD is a strong tower; the righteous run into it and are safe" (Prov 18:10). "The house of the wicked is destroyed, but the tent of the upright flourishes" (Prov 14:11). "Those who guard their mouths preserve their lives; those who open wide their lips come to ruin" (Prov 13:3). "The mouth of the righteous is a fountain of life" (Prov 10:11*a*). The one who heeds instruction is "on the path to life" (Prov 10:17). "The wicked earn no real gain, but those who sow righteousness get a true reward" (Prov 11:18). "A gentle tongue is a tree of life, but perverseness in it breaks the spirit" (Prov 15:4). "The violence of the wicked will sweep them away, because they refuse to do what is just" (Prov 21:7). Wisdom is "a tree of life to those who lay hold of her; those who hold her fast are called happy" (Prov 3:18). "My child, . . . keep sound wisdom and prudence, and they will be life for your soul and adornment for your neck (Prov 3:21-22). "My child, be attentive to my words. . . . For they are life to those who find them, and healing to all their flesh" (Prov 4:20, 22).

Week Six: We Exchange Our Childhood God for a God for Grown-ups

Job exchanges one set of responses to his undeserved sufferings for another. He exchanges passive acceptance, blaming self, or blaming God for an active search for God. Ultimately, he sacrifices his current notion of God as a God who is in control of everything, who has placed human beings at the very center of the universe, and who distributes divine retribution according to precise stipulations. He exchanges this human-shaped understanding of God for an encounter with the God he was not raised to expect, a God who may not micromanage the world's affairs, a God who affirms that divine retribution is a human invention, a God who has a lot of other things to be concerned about besides human beings. There is one thing about this God that is beyond dispute and uncertainty: this God will be present with us in times of trial and pain. This God will always show up.

Week Seven: We Exchange Complaints for Gratitude

We have seen how Qohelet initially listens to an inward voice that repeatedly expresses its disappointment with life for not living up to traditional wisdom's affirmation that good actions lead to good fortune. He eschews denial and whining, however, exchanging them for facing into the harsh realities of the limitations of human knowledge, the mystery of God, and the sure approach of death. Having done so, he is able to find peace and even joy in the present moment, as fleeting and fragile as it is. He is able to exchange discontentment and resentment for gratitude.

"Jesus' Uncomfortable Questions"

When I was growing up, my three siblings and I knew that our mother had the hearing of a bird dog. She heard things we didn't even remember saying, but we knew we had thought them! Jesus' spiritual hearing was divinely acute. He was always listening with his heart and had an uncanny ability to read the hearts of others. As he reads our hearts, he calls us to exchange fear, self-centeredness, and evil for faith, love of God and neighbor, and righteousness. If we are listening with our hearts, we will be able to hear the wisdom he has to direct and redirect our lives.

A moving series could be done on "Jesus' Uncomfortable Questions."

Week One: "Why do you raise such questions in your hearts?" (Mark 2:8)

Listeners would be called on to exchange skepticism for obedience.

Week Two: "Who do you say that I am?" (Mark 8:29)

Listeners would be challenged to exchange unthinking lip service to their faith to a genuine, full-hearted confession of who they believe Jesus to be.

Week Three: "Why do you argue over who is greatest?" (see Mark 9:33)

Listeners would be called on to exchange motives of self-aggrandizement for discipleship not motivated by desire for reward.

Week Four: "What is the one thing you lack?" (see Mark 10:21)

This week's message would be based on Jesus' terse assessment of the rich man's spiritual life. "You lack one thing" (Mark 10:21). Listeners would be challenged to exchange a surface desire to follow Jesus with a genuine following and would be asked, "What would it take? What would you have to give or give up?"

Week Five: "Where is your faith?" (see Luke 8:25)

Listeners would be challenged to ask themselves Jesus' questions in the midst of whatever trials life is handing them. The speaker could point them to positive examples from the Gospels of people with faith. These include the four friends of the paralytic (Mark 2:5), the centurion (Luke 7:9), and the woman with a flow of blood (Luke 8:48).

Week Six: "What is your name?" (Luke 8:30)

This week would deal with the chilling question Jesus asks the demons tormenting the young man of Gerasene. Listeners would be challenged and inspired to name the legion that torments them and exchange it for the peace of Christ that gives them a new name: disciple, seeker of wisdom.

Meditation on the Listening Heart

"Give Me a Listening Heart"

Scriptures: 1 Kgs 3:3-12; Ps 34:1-10; Mark 10:46-52

Several years ago, a friend of mine was about to start a new position, moving from associate pastor to senior pastor. He told me, "I dreamed I was a little boy with Daddy's briefcase walking into work the first day." We may put on our game face during the daylight hours, but after midnight, in our dreams, our fears come out. That's what happened to people in the Bible, too.

Solomon's dream in 1 Kgs 3 was similar. "You have made me king to fill Big Daddy's shoes, and I am only a child. There are so many of them and just one of me. . . . Help!"

I wonder if Bartimaeus had a recurring dream in which he was an old, old man, still with veiled, sightless eyes, still sitting on his cloak, with it all spread around him to catch the coins passersby tossed at him. Nothing changed; he was just old and blind and alone.

God instructs Solomon, "Ask what I should give you" (1 Kgs 3:5).

Jesus asks Bartimaeus, "What do you want me to do for you?" (Mark 10:51).

When he turns to you, what's your answer? "I want things to stay just like they are." "I want everything to work out painlessly and perfectly for me and my family." "I want to reach my dreams without making any sacrifices."

Bartimaeus has the right answer to Jesus. "Too long I have lived in this dark and enclosed place. Too long I have focused on my own sufferings and the unfairness of it all. Let me see again so I can emerge from this prison."

Solomon has the right answer to God. "I am overwhelmed by my new responsibilities. Give me a listening mind, or a hearing heart." It doesn't much matter how you translate it, because for the Hebrew mind, the heart was the source not just of emotions but of thought and decision making as well. Solomon was saying something like, "Help me to give my full attention to the encounters with people that lie ahead of me, when I will be called on to judge wisely. Help me to listen attentively to what they say and to what God is saying when we are face to face."

Many adults remember *Highlights* magazine, a magazine for children often found in doctors' waiting rooms. Each issue featured a "Can You Find?" page that featured a picture in which several everyday objects were hidden. The wisdom of Proverbs promises us that if we look carefully, if we listen with our hearts, we'll find not an apple or a bat or a cupcake, but patterns that show us how best to live. "Like somebody who takes a passing dog by the ears is one who meddles in the quarrel of another" (Prov 26:17). "Like a city breached, without walls, is one who lacks self-control" (Prov 25:28). The sages of Israel were always listening for wisdom.

Don't you imagine that Jesus had plenty of his own fears to preoccupy him on his way to Jerusalem? "Oh God, I'm afraid they're going to kill me. I don't want to die. Oh God, I don't want to suffer. Oh God, I'm afraid they're going to kill me." In light of that, the three most beautiful words in the passage to me are these: *Jesus stood still* (Mark 10:49).

How typical of Jesus is this action! He always notices our fears: whether we are terrified in our storm-battered boat, kneeling at his feet, worn out with illness or sorrow, not thinking ourselves worthy to so much as touch the hem of his cloak, or cowering behind locked doors because all our hopes are presumed dead. Our risen Jesus always passes through the thickest wall of our fears and stands before us. With these words on his lips: "Take heart. I am with you. Be healed of your diseases. Do not be afraid." *Jesus stood still.*

How typical of Jesus is his command to anyone who would prevent another's coming to him. Act like a poor, blind person in this society should; says the crowd, "Sit down and shut up!" "Call him here," says Jesus.

How typical of Jesus is his question to Bartimaeus that respects Bartimaeus's ability to articulate and choose. It's as if Jesus says, "The choice of response is yours." "What do you want me to do for you?" he asks Bartimaeus (Mark 10:51).

Many years ago when I was serving a church in Pennsylvania, a parishioner called me around 10:30 PM. "I'm so sorry to bother you. My nephew needs to talk to somebody really badly. He is not a churchgoer but he said he wanted to talk to my pastor." A half hour later I sat in my living room across from a young man in his late twenties, pale as a ghost, with a red gash in his forehead. He launched into a story that you have heard all too often: He'd had several drinks out with his friends, then he and his friend had left to go home, with him driving, and he was now sitting here with one surface head wound while his buddy was fighting for his life in the ICU. While he talked he picked up the big Bible we had on the coffee table, the kind with the face of Jesus on the front. He started tracing the face of Jesus while he told his tale. Around the face, tracing his hair, circling his eyes, down the line of his nose, the outline of his lips, his ears, back around the route, over and over. Suddenly, he looked up at me, his eyes wet, and blurted out, "Jesus Christ, what am I going to do?"

There are a lot of people out there in the pews, in hospital waiting rooms, on reservations, in upscale neighborhoods, in Section 8 housing, saying the name of Jesus, halfway between a curse and a prayer; people who think cursing is all that's left for them, because it's too late for them to start praying. People who don't pray anymore because the path of their life has gotten so far off the map, because people like them have no futures, because peace of mind is a thing of the past.

Are we paying enough attention to notice and offer the gospel they need? The news that it's not too late to fear the Lord? That whenever we turn to God, trembling, receptive, repentant, God comes to meet us bearing gifts? A peace that seems impossible under the circumstances, a joy we could not possibly have earned, and some directions that are a whole lot more reliable than the wandering around we've been doing. Can we tell them from our own experience that the Lord is listening with his heart? The Lord is asking from his heart *What do you want me to do for you?*

The man had read all the statistics on Alzheimer's disease, knew the clinical symptoms, had been to a couple of workshops on nursing care for sufferers. The center he administered had just finished a new Alzheimer's wing. It was brand new with all the modern conveniences. Then he saw them, a couple coming down the spotless hallway, the woman walking with the assistance of her husband, her eyes filled with confusion and fear, looking around at the unfamiliar surroundings of her new home. He greeted them warmly, with the hearty assurance, "Things seem a little strange now, but you'll feel at home in no time." Two weeks later he noticed the woman, Mary, still had fear in her eyes. Her children and husband brought in memorabilia from home to brighten up her room. An afghan, family pictures, a favorite lamp. He noticed that Mary came to meals but didn't stay in the common rooms any longer than she had to. Neither did the other guests. He decided to talk with colleagues at other centers. He made several visits to the other centers and noted that some of them had "memory lane rooms": rooms that were decorated to reflect the time in which many of these people mentally lived—the 1950s. So he came home and decorated the whole wing that way. He put a Judy Garland movie in the DVD player. He got a small CD player and kept a stack of big band CDs next to it. The Campbell Soup Kids emblem graced the wall.

The last time he walked down the hall, many of the guests' rooms were empty, including Mary's. She was sitting with her friends in their living room, listening to Tommy Dorsey, and he noticed there was not nearly so much fear in her eyes.

There is someone in your life and mine waiting for us to notice him and in that noticing to unleash a divine repair. I wonder who. . . .

The listening heart describes our ministry in a nutshell: being attentive to others' pain and fear and inviting them into wholeness and healing, to follow, with us, the path of devotion to Jesus Christ. The life of the listening heart is not an easy path. We hear things we would rather not hear, learn things it is easier not to know, and feel things it is more comfortable not to feel. So that's how it feels to be fourteen and without a future except the needle. So that's how it feels to live in fear of your boyfriend's fist. To hope for a last-minute pardon from the governor. To dread your daddy's visits to your room. We go places we never thought we'd go. We cry tears we would rather not cry. Sometimes we lie awake when we would rather be sleeping just because someone else is in too much pain to sleep. Mystic Henry Nouwen defines Christian maturity as "the ability and willingness to be led where you would rather not go."[4] He continues, "The way of the Christian leader is not the way of upward mobility in which our world has invested so much, but the way of downward mobility ending on the cross."[5]

Not everyone wants to live that way. Just before the story of Bartimaeus is the story of two disciples, James and John, the sons of Zebedee. They came forward to Jesus and said to him, "Teacher, we want you to do for us whatever we ask of you" (Mark 10:35). He said to them, "What is it you want me to do for you?" (Mark 10:37). They said to him, "Grant us to sit, one at your right hand and one at your left, in your glory." Well that's one vision for ministry.

But here's another. "What do you want me to do for you?" Jesus asks Bartimaeus. "My teacher, let me see again," says the blind man. "Immediately he regained his sight and followed [Jesus] on the way [*to Jerusalem*]" (Mark 10:51-52, emphasis added).

CHAPTER SIX

THE THIRD PILLAR OF WISDOM: THE COOL SPIRIT

"One who spares words is knowledgeable; one who is cool in spirit has understanding." (Prov 17:27)

In the second century C.E., a rabbinic sage, Rabbi Meir, made a connection between the listening heart and the cool spirit.

> Through attention to Reality
> Comes self-control and discernment
> Secrets are revealed,
> And one becomes an ever-fresh spring of wisdom.[1]

The Sages of Hebrew Scriptures

Self-Control: The Hallmark of the Wise Person

Self-control, in this context, is a misnomer. For the sages, such discipline flowed from living connected to God through the fear of the Lord. The fear of the Lord means trusting our present and our future into the hands of God. The listening heart listens to others for signs of hurt and the need for healing. The third pillar of wisdom, the "cool spirit," rests on the ability to forego short-term gratification for longer-term benefit.

One of the quintessential traits of the fool is the lack of self-control. Self-control relates to a spectrum of behaviors: speech and silence, hard work, appetites for food and drink, and sexual temptation. The sages did not debate the relative role of nature and nurture. They did not discuss the dynamics of addiction and disease. They did not consider how family anger and violence often have their roots in childhood abuse that creates adult abusers. As contemporary wisdom teachers, we need to understand those dynamics. It is also useful for us to keep in mind the uncompromising cautions of Israel's sages. For Proverbs simply lists and describes negative behaviors and their results and warns the young, in the strongest possible terms, to avoid them.

When self-control is lacking, the result is behaviors that produce strife: drunkenness, quarreling, anger, hatred, and greed. "Those who are hot-tempered stir up strife, but those who are slow to anger calm contention" (Prov 15:18). "Hatred stirs up strife, but love covers all offenses" (Prov 10:12). Greed is the breeding ground for a whole battery of crimes against individuals and society. It stems, like anger and hatred, from a breakdown of self-control. The wise teachers of Israel characterized these actions, and the attitudes from which they stem, as typical of the vicious fool (*nabal*).[2]

All of these behaviors disrupt the harmony of interpersonal relationships and, with it, the orderly functioning of society. If these behaviors are allowed to persist, they tear society apart. To lack self-control is to be antisocial and to live in a way that is incompatible with the fear of the Lord.[3] Throughout Proverbs those who live by wisdom are described as following a path (4:18; 5:6; 10:17; 12:28; 15:19, 24). Self-control is a crucial communal value. It helps ensure that the community is traveling along together on the path of Wisdom that leads to *shalom*, peace with justice.[4]

A young African American pastor in an inner-city Dallas church spoke of the role of his mother in teaching him the value of a cool spirit.

> My mother was a big influence on me. She used to say, "Don't burn your bridges." "Be careful about the company you keep." "Birds of a feather flock together." She was a walking book of Proverbs. "My mother always taught me" is something I say a lot in my preaching, and when I do, the older people nod their heads.

An anonymous sage once said that "discipline puts back in its place that something in us which should serve but wants to rule."[5] Self-control is particularly important in leaders. Without it, the king might forget to fulfill his communal responsibilities to speak for the silent, the poor, and the needy and to champion the rights of those left desolate (21:8, 9). Self-indulgence in a ruler harms the whole community.[6]

The "Cool Man"

The ideal of the sages of Proverbs is the one who is "cool in spirit" (17:27). Primarily used to refer to self-control in matters of speech, it also is an apt description for one who exercises it across a broad spectrum of situations. Injunctions to self-restraint appear in the didactic literature of other ancient Near Eastern cultures, especially that of Egyptian origin. The sayings of Prov 22:20–24:22 are likely dependent on *The Instruction of Amenemope*, an Egyptian collection of wise advice for young courtiers that predates Proverbs, probably dating to 1200 B.C.E.[7]

Frequent in *The Instruction of Amenemope* and other Egyptian writings is the contrast between the one who is "slow to anger" and the "heated man." This theme is found in Prov 15:18; 22:24; and 29:22.[8]

In Prov 17:27, the expressive phrase "cool in spirit" is used to indicate self-control in speaking: "One who spares words is knowledgeable; one who is cool in spirit has understanding."

The cool spirit has at its core the ability to control oneself, a theme that runs through the Proverbs collection (see especially 10:1-21; 16; and 25:1–29:27). The "cool man" values self-control as the leash that restrains destructive emotions and the actions to which they give rise.

> Like a city breached, without walls,
>   is one who lacks self-control. (Prov 25:28)

The value of self-control in matters of the temper spans religious boundaries. There is a story about Buddha that makes this clear. It seems a man had heard of the reputation Buddha had for being peaceful and nonviolent regardless of what he encountered in life. This man decided to test the divine one, and he traveled a long distance to be in his presence. For three days he was rude and obnoxious to the Buddha. He criticized and found fault with everything the Buddha said or did. He verbally abused the Buddha, attempting to get him to react angrily. Yet the Buddha never faltered. Each time he responded with love and kindness. Finally the man could take it no longer. "How could you be so peaceful and kind when all I've ever said to you was antagonistic?" he asked. The

Buddha's response was in the form of a question to the man. "If someone offers you a gift, and you do not accept that gift, to whom does the gift belong?" The man had his answer.[9]

In Proverbs, the "cool man" avoids public intoxication (Prov 23:20-21) and foolish companions (Prov 13:20).[10] The "cool man" (Prov 17:27) will not give way to fits of temper and will ignore insults (Prov 12:16). He resists sexual temptation and honors the marital relationship. The one who lacks self-control in such matters is compared with a person carrying "fire in one's clothes" or "walking on hot coals" (see Prov 6:27-29).

Hard Work

The "cool man" or disciplined person embraces hard work. Hard work is another demonstration of self-control. The sages admonished their students to be diligent and not to despise discipline and correction (Prov 1:7b). They warned them not to sleep too much. The sages learned these lessons in part from observing the animal kingdom (Prov 6:6; 30:24-31) as well as the human realm (Prov 24:30-34).[11] From their observations they deduced that actions have consequences and that the consequences of diligence are preferable to those of sloth.

John Wesley, the founder, along with his brother Charles, of the Methodist movement in England in the 1700s, was an enthusiastic advocate of hard work. "It is a great thing to seize and improve the very now. You cannot live on what God did yesterday. The more labor the more blessing."[12]

The sages of Proverbs affirmed that hard work is the road to wealth (12:27; 13:4; 14:23; 20:13). While wealth doesn't necessarily bring happiness (16:16; 22:1-2), it is essential to security (10:15; 18:11). Its possession can contribute to the peaceful, prosperous life and may be a sign of divine blessing (10:22; 13:21, 25; 15:6; 22:4).[13]

Cool Speech

The sages realized that speech was an area of human life that demanded rigorous self-control. "Death and life are in the power of the tongue" (Prov 18:21). "Truthful lips endure forever, but a lying tongue lasts only a moment" (Prov 12:19). "It is better to be poor than a liar"

(Prov 19:22b). The "cool man" controls his speech. He uses it sparingly and carefully considers each word.

> Those who guard their mouths preserve their lives;
> those who open wide their lips come to ruin. (Prov 13:3)

> The mind of the righteous ponders how to answer,
> but the mouth of the wicked pours out evil. (Prov 15:28)

For the sake of harmony in society the wise person's speech avoids provocative and harsh words.

> A gentle tongue is a tree of life. (Prov 15:4a)

> A soft answer turns away wrath, but a harsh word stirs up anger. (Prov 15:1)

Knowing when to be silent and listen is an important aspect of self-control (Prov 18:15b). It is especially difficult to maintain silence when one is being criticized. The wise person does not resent criticism but listens to it and evaluates it.

> Whoever loves discipline loves knowledge, but those who hate to be rebuked are stupid. (Prov 12:1)

The wise person refrains from boasting.

> If you have been foolish, exalting yourself,
> or if you have been devising evil,
> put your hand on your mouth. (Prov 30:32)

With regard to his speech, the "cool man" confines himself to saying what he knows (Prov 20:15). He avoids slander, gossip, and quarreling (Prov 10:18; 11:12-13; 26:21). He avoids unnecessary involvement in the quarrels of others (Prov 26:17). He is a good listener (Prov 12:15; 18:13; 25:12). Just knowing when to stay silent can work wonders, even for one of limited talent:

> Even fools who keep silent are considered wise,
> When they close their lips, they are deemed intelligent. (Prov 17:28)[14]

The fool, the "hot man," is one who does not know when to keep quiet, and who has no control over his tongue (Prov 10:8, 14; 12:23; 18:2).

Learning by Doing

How does one gain self-discipline? Self-control and self-discipline must be earned by practice. Self-control is described both as a gift (from God and Woman Wisdom) and also as an accomplishment that comes from earnest and lasting effort by the learner (Prov 2–7).[15] Self-control is not just a private virtue. The learner's self-discipline is fostered and modeled by family, mentors, and teachers. It is learned from the support and discipline of one's family, as in the case of King Lemuel's mother and the "father and mother" referred to so often in Prov 1–7. The learner's self-discipline has beneficial effects on the whole community. Conversely, the fool's lack of impulse control can do harm to many (Prov 10:14).

The Cool Spirit of Ecclesiastes

While Job is all about a passion for vindication, Qohelet is all about being cool. Qohelet, the name given to the "gatherer" of the wisdom reflections and sayings in Ecclesiastes, was a cool character. Lacking the passionate anger of Job, Ecclesiastes is characterized by melancholy and a depiction of God as distant. This is a lean, taut book, knit together with tremendous literary discipline. The author's agenda is the deliberate subversion of all the major tenets of traditional wisdom through the employment of its own genres of reflection and proverbial sayings. He repeatedly juxtaposes traditional assurances with subversive versions of his own coinage (see especially chapter 7).

He was disappointed that the fear of the Lord doesn't always lead to knowledge that is useful for figuring out life, but instead bumps up against the limitations of human wisdom (Eccl 1:17-18). He was disappointed that hard work and wise living do not exempt one from misfortune and death (Eccl 2:14b-17; 8:14-15; 9:11-12). He was disappointed that the rich oppress the poor and the powerless (Eccl 4:1-3). Though he does admit to feeling anger and despair (Eccl 2:17, 20), he gives in to it only temporarily. His collection of sayings and reflections is not an undisciplined outpouring of cynicism, anger, pessimism, and despair. He is able to rein in those emotions. He is able to channel them into a realistic view of life that focuses on gratitude for the good gifts of wisdom, food, drink, work, and human companionship in each passing moment (Eccl 2:13-14a; 2:24-25; 9:7-8).

Qohelet counsels self-discipline with regard to speech and the accumulation of wealth in terms reminiscent of Proverbs' more conventional wisdom collection.

> Words spoken by the wise bring them favor,
>   but the lips of fools consume them.
> The words of their mouths begin in foolishness,
>   and their talk ends in wicked madness;
> yet fools talk on and on. (Eccl 10:12-14)

> Better is a handful with quiet than two handfuls with toil, and a chasing after wind. (Eccl 4:6)

> Do not let your mouth lead you into sin. (Eccl 5:6a)

> If the anger of the ruler rises against you, do not leave your post,
>   for calmness will undo great offenses. (Eccl 10:4)

Qohelet warns against being rash and greedy for gain. Such attitudes and actions are futile—they cannot increase our good and so they are just so much wasted energy. They distract us from enjoying our portion in the present moment, the only good that life holds in Qohelet's view.

> The lover of money will not be satisfied with money; nor the lover of
> wealth, with gain. This also is vanity.
>   When goods increase, those who eat them increase; and what gain
> has their owner but to see them with his eyes? (Eccl 5:10-11)

Throughout the book he juxtaposes positive statements about wisdom and its value with grimly realistic statements of the inequities of life that seem to undercut its value. "Then I saw that wisdom excels folly as light excels darkness. The wise have eyes in their head, but fools walk in darkness. Yet I perceived that the same fate befalls all of them" (Eccl 2:13-14). This is not just a ploy to confuse the reader. Nor is it, in my view, evidence of a later editor who inserted positive statements about wisdom to blunt the sword of Qohelet's cynicism. Qohelet juxtaposes conventional and subversive wisdom because he wants us to live with two truths in sight. First, the "cool man" can avoid many of the pitfalls of life by disciplining his appetites. Conventional wisdom does have value. Second, there are some events and conditions the coolest of the cool cannot avoid. The context of the "cool man's life" is the limitation of human knowledge and the mystery of God (Eccl 5:1-7), the unpredictability of life (Eccl 9:11, 12), and the inequities of social systems (Eccl 4:1-3). All the more reason, Qohelet believes, to be cool. It does no good not to be. There is great value in disciplining oneself to focus on the present with a grateful heart and not be buffeted by heated waves of anxiety and anger over the inequities and unpredictabilities of life.

The Cool Spirit of Jesus the Sage

Conventional wisdom on self-control with regard to appetites, speech, and hard work does not figure in Jesus' teachings. He does not talk about when to speak and when to be silent, a major theme in Proverbs. He has much more to say about listening than speaking![16] His concern is that people hear his words and act on them (Matt 7:24). He does not talk about avoiding foolish companions. In fact, he dined with those society had labeled "expendables" more often than not.[17] He offers no conventional wisdom about moderation in food and drink.

Still, there is some continuity between the sages of Proverbs and Jesus the sage with regard to this wisdom virtue of self-control. Both warn against greed; both discern that the heart is the wellspring of conduct, and both deal with how one is to relate to the poor. Proverbs enjoins respectful charity to the poor (14:21, 31). Jesus goes a step further and, with his life and death, as well as his teachings, exemplifies identification with the poor.

The self-control it takes to be a disciple of Jesus, however, springs from a different motivation from that of Israel's sages. Generally, the sages of Proverbs commended self-control as a means of stabilizing society. Jesus commended it, through example as much as through teaching, as a means of challenging and subverting oppressive social and political traditions and pointing toward an inbreaking kingdom of God.

Not only is the motive for self-discipline different when we contrast Proverbs' teachings with those of Jesus, but so are the arenas in which one is to exercise self-control. Nowhere are the differences and similarities more clearly represented than in the Sermon on the Mount in Matthew's Gospel. We have seen how the Hebrew sages' students were to exercise self-restraint in food, drink, sexual expression, temper, and speech. Jesus

114

is in agreement with the sages on the need to restrain oneself from anger (5:21-22) and adultery (5:27) and gullibility with regard to false teachers (7:15-16).

However, he emphasizes several examples of self-discipline that are almost at odds with the advice of conventional proverbial wisdom. Proverbial wisdom underscores the importance of planning ahead and hard work as means to a degree of prosperity and security. It highlights the importance of prudent, close-mouthed public behavior as a means to a good reputation. Jesus emphasizes that his followers were to restrain themselves from worry about the necessities of life (6:27-39) and resist a preoccupation with personal security (16:24-26). They were to avoid displays of public piety (6:1), materialism (6:19), judging others (7:1), and retaliation (5:38). Proverbs is concerned that the young avoid those who would hinder them in their pursuit of wisdom. Jesus has much more to say about a kind of restraint never mentioned in Proverbs. Jesus' disciples were to restrain themselves from a tendency to hinder *others* in their approach to God (Matt 18:10-14; Mark 9:33-37).

Every case of restraining a negative quality involves replacing it with its positive counterpart. God helps us replace worry with trust, preoccupation with security with joyful risk-taking, verbose displays of public piety with private prayer and fasting, materialism with storing up treasures in heaven, judging others with forgiveness, retaliating against our enemies with loving them, gullibility regarding false teachers with belief in Jesus and listening to his teachings and acting upon them.

The students of Israel's sages learned self-control not only by practicing it but also by observing the lives of their teachers. So we can learn about self-control not only from Jesus' teachings but also from his life. Here is a subversive sage with a cool character—one who did not act or speak impulsively. He responded spontaneously but always strategically. Instances of Jesus' own self-control abound in the Gospels. He resisted the temptation of Satan to allow greed and ego to get out of hand and become his motivation. Far more than once, he exercised the "cool man's" ability to ignore an insult. His followers were not always so strong. When one of his followers sliced off the ear of one of the high priest's slaves in the Garden of Gethsemane, Jesus pointed out the folly of anger as a way of life (Matt 26:51-52; Luke 22:51).

Motivated by compassion, Jesus controlled his own fatigue and hunger, rising to the occasion when human need surrounded him (Mark 6:30-44). His symbolic action of turning over the tables in the temple was motivated by a sense that God was being done an injustice, not that he himself was being issued a personal affront. The action, though dramatic, did not take the form of violence against other people.

A pastor from a Japanese Christian church in San Diego told me this.

> When you talk about the "cool spirit," that's a very Buddhist way, and it's often described as being cool. Whereas Jesus' way of dealing with suffering is not to withdraw but to engage the suffering, to take it on. Instead of a relationship of coolness with the world, it's a hot relationship. Not in terms of temper, but in terms of involvement. That Asian or Buddhistic withdrawal is a very helpful kind of management tool in terms of our personal lives. But ultimately, as Christians, our testimony is engaging and sharing in other people's suffering. There is really a warmth to that that is different from the coolness of Buddhism. Often we talk in our senior Bible study on Wednesdays about how oftentimes Buddhistic behavior and morality can look very similar to Christian behavior and morality. The difference is not in what we do and how we treat the other person, but in the reasons for that treatment.

> I'm not trying to get my people to actually behave all that differently. My mother came to the Lord just before she died of cancer. My whole life growing up, she was the most moral, ethical, gentle, understanding person I knew, even more so than most people who know Christ. And so all my life I knew that it is possible for non-Christian people to be very moral and very caring based on the example of my mother.

While Proverbs acknowledges that there were times when harsh speech and rebuke were called for (10:10; 25:12; 28:23), it mostly favors conciliatory speech and silence as modes of ensuring community harmony. It favors conciliatory speech toward rulers and social superiors as a means of survival (20:2; 22:11). Jesus' teachings show a pattern of challenging speech to religious and political authorities and comforting, conciliatory speech to those on the social margins, the desperate and the ill.[18] An excellent example comes to us in Luke 7:36-50 when we contrast his challenging words to Simon with his comforting words to the woman.

Throughout the Proverbs collection there is an insistence that the heart is the source of actions and speech. Proverbs reminds us, "Keep your heart with all vigilance, for from it flow the springs of life" (4:23), and "The thoughts of the righteous are just" (12:5a), and "Whoever is slow to anger has great understanding" (14:29a). The cool spirit is very much a matter of the inward person, the heart, the seedbed of volition, emotion, and thought. Still, many of the sayings in Proverbs define self-restraint as the restraint of destructive actions. Jesus defines self-restraint as the control of violent, destructive thoughts wherein actions such as violence and adultery originate (Matt 15:19; Mark 7:21-23).

Self-discipline of the inward life is not merely preventative. It is proactive. Jesus advocates the cultivation of an inner life that will result in unconventional actions, actions that challenge traditional mores. Such actions, if practiced over time, transform personal and social relationships into embodiments of the kingdom that is at hand. In Jesus' teachings as well as in his interactions with people, this focus on the inward life is clear. Loving one's enemies results not in retaliation but in forgiveness. Striving for God's kingdom and righteousness results not in a paralyzing preoccupation with personal security but in a carefree life that trusts God for provisions for each present day. Being pure in heart results not in ritual purity but in the purity of the words that issue from our mouths.

Jesus had a cool head. But he used it not to promote his reputation but to strategically convey his subversive teachings. Jesus offers proverbial sayings to live by, but they are paradoxical and life-shaking. Proverbs tells us self-control can bring us security and life. Jesus tells us that if we would save our life we must lose it. Proverbs tells us that if we exercise self-control we will have a good reputation. Jesus says "Blessed are those who are persecuted for righteousness' sake" (Matt 5:10). Proverbs warns against harsh words that stir up wrath. When the occasion called for plain speaking, Jesus did not care whose hackles he raised. Proverbs advocated strategic speech for the purpose of social stability. Jesus exercised it to subvert exclusionary religious norms.

Injunctions to self-control anchor the world's great religions. Confucianism counsels "Nothing in excess," a way of life that charts a middle course between unworkable extremes and brings harmony and balance to family and social relationships.[19] Sufism, a manifestation of Islam especially focused on one's present, inward life, counsels the control of one's anger and addictions as a way of subduing the ego (*nafs*) that impedes one's surrender to Allah. Hinduism offers the discipline of Yoga, with its emphasis on diet, posture, breathing, and concentration as a means of connecting with *Atman*. *Atman* is that dimension of the human self that reflects *Brahman*, the hidden ground of all existence that pervades, sustains, and inspires human life.[20] Buddhism recommends self-control in matters of speech and behavior. Speech should be both true and charitable. Those who follow "The Way" seek the gradual liberation from delusions and cravings and the attainment of *nirvana*, eternal and imponderable peace. Such followers should practice gentle, caring actions and eschew anger, unchastity, and the consumption of intoxicants.[21]

John Wesley repeatedly preached and taught that the Christian life is a gift of grace. He warned his followers not to forget that "we are saved *by faith,* producing all *inward* holiness, not by works, by any externals whatever."[22] At the same time he insisted that the Christian life also involved a concerted, consistent human response. One made use of what he called the "means of grace": searching the Scriptures, public and private prayer, worship and the sacraments, attendance at societies, small groups for spiritual accountability, and acts of charity. Responding intentionally to God's grace meant self-discipline. In one of his letters he wrote, "Better forty members should be lost than our discipline lost: They are no Methodists that will bear no restraints."[23]

For Christians, ironically, a key craving we need to get control over is our compulsion to be in control. This, I think, is part of what Jesus meant when he coined the aphorism "For those who want to save their life will lose it" (Matt 16:25; Mark 8:35; Luke 9:24). We need to give control over to God.

A United Methodist pastor serving a church in central Texas made a connection between faith and relinquishment of control. He said,

> To be a person of faith who lives by grace, you can't be in control. You have to relinquish that. Of course, we give our best to the task at hand, but we are not completely in control of life. We must have the ability to laugh at ourselves. People make faith a set of religious principles, a program, and they miss the point. It's about living life in a fulsome way. It is like people planning or going to a wedding. They get all fussy with the pictures and the clothing, and they completely miss the experience. It's like parents so hell-bent on making something out of their children and their children making something out of themselves that they miss the relationship.

The virtue of a cool spirit is crucial to the exercise of the subversive voice in our teaching and preaching. Possessing a cool spirit contributes to one's credibility in the community. By exercising impulse control in temper, speech, physical appetites, and relationships, the sage gains the respect of the community. He or she earns a reputation for morality, moderation, and discipline. This is a foundation that takes time to construct. It is a groundwork that must be laid if we seek to raise our subversive voices; that is, to articulate strategic, credible, and premeditated challenges to the status quo.

CHAPTER SEVEN

TEACHING AND PREACHING WITH A COOL SPIRIT

The purpose of teaching and preaching with a cool spirit is to exchange the yoke of our appetites for the yoke of the fear of the Lord. The goal is not to become cold-hearted or dispassionate in our enjoyment of life or our pursuit of justice. The goal is to allow our passion for God to take the driver's seat and operate the control panel of our other passions.

The virtue of a cool spirit is most obvious when it is missing. It manifests itself as impulse control, and as an instinct for when self-revelation is appropriate and when it crosses the line. Other manifestations of a cool spirit are appropriately directed anger; the ability to hold one's temper; resistance to the excesses and idolatries of contemporary culture; and the power to resist addictions, whether to things, work, others' approval, power, possessions, or substances. The cool spirit might also assert itself in the nudge to recognize that we are out of control and to seek help in the face of an uncontrollable addiction that hurts others as well as ourselves. The cool spirit brings with it a stringent willingness to be honest with oneself, sifting through rationalizations to one's true motives and abiding faults. Additional evidence of possessing both the fear of the Lord and the cool spirit are having appropriate physical boundaries and the ability to avoid the temptation to misuse one's power.

Preaching and Teaching with a Cool Spirit: Qualities of Sermons and Lessons from a Cool Spirit

Talk Less, Say More

Regarding the sermon or lesson itself, a cool spirit, a spirit of restraint, leads the speaker to abide by the Vermont proverb: "Talk less, say more." It would lead one to eschew sentimentality over explanation, inappropriate self-exposure, and a penchant for telling people what they want to hear.

The use of pauses is a sign of the cool spirit in preaching and teaching. So is restraint in knowing how much material to include in a sermon. The cool spirit leads us not to try to cram too much information in one sermon. It also leads us to choose our battles and our timing in addressing sensitive, potentially divisive topics.

Let Proverbs and Parables Do Our Preaching and Teaching for Us

If we would embody and teach the wisdom virtue of the cool spirit, it would make sense that we would choose to do so in proverbs and parables. Why? Because they are terse, employing only as many words as necessary. They are characterized by a certain self-containment and refusal to use extra verbiage in order to force listeners into certain applications. Proverbs and parables are respectful of the wisdom of the listener, trusting hearers to place them in context in their own lives. They do not exceed their limits and try to impose themselves categorically and universally. Their mode of operation is restraint. Proverbs and parables are not concerned with imposing a unilateral interpretation on everyone within earshot. They want to undermine those very dynamics to do what good novelists do, provide more scene and less summary.

Resist Temptation

When we teach and preach with a cool spirit, we resist the urge to be the answer giver when it is more faithful to let people struggle with the questions. We resist the temptation to bring false closure to unresolved issues. We resist our urge to tell people what they want to hear, that things will always and quickly turn out fine if they just have faith. We are able to curb our appetite for the approval of others and speak an unpopular but faithful word.

Bring the Gift of Preparation, Sustained Thought about the Topic

When we teach and preach with a cool spirit, our session with people has been preceded by times of sustained thought and preparation. We have the discipline to structure such time into our busy lives.

Capable of Setting Boundaries

In describing a friend, I once heard someone say, "She is always in one of two conditions: either a state of frenetic activity or immobile, sick in bed." The cool spirit exercises the common sense to honor our limits and care for our health—emotional, spiritual, physical, intellectual—so that the demands of life do not destroy us. Jesus was able to maintain his composure because of frequent withdrawals to quiet places to commune with God. We cannot expect to have self-control unless we first employ it to seek out times of prayer with God.

One Day at a Time

We know that when trying to break a bad habit, we can make progress, and then, when we think we have won the battle, we slide back again. The virtue of the cool spirit knows that the battle is won on a daily—somedays an hourly—basis. Discipline and composure pave the way for the energy and intensity the sage needs to observe, teach, and challenge.

A Unitarian pastor from a church in Dallas expressed an aspect of the cool spirit in this way.

> I have a larger vision of things than I used to. I am not as "kidnapped" as I used to be by people's dilemmas. They want me to get down there with them. They want me to be their savior. I keep a cool head in a crisis.

Preaching about the Cool Spirit: Suggestion for a Thematic Series

I can imagine a series of lessons or sermons that highlights foolish actions and alternatives that come from living with a cool spirit.

You May Be a Fool If Your Lack of Restraint Leads You to Engage in the Following Attitudes and Actions

Proverbs Version

You blurt out angry words that make bad situations worse or ruin good ones (Prov 15:1, 4, 18; 16:32; 17:27; 22:24; 29:22).

You don't know the value of judicious, pleasant speech (Prov 16:21, 23, 24).

You slander others (Prov 10:18).

You gossip, ruining others' reputations (Prov 11:12-13).

You pick fights (Prov 26:21).

You say dishonest things (Prov 12:19; 19:22).

You blather on, saying little of importance (Prov 10:8; 12:23; 13:3; 18:2).

You brag and boast about your accomplishments (Prov 30:32).

You can't ignore an insult (Prov 12:16).

You have not learned the importance of listening (Prov 17:28; 18:2).

You are a know-it-all (Prov 12:15; 18:13).

You think having lots of material possessions will make you happy and contented (Prov 15:16; 16:16-19; 17:1).

You place gaining money above your integrity and relationships (Prov 17:23).

You cannot control yourself in certain areas of your life. This is having a negative effect, and you are not doing anything about it (Prov 6:6-11; 23:29-35; 24:30-34; 25:28).

You lack self-control (Prov 25:27-28).

You are lazy (Prov 6:6; 18:9; 24:30-34; 26:14; 30:24-31).

You are unfaithful to primary relationships and betray the one closest to you (Prov 6:27-29).

You keep company with people who bring out the worst in you (Prov 13:20).

You enjoy spoiling the good fortune and happiness of others through deceitful speech and actions (Prov 16:27-30; 17:19, 23; 18:6-8).

You meddle in other people's concerns that are none of your business (Prov 26:17).

You cannot stand to be corrected (Prov 1:7b; 25:11-12).
You disdain those who are poor (Prov 17:5).
You hold grudges (Prov 17:9).

Qohelet's Version

You're always looking for a future lucky break rather than dealing with the unchanging realities of the present (Eccl 1:4-11).

You think your hard work can bring security (Eccl 2:18-22; 9:11-12).

You think wealth will bring you contentment (Eccl 5:10-12).

You think your accomplishments can bring you a lasting memory (Eccl 2:16-22).

You think your wise living can help you escape from death (Eccl 3:16-22).

You think you can know all there is to know about life and God (Eccl 5:1-7; 8:10-17).

You are impatient and try to force events to premature conclusions (Eccl 3:1-8).

You live as if you will never get old (Eccl 12:1-8).

You think you can live life without coming in contact with tragedy and injustice (Eccl 4:1-7).

Jesus' Version

You think you can harbor evil, foolish thoughts and they will stay your little secret (Matt 5:21-22, 27-29).

You think wealth can bring you lasting benefit (Matt 6:29).

You are gullible to false teachers and resistant to Jesus' message (Matt 7:15-16).

You think obsessive worry does any good (Matt 6:25-34).

You are preoccupied with personal security (Matt 16:24-26).

Your desire to be well thought of leads you to engage in displays of public religiosity (Matt 6:2).

You believe you are in a position to judge others (Matt 7:1).

You believe you are entitled to retaliate for wrongs done to you (Matt 5:38).

You hinder the approach of others to God (Matt 18:10-14; Mark 9:33-37).

You cannot ignore an insult (Matt 26:51-52; Luke 22:51).

You have no trouble sleeping while others face suffering (Matt 26:36-46; Luke 22:45-46).

Meditation on the Cool Spirit

"What Kind of Fool Are You?"[1]

Scriptures: Prov 1:4; 15:12; 17:21; 1 Cor 1:18-31

The book of Proverbs might also be called "Self-Control for Dummies." When we lack self-control, we become fools. And there are, in Proverbs, several answers to the question "What kind of fool am I?"

Imagine we are in a portrait gallery looking at portraits of each kind of fool in turn.

The Gullible Fool (*the Peti*)

Let's stop first in front of the gullible fool (*peti*). One of the goals of the Proverbs collection is to "teach shrewdness to the simple" (the *peti*).[2]

Note the open, gullible look on his face. He doesn't know the importance of self-control to gain wisdom, so he is, in effect, just waiting for someone or something else to take control of his life. "The simple believe everything" (14:15*a*). "Waywardness kills the simple (1:32*a*). He is still teachable but somebody better get to him with some wisdom fast. (1:22; 7:7; 8:5; 9:4, 6, 16).

In the background of this portrait of the *peti* are a group of people standing around. They are the gullible fools in Paul's church at Corinth. They are sitting ducks for false teachers. Anyone who looks good and sounds good will impress them. Somebody better get to the gullible fool with wisdom fast!

The Know-It-All Fool (*the Lutz*)

Our next stop is in front of the portrait of the *lutz*. (Note the big mouth and the small ears.) The NRSV translates this kind of fool as a "scoffer." My Hebrew-English lexicon calls him a "scorner" (Prov 13:1-2; 14:6, 8; 15:12). He enjoys hearing himself talk. As a philosopher once said, "The opposite of wisdom is not stupidity. It is knowing it all."

The *lutz* has become unteachable. He cannot control his own arrogance. He scorns the opinions and direction of those who are wiser. His attention is so focused on the sounds of his own voice that he cannot discipline himself to listen to anyone else.

See the lineup of good looking, confident people in the background of this picture? These are the *lutzes* of the Corinthian church: the false teachers that wormed their way in the minute Paul left. Paul calls them the "super apostles," better looking and taller than Paul, with a more commanding presence. No calluses on their hands from tent-making. Ecstatic experiences. Special religious knowledge. They know it all.

It is a dangerous group dynamic when *lutzes* lead *petis,* when the know-it-alls grasp authority to teach the gullible.

The Malicious Fool (*the Nabal*)

And finally we stop before the portrait of the kind of fool described by the Hebrew word *nabal.* Note the cold eyes and the cruel smirk. The *nabal* is far advanced in the school of folly. He cannot control his own malice. He cannot control his appetite for the misery of others. When you fail, he feels better. So much better that, while posing as your friend, he works behind the scenes to ensure your downfall.

This is Paul's fear for the Corinthians. That, in their gullibility, they will come under the influence of know-it-alls and malicious, self-serving people who misrepresent the gospel.

Proverbs makes it all seem so clear. It promises that if we exercise self-control and make wise choices, we will be able to gain a large measure of control over our health, longevity, reputation, prosperity, and relationships. It will be obvious to everyone that we are wise. If we lack self-control and make foolish choices, we will not flourish and everyone will be able to tell. If this is true, then, we should easily be able to look in the mirror and tell whether we're wise or foolish. We should be able to look at the diplomas on our walls, our bank accounts, our cholesterol levels, and our children's report cards and tell if we're wise or fools. Communities could give themselves the same test. What are real estate values here? How far or near are we to toxic waste dumps and chemical plants? What is the annual amount spent by the state on the education of each school-age child in our school districts?

Paul thinks it is not nearly that easy.

One summer during her college years, a friend of mine worked at a toy factory in Burlington, New Jersey. Once, her job crew was assigned to assemble tops. These were large, plastic tops that had a farm scene on a little platform at the bottom. On one side of the platform there was a cow and a sheep, and on the other side there was a cow and a goat. Her particular job was to place the little plastic farm animals on the platform, clicking them onto the knobs on the base. The animals came all lumped together in one huge plastic bag. The first girl had the job of digging out all the cows. My friend's job was to dig out all the sheep and goats and separate them into two piles on the assembly line table and then snap them into place in the farm scene, as quickly and efficiently as possible.

In this passage from First Corinthians it is as if Paul took the handle of this top and started pushing on it so that the farm scene began to spin faster and faster before our eyes. Sheep, Goat. Wise Fool. Sheep. Goat. Wise. Fool. Geep. Shoat. Fise. Wool. Geep. Shoat. Fise. Wool.

According to Paul, it is possible for someone to be a fool within and still give the appearance of possessing wisdom by conventional standards. According to Paul, it is possible for someone to be wise within and be judged a failure in the eyes of the world. For Paul, Jesus, in his teachings, death, and resurrection, has reframed conventional definitions of wisdom and folly.

We saw in Proverbs, Job, and Ecclesiastes that being wise boils down to trusting God's Wisdom as a divine gift to which we respond with trust and trembling, the fear of the Lord.

For Paul, the source of a wise life is God's act for our salvation in the resurrection of God's Son Jesus who "became for us wisdom from God" (1 Cor 1:30). This wisdom is, ultimately, not based on the precepts of common sense born out of the observation of daily life, but on a humiliating death that appears to completely refute conventional expectations. The acquisition of this wisdom is, ultimately, not dependent on the exercise of self-control toward measurable ends. Rather, it is unleashed in our lives when we relinquish control in favor of a risky reliance on the teachings and presence of a crucified Messiah, a sacrificial sage. This wisdom goes against cultural convention. It leaves no room for the boasting rights that motivate too many of our religious accomplishments.

You May Be a Fool If . . .

How are we to know where we stand? You've probably heard politically incorrect "You might be a redneck if…" jokes. Paul presents us with three self-checks in 1 Cor 2:6-16. Three signs that "you may be a fool if…."[3]

You Meditate on the Cross

You may be a fool if, in the past month, you have been meditating on the cross without meaning to. When you close your eyes do you see the outline of the cross? Have you seen its imprint in the faces of the suffering victims' families, refugee children with wide eyes like sad saucers, firefighters, rescue workers, and the young, thin-shouldered boys and men crowded on trucks in dusty clothing clutching their guns?

In prayer do you ever find yourself standing before the cross offering our Lord prayers of thanks and encouragement? Do you find yourself affirming that which is far from obvious? Things like "in weakness there is strength"; "in death there is life"; "love is stronger than death"?

If so, you are well on your way to being a fool by Paul's definition.

You Rely on the Holy Spirit

The second sign that you may be a fool is if, in the past few weeks, you have found yourself praying more than usual, for others, for wisdom, for God. That means you are coming to an even deeper sense of your need for God in your ministry of teaching and preaching. It means you are living out the first Beatitude, "Blessed are the poor in spirit" (Matt 5:3). The NEB rendering is "How blest are those who know their need of God." This is echoed in the Christian mystical tradition that tells us that our greatest perfection is to need God.[4]

And if you start recognizing your need for God more, you're going to get more disciplined about quiet times of prayer. And if you continue or begin to set aside quiet times of prayer, you are going to be listening to yourself breathe. And once you start listening to yourself breathe, you cannot help being reminded of the Holy Spirit that animates your spirit. And it is a short step from there to your experiencing, in prayer, a growing awareness of your reliance on that Spirit.

You Are Motivated by Love for God/Others

And if, in a time of prayer, you should feel as if your personal anxieties are dropping away, replaced by a sense of being loved and a spontaneous love for those around you, you have placed yourself in a very dangerous position—you are about to unwrap the riskiest of gifts.

That gift is "the mind of Christ," and it is the third sign that you may be a fool. Paul warns us in 1 Cor 2:16 that it could come to us.

"To partake of the mind of Christ" is to be so overcome with love for God and others that you are willing to risk everything, in faith that God holds your future.

Meditating on the cross instead of on trivialities is bad enough; relying on the Holy Spirit rather than knowing it all yourself is bad enough; but if you also have this third symptom of foolishness, the mind of Christ, then you have probably already exchanged fear for faith in God. There may be no turning back. You may already be what Paul calls "mature" or complete (1 Cor 2:6). You may already be a total fool.

Congratulations!

CHAPTER EIGHT

THE FOURTH PILLAR OF WISDOM: THE SUBVERSIVE VOICE

"You have heard that it was said . . . but I say to you. . . . " (Matt 5:21-22)

In his autobiography, frontier preacher Peter Cartwright (1785–1872) tells the story of an incident in his charge in Marietta, Ohio, when he served as a subversive sage.

There was here in Marietta a preacher by the name of A. Sargent . . . [who] assumed the name of Halcyon Church, and proclaimed himself the millennial messenger. He professed to see visions, fall into trances, and to converse with angels. His followers were numerous in the town and country. . . .

On Sunday night, at our camp-meeting, Sargent got some powder, and lit a cigar, and then walked down to the bank of the river, one hundred yards, where stood a large stump. He put his powder on the stump, and touched it with his cigar. The flash of the powder was seen by many at the camp; at least the light. When the powder flashed, down fell Sargent; there he lay a good while. In the meantime, the people found him lying there, and gathered around him. At length he came to, and said he had a message from God to us Methodists. He said God had come down to him in a flash of light, and he fell under the power of God, and thus received his vision.

Seeing so many gathered around him there, I took a light, and went down to see what was going on. As soon as I came near the stump, I

129

smelled the sulphur of the powder; and stepping up to the stump, there was clearly the sign of powder, and hard by lay the cigar with which he had ignited it. He was now busy delivering his message. I stepped up to him, and asked him if an angel had appeared to him in that flash of light.

He said, "Yes."

Said I, "Sargent, did not that angel smell of brimstone?"

"Why," said he, "do you ask me such a foolish question?"

"Because," said I, "if an angel has spoken to you at all, he was from the lake that burneth with fire and brimstone!" and raising my voice, I said, "I smell sulphur now!" I walked up to the stump, and called on the people to come and see for themselves. The people rushed up, and soon saw through the trick, and began to abuse Sargent for a vile impostor. He soon left, and we were troubled no more with him or his brimstone angels."[1]

Subversive sages, as we shall see, with varying degrees of subtlety, do what Peter Cartwright did. They expose as human constructs that we humans like to call divine wisdom.

The Sages of Hebrew Scriptures

To use the terms *subversive* and *sage* in the same breath may seem like an oxymoron. For sages so often serve to stabilize the community by inculcating respect for the authority of traditional wisdom. To subvert something, by contrast, means to undermine it, to disturb its equilibrium, or to overthrow it. We may judge a person who subverts tradition to have some kind of "problem with authority."

To call someone a subversive sage is to commend him or her for his or her respect for authority: God's. The sages' search for wisdom was undergirded by two precepts that punctuate the book of Proverbs: the gracious freedom of a Sovereign God whose divine order is only partially revealed in creation, and the limitations of human knowledge. These precepts are the guarantors of biblical wisdom's integrity from generation to generation.

It is all too easy for human sages in any age to forget those two precepts and promote our observations about acts and their consequences into universal rules. Then the listening heart closes its ears, because we must ignore much of the evidence around us to maintain the vision of order we have constructed. We have to ignore the diligent people who, because of a poor economy, are laid off and evicted from their homes.[2] We have to distance ourselves from the fact that there are people who, despite their healthy lifestyles, contract debilitating diseases.

The sages of Proverbs acknowledge these discrepancies between rule and exception in the "limit proverbs." "The human mind may devise many plans, but it is the purpose of the LORD that will be established (Prov 19:21).[3]

The sages responsible for the books of Job and Ecclesiastes deserve the high compliment of being called subversive sages. When a body of wisdom began making universal claims for its partial generalizations, the sages employed the pedagogical tools of the wisdom enterprise to subvert its arrogance: proverbs, admonitions, reflections, and parables. So Qohelet coins a subversive proverb. "The wise have eyes in their head, but fools walk in darkness. Yet I perceived that the same fate befalls all of them" (Eccl 2:14). So Jesus says, "It is not what goes into the mouth that defiles a person, but it is what comes out of the mouth that defiles"(Matt 15:11). Speaking out strategically and cannily to undermine oppressive conventional wisdom is what is meant by the "subversive voice."

The subversive voice functions in a dynamic unity with the other three wisdom virtues. The fear of the Lord supplies the moral courage to speak out despite the opposition of others. The listening heart provides the connection with others' suffering that activates the subversive voice. The cool spirit provides the reins we can tighten on our tempers and the discipline to choose our battles.

Mujerista theologian Ada María Isasi-Díaz summarizes the principles by which the subversive sage lives as she describes the presuppositions for her vocation of helping to shape a Hispanic Women's Theology.

1. When in doubt, I act; for if I do not, possibilities will never unfold.

2. Risk is part of life. So I do not attempt to avoid it. I am afraid but not paralyzed....

4. My goal, my hope, is the creation of the community and its common good: that is what the "reign of God" is all about. The common good is always being understood afresh and cannot fall under ideological control. Therefore, leadership belongs to the community, and to hold those who exercise it accountable is both the right and obligation of the community.[4]

The Subversive Voice of Job

The book of Job is a complex mosaic composed of several literary strands, each of which has its own unique subversive message. The first two chapters and 42:7-17 are most likely from the early monarchial period. They originally outlined a traditional story of the divine testing and vindication of a righteous man. The poetic dialogues (3–31; 38:1–42:6) may have been written soon after the Babylonian invasion of 586 B.C.E. That event would have provided a local catalyst for a crisis of intellect and faith.[5] The poetic sections subvert the older narrative's theology of suffering as divine testing. During the postexilic period, two additions were made to this now twice-told tale: the speeches of Elihu (32–37) and the poem on the inaccessibility of Wisdom (chap. 28).[6]

The original narrative begins to subvert the reader's confidence that God is consistent and righteous. This is in response to Satan's challenge of the wise man's motives for living wisely: he suggests that Job's motive for moral virtue and piety is self-interest. Job serves God because God prospers him. This initial depiction of a suspicious and capricious God is disturbing. Job's own monologues proceed to voice his growing suspicion that God may indeed be faithless and capricious.

Traditional wisdom affirmed that people had the capacity to take up the path of wisdom and to incorporate it into their own lives. Job's friends' poetic discourse asserts that this capacity is severely limited due to innate human sinfulness (5:7). Since all, including the wise, are sinners, the only hope for redemption lies in "seeking God, repenting, confessing one's sins and praying for salvation."[7] Job refuses to apply this understanding to his own life.

Though he increasingly attributes his sufferings to God's hand, he does not abandon moral virtue and piety. His actions subvert Satan's initial assessment of him as one who serves God only for what he can get out of it. God's response out of the whirlwind to Job subverts the notion that God is subject to traditional wisdom's construals of a cause-and-effect world of moral retribution. Job's final act of moral virtue and piety occurs when he intercedes for his friends.

Recent scholarship by J. David Pleins, Gustavo Gutierrez, and Walter Brueggemann points out that the book of Job is undergirded by a social vision that subverts Proverbs' elitist attribution of poverty to laziness.

Job's friends accuse Job of exploiting the poor. This accusation is voiced by Eliphaz the Temanite in Job 22:5-7, 9-11, especially in 22:6-7.[8]

> You have exacted pledges from your family for no reason,
>   and stripped the naked of their clothing.
> You have given no water to the weary to drink,
>   and you have withheld bread from the hungry. (22:6-7).

A prominent strand of thought in Proverbs attributes poverty to laziness and wealth to hard work. Job views poverty as the result of oppression by the wealthy and wealth as the result of the exploitation of the poor. The writer of Job asserts that the wealthy steal the land and livestock of the poor, driving them from their land into hiding (Job 24:2-4).[9]

Job rejects his friends' accusation that he is suffering because he amassed his wealth by exploitation. He claims that, on the contrary, he rescued the poor and the fatherless (29:12, 16). Though his reputation is in shambles, Job claims that he had true compassion for the poor.[10]

Gustavo Gutierrez, in his book on Job, asserts that Job's experiences fit him to be an advocate for the poor and a critic of his social world. Job's attitude toward poverty moves him closer to the prophets than to traditional wisdom represented by Proverbs.[11] For Job speaks, not just as a prophetic advocate for the poor, but out of the ash heap of impoverished suffering (2:8). A dimension of human experience is opened up that is absent from Proverbs: human grief. Job exudes a vulnerability to the harshness of life. Its verses bear the "scars of the journey."[12]

The prophets were confident about God's readiness to judge society. But the writer of the dialogues of Job probes the sufferer's resentment at God's inaction in the face of massive injustices that have no relief in sight. The friends affirm that God does listen to human grief and at times will intervene to right injustice (36:5-7). In their view, we can cry out to God for justice, but not condemn God for inaction (34:29). Job struggles to continue speaking well of God in the face of his suffering and God's silence.[13]

When God finally speaks, it is in response to the presumption of Job and his friends that they understand God. God's speeches in chapters 38–41 tell of creation in all its freedom and power: the beauties and grandeur of landscape and weather, animals and birds, and the formidable beasts of land and water. God will not tolerate disrespect of his judgment and justice, whose comprehension lies beyond human capabilities and categories.[14]

The author(s) of Job do not offer a neat solution to the "problem of evil." As a creative educational work built around dialogue, the book of Job explores numerous possible explanations for suffering. Perhaps it is the product of a divine contest (1–2) or a built-in component of the human condition (4:1-5; 5:6-7; 7:1-6; 15:14-16; 25:4-6). It may be the result of wrongdoing (4:6-11; 8:11-13; 11:5-6, 13-16; 15:25-35; 18; 20:15-22; 22:5-11; 27:13-23), the outcome of divine discipline (5:17-27; 11:7-12; 40:8-14; 42:1-6), or the result of God's malice (7:17-21; 9:1-14; 12:12-25; 19:6-14; 30:19-31). Maybe it is the result of bad theology (13:1-12; 42:7-8). It may also be the result of the exploitation of one social group by another, an assertion meant to lead not to philosophic answers but to commitment and protest.[15]

The writer entertains many options for explaining innocent suffering. Thereby he draws the reader into an encounter with God by speculating on the many ways God might see the situation. No one solution is satisfactory. We as readers bear the responsibility to continue to seek answers, for Job, for our communities, and for ourselves.[16] Writing amid and in response to Israel's postexilic dislocations, Job encourages readers to look for God in the realities of suffering, grief, and painful silence. There God will be present and will speak. God may not be heard in abstract, time-honored wisdom systems. Rather, God can be found in the struggles of grief beyond words.

The Subversive Voice of Ecclesiastes

The sages responsible for Ecclesiastes used their listening hearts to alert themselves to the pain and injustices of life. Death, inevitable for wise and fool alike, the sufferings of the poor oppressed by the rich, our constant vulnerability to accidents and reversals of fortune, and the debilitating effects of old age—all these conditions were rife with suffering. All of them were topics traditional wisdom preferred to downplay. Qohelet's acute, unflinching alertness to life around him and within him led him to subvert the major tenets of traditional wisdom.

Proverbs: "The Fear of the Lord Is the Beginning of Knowledge."

Qohelet: "Fear God!"

Proverbs understands the fear of the Lord as the beginning of wisdom, the promise that God will reveal aspects of the order of life to the earnest seeker. Qohelet views God as distant and largely unknowable. He enjoins his students to "fear God," which for him means, "Accept the fact that your human faculties are limited, and don't dishonor God by overstepping your bounds." "With many dreams come vanities and a multitude of words; but fear God" (5:7). For Qohelet, to fear God is not the first step on a journey of discovery, but a response to the fact that God is unknowable in human experience. We are to fear God because God is distant and mysterious and dispenses certain functions at certain times (3:1-8, 11). God desires awe from human beings (3:14) and such awe ranks higher for Qohelet than justice or wisdom (5:6; 7:18). For him it is the pinnacle of wisdom: the recognition of human limitation.[17]

Proverbs: "Wisdom Leads to Order and Life."

Qohelet: "The Pursuit of Wisdom Is *Hebel* (Vanity)."

The sages of Proverbs saw patterns of cause and effect around them whereby a wise life led to happy consequences (long life, good health, good reputation, and large, harmonious family). Qohelet is attentive to the scenes from his own life and others' lives in which those who hold such expectations are repeatedly disappointed. The wise age and die just like the fools (2:16-17); the righteous poor are oppressed by rich fools (4:1-3), and all our precautions cannot save us from the accidents and tragedies of an unpredictable life (9:11-12; 10:8, 9). He calls the repeated disappointment of traditional wisdom's promises, not order, but vanity, *hebel*, Hebrew for vapor (2:17).[18]

Proverbs: "Wisdom Is a Gift from God."

Qohelet: "Our Portion *(Heleq)* Is God's Only Gift."

Traditionally, wisdom was viewed as a gift from God. God has placed clues to how human beings are to live in the patterns of the created order. Qolehet's understanding of the gift we've been given is less comprehensive and attainable. The gift he perceives in life is what he calls our portion *(heleq)*. It is a reference to a plot and can be understood literally, as the plot of land one tills, or metaphorically, as one's lot in life, with its attendant joys and sorrows. A distant, unknowable God gives us each a portion—of relationships, work, and food and drink—and the joys and sorrows they hold. To focus on those joys with gratitude in the present moment is to make the most of our portion in life (8:15; 9:7-10). This is Qohelet's definition of living wisely.

The Subversive Voice of Jesus the Sage

There are about 102 proverbial sayings in the Synoptic Gospels and over 40 parables. The predominance of these wisdom genres in Jesus' synoptic teachings strongly suggests that one important role Jesus chose for himself was that of a sage or wisdom teacher.[19] The Gospel of John depicts Jesus as an expression of the Word and Wisdom of God. Jesus' habitual manner of speech in this Gospel is in "I am" sayings, poetic discourses more characteristic of Woman Wisdom in Prov 1 and 8 than the shorter wisdom sayings of the rest of Proverbs. While John's Gospel may also include over 30 proverbs or aphorisms, their close relationship to the themes of the Fourth Gospel suggests that they point behind it to the evangelist and his community. At any rate, our emphasis will be on Jesus' proverbs and parables as depicted in the Synoptic Gospels.[20]

The synoptic Jesus dressed his aphorisms (sayings that are proverbial in form but whose author we can identify) in the garb of *meshalim*. We have pointed out before that both proverbs and parables belong to the genre of *mashal* (plural *meshalim*).[21] This genre encompasses a number of wisdom forms, from proverbs and analogies to parables. These members of the *mashal* family share a couple of prominent family traits. One is that they are memorable, employing metaphor, vivid images, and concrete language. Another is that they elicit involvement, enticing listeners to evaluate their present situation in light of a particular saying, simile, or narrative.[22]

The search for the "original sayings" of Jesus, free from ecclesial interpretation, is problematic at best and futile at worst. The search for teachings that reflect the spirit of Jesus' message is a more modest and helpful enterprise. Several criteria have proved fruitful in this latter effort. The first is the criterion of embarrassment or contradiction, which focuses on those sayings or actions that would have created difficulty or embarrassment for the early church. The second, and perhaps the most problematic, is the criterion of discontinuity or dissimilarity that focuses on the words or deeds of Jesus that cannot be derived either from Judaism at the time of Jesus or from the early church after him.[23] The third is the criterion of multiple attestations. The fourth is the criterion of coherence or consistency. The final criterion is that of rejection and execution. It directs our attention to the historical fact that Jesus met with a violent end at the hands of Jewish and Roman officials and then asks, "What historical words and deeds of Jesus can explain his trial and crucifixion as 'King of the Jews'?"[24]

Listening Strategies for Discerning Jesus' Subversive Voice

As we listen to Jesus' proverbial synoptic sayings, sometimes we will hear echoes of the traditional wisdom of Proverbs and the Greco-Roman world. Sometimes we will hear the sound of silence, as he refrains from dealing with conventional themes. And sometimes we will hear a haunting, edgy melody coming through in a minor key, the sound of Jesus' subversive voice.[25] Jesus seems to have uttered sayings that sound like traditional proverbs, anonymous expressions of common wisdom that do nothing to rock the status quo. It is clear that he also, at times, coined aphorisms. Aphorisms are distinguishable from proverbs in that we know who their author was and that they often subvert traditional values.[26]

Listening Strategy #1: Listen for Commonplace Proverbs That Serve Uncommon Purposes

Jesus often quotes sayings that sound like they could have come straight out of the book of Proverbs. They echo themes of the wisdom traditions of the ancient Near East as well as of his contemporary Greco-Roman milieu.

For example,

> Nothing is covered up that will not be revealed.
> The sick need doctors, not the well.
> No one can serve two masters.
> Let the day's own trouble be sufficient for the day.
> The measure you give will be the measure you get back.
> Many are called, but few are chosen.
> A tree is known by its fruits.
> One's life does not consist in the abundance of one's possessions.
> A city set on a hill cannot be hid.
> All that defiles comes from within.
> Out of the abundance of the heart the mouth speaks.[27]

Jesus uses traditional sayings for nontraditional purposes. He does not use them to make his preaching more interesting or to prod his listeners to ponder life in general. He uses them to point listeners toward a life of discipleship that often means challenging common wisdom.

When he says that what is hidden now will be revealed, his purpose is to allay his disciples' fear of the enemies of the gospel (Matt 10:26). When he reminds his listeners that the sick don't need doctors, but the well, he is defending his choice of table companions to the scribes (Mark 2:17). When he reminds listeners in Mark 4:23-25 that "the measure you give will be the measure you get," he is not just making a general observation such as "What goes around comes around." He is offering an incentive to people to pay attention to and internalize his teachings. In Matthew and Luke he is warning them that they will be judged by the same standard with which they judge others (Matt 7:2; Luke 6:37-38).

When Jesus points out that "many are called, but few are chosen," he is expressing the fact that, while everyone is invited to God's banquet, not everybody's response is rightly motivated (Matt 22:14).

When Jesus tells us, "Do not worry about tomorrow, for tomorrow will bring worries of its own" (Matt 6:34), he is not just making the point that the future is unknown (see Prov 27:1). He is encouraging us to take the risk of having faith in a God who, while he demands all, also provides all.

When he decries hypocrisy with talk of log and speck (Matt 7:5), he is warning that we will be judged by the standards of our own hypocrisy. Blessedness consists of a merciful attitude toward others based on our admission of our own weaknesses and our affirmation of God's mercy to everyone.

Greco-Roman wisdom understood that one can't have divided loyalties. The parable of the Dishonest Steward in Luke ends with this proverb: "You cannot serve God and wealth" (Luke 16:13b; Matt 6:24b).

Common human wisdom pointed out that life is more than just possessions, as expressed in Prov 11:28, though material prosperity was a positive condition that often resulted from wise living (Prov 3:15). Jesus' teachings reveal a radical suspicion of wealth. "Be on your guard against all kinds of greed; for one's life does not consist in the abundance of possessions" (Luke 12:15). This is immediately followed by the parable of the Rich Fool. It ends with the warning that it will not go well with those who "store up treasures for themselves but are not rich toward God" (12:21). Greed destroys community and distracts followers from God.

Common wisdom acknowledges that a tree is known by its fruits. Jesus uses the proverb to warn against false prophets (Matt 7:20) and to encourage hearers to build their lives on the foundation of his teachings (Luke 6:43).

Common wisdom knew full well that "a city built on a hill cannot be hid" (Matt 5:14). Jesus used this saying to buttress his call to his followers to let their light shine in the world so their good works will glorify God.

Common wisdom knew that one's character was the wellspring of one's speech and, therefore, what defiles comes from within. Jesus employed this insight to challenge a myopic focus on ritual purity (Matt 15:10-11).

Jesus clearly respected the commonsense proverbs of traditional wisdom. He recognized their vitality and their persuasiveness. For that reason he borrowed from them whenever he could and wove them into his own message. They were there to commend attentiveness to his own teachings, and to challenge current practices.[28]

Listening Strategy #2: Listen for the Sound of Silence

We can hear something of Jesus' subversive voice by asking, "What themes of conventional wisdom did Jesus neglect?"

His wisdom sayings lack any admonitions to seek wisdom, an injunction basic to the wisdom tradition as a whole (Prov 1; 7; Job 38). He does not commend wisdom as being more precious than jewels (Prov 3:15; 8:11). He does not commend the wisdom of foresight. He doesn't equate the wise with the living and the foolish and the ignorant with the dead. He does not talk about the rewards of wisdom. He does not promise that cultivating wisdom will help us to make sense of life.[29]

He includes no character-building proverbs, sayings that tell us that we ought not to take pride in our looks but in the beauty of our habits and character. He does not insist that hard work is the road to excellence. He does not dwell on the folly of anger, with the exception of Matt 5:22, nor on the importance of trustworthiness. He offers no proverbs about money, its importance, its seductiveness, or its proper use. He does not talk much about proper speech, one of the major themes of Proverbs.[30] He has much more to say about listening than he does about speaking. There is nothing about friendship, a central theme of biblical and Greco-Roman wisdom. He does not talk about avoiding evil companions and fools, a major theme in Proverbs. He was constantly criticized for the company he kept.

He is silent on the subject of the dangers of alcohol, a commonplace theme in the wisdom of the ancient world.[31] Jesus says little about family relationships, marriage, and parenthood. He has absolutely no conventional "wisdom" about women, decrying their innate inferiority and the bad influence they exercise over males. Proverbs and Sirach are full of negative comments about women. Says Carlston: "Jesus' countercultural stance on this matter is as refreshing as it is certain."[32]

Jesus' wisdom is characterized by an absence of the Golden Mean, the sense of balance and restraint that is characteristic of so much of the wisdom tradition.[33]

Listening Strategy #3: Listen for That Which Puzzles and Provokes

EQUATIONS YOU CAN'T SOLVE: (Paradox)
The Equation of Opposites

- Antithetical Sayings in Proverbs
- Jesus' Version of Antithetical Sayings: Paradoxical Sayings
- "Blessed are you" Sayings in the Hebrew Scriptures
- Jesus' Version of "Blessed are you" Sayings: Paradoxical Beatitudes
- Already, but not yet

ADVICE YOU CAN'T FOLLOW: (Hyperbole)
Extreme and Impractical Admonitions

- Admonitions in Proverbs
- Jesus' Version of Admonitions: Focal Instances

QUESTIONS YOU CAN'T ANSWER: (Impossible Questions)

- Rhetorical Questions in Proverbs
- Jesus' Version of Rhetorical Questions

Jesus dresses his aphorisms in the garb of a variety of *meshalim*. They include antithetical sayings, "blessed are they who . . . " sayings, "better than" sayings, admonitions, and rhetorical questions. These forms are the stock-in-trade of the Wisdom literature of the Hebrew Scriptures. As we shall see, Jesus infuses traditional forms with subversive import.

Jesus is a master at coining subversive sayings that wear the disguise of a proverb.[34]

EQUATIONS YOU CAN'T SOLVE: (Paradox)
The Equation of Opposites

Antithetical Sayings in Proverbs: The Opposites Game

A form prominent in traditional proverbs collections is the antithetical or oppositional proverb, in which the second line contrasts or opposes the first.[35] This is the primary form of the proverbs in Proverbs 10–15.

"A wise child makes a glad father, but a foolish child is a mother's grief" (10:1; see also 10:31 and 11:17). Such proverbs show the antithesis between two different types of people or two different ways of life. They make clear-cut contrasts between wisdom and folly, good and evil, rich and poor, success and failure. They avoid paradox and enigma in favor of cut-and-dried choices of good over evil.[36]

The kind of antithesis that provides the background for Jesus' synoptic paradoxes is the antithesis that expresses a reversal of situation. "A person's pride will bring humiliation, but one who is lowly in spirit will obtain honor" (Prov 29:23).

A very widespread usage, the antithesis expresses the disastrous consequences of exceeding one's role. "He that exalts himself shall be humbled," in commonsense wisdom is a warning against what the Greeks called *hybris*, a stepping out of place. Similar warnings appear in wisdom sayings from Israel's ancient Near Eastern neighbors.[37]

"All who exalt themselves will be humbled, and those who humble themselves will be exalted" (Luke 14:11; see also Luke18:14; Matt 23:12).

"Many who are first will be last, and the last will be first" (Mark 10:31; see also Matt 19:30; 20:16; Luke 13:30).

"What will it profit them, to gain the whole world and forfeit their life?" (Mark 8:36; Luke 9:25).

"Whoever wishes to become great among you must be your servant, and whoever wishes to be first among you must be slave of all" (Mark 10:43-44; Luke 22:26; see also Matt 20:26-27).

Jesus' Version of Anthithetical Sayings: Paradoxical Sayings

When an antithesis or oppositional saying is sharpened and intensified to the point that it equates opposites, it becomes paradoxical. It provokes the listener into figuring out in what situations in his or her life the equated opposites are, or could be, a reality. This kind of form is absent from Proverbs, but occurs in Ecclesiastes (1:18; 7:1*b*, 4). Rather than commend balanced foresight, Jesus' teachings disregard compromise and commonsense. The result is a number of provocative paradoxical statements that go to extremes in making their point.[38]

"Those who try to make their life secure will lose it, but those who lose their life will keep it" (Luke 17:33; see also Mark 8:35; John 12:25). This dynamic is what New Testament scholar William Beardslee calls "the distinctive intensification of proverbial wisdom in the Synoptic tradition." The paradox negates the project of seeking security as the purpose of life, insisting that life is conferred through this paradoxical route.[39]

Other examples of paradoxes are

> To those who have, more will be given; and from those who do not have, even what they seem to have will be taken away (Luke 8:18; see also Matt 13:12; Mark 4:25; Luke 12:48*b*).

> The greatest among you must become like the youngest, and the leader like one who serves (Luke 22:26; see also Matt 20:26; Mark 10:43).

> What is prized by human beings is an abomination in the sight of God (Luke 16:15*b*).

> It is not what goes into the mouth that defiles a person, but it is what comes out of the mouth that defiles (Matt 15:11; see also Mark 7:15).[40]

Conventional wisdom sayings pair good behavior with good results and foolish behavior with disastrous results. Jesus' paradoxical proverbs pair what is viewed as good by conventional wisdom with disastrous results and what is viewed negatively with positive outcomes.

By their pairing of opposites they disorient us to our habitual goals of seeking order and harmony. They subvert conventional wisdom's notions of wisdom and folly and subvert our quest for the orderly life.[41]

"Blessed are you" Sayings in the Hebrew Scriptures

Occurring almost exclusively in the Psalms and Wisdom literature, Beatitudes or "blessed are those who . . . " sayings are declarations of well-being to those who engage in life-enhancing behavior. Such behaviors include studying and obeying torah (Ps 1; Prov 29:18), caring for the poor (Ps 41:2; Prov 14:21), trusting in God (Pss 112:1; 128:1; Prov 16:20), fearing God (Prov 28:14), finding wisdom (Prov 3:13), and listening to wisdom (Prov 8:33-36). The state of blessing largely refers to blessings that lie in store for individuals in the future. Comforted and strengthened by that future assurance, one can begin to live in a sphere of blessed well-being now (Ps 41:2-4). The sages believed that when one engages in wise behavior, one enhances one's own life and others' lives and is surrounded by a sphere of well-being.[42]

Jesus' Version of "Blessed are you" Sayings: Paradoxical Beatitudes

Jesus' Beatitudes or pronouncements of blessing are paradoxical, pairing attitudes and circumstances we think of as undesirable with positive consequences. They are clustered in Luke's Great Sermon and Matthew's Sermon on the Mount, but they appear elsewhere in the Gospels as well (Matt 11:6; 13:16; 16:17; 24:46).[43] Luke's formulation of the Beatitudes in his Great Sermon proclaim a state of blessedness for the "poor," the "sad," the "hungry," and the "hated," categories of people hardly considered blessed by conventional wisdom. Matthew blunts the subversive edge of these sayings by adding "poor in spirit" and "hunger and thirst for righteousness." His version of the sayings allows virtue to have its reward.[44]

The Beatitudes in Matt 5:3-12 are not intended to burden the faithful with moral imperatives. Instead, they aim to bring solace. By exhibiting to the religious imagination the good things of the life to come, they compensate those who are, because of their commitment to Jesus, suffering in this world.[45] The Beatitudes are the result of Jesus' own experience of persecution because of his involvement with the expendables, those on the social margins. Matthew turns the message toward the spiritual, eschatological, and the ethical, but the Beatitudes also refer to the physical state of those who are poor, hungry, thirsty, and persecuted.[46]

Matthean scholar Dale Allison points out that the Beatitudes were meant to startle hearers. Simple observation of the world as it is informs us that the rich, not the poor, are blessed; that those who are happy, not those who mourn, are blessed; that those who have power, not the meek, are blessed; that those who are filled, not the hungry and thirsty, are blessed; and that those who are well treated, not those who are persecuted, are blessed. The Beatitudes have things backward. To take them seriously is to call into question our ordinary values.[47]

Matthew's Beatitudes are not conditions for those who would enter the kingdom of heaven. They are not primarily to be seen as imperatives, though there is an element of this in the fifth, sixth, and seventh Beatitude. The ethical imperative of the Beatitudes is balanced by the elements of consolation and promise.[48]

Already, but Not Yet

The Beatitudes' referent is partly the future, for the desired state is not yet fulfilled and will only be fully realized in the time to come. The Greek language can use a present tense to indicate a circumstance that, although it has not yet occurred, is regarded as so certain that it is spoken of as having already happened (Matt 26:2). This is the case in the last line of Matthew's Beatitudes. The reward is yet to be bestowed, but its secure reality is here conveyed through a present tense. "Rejoice and be glad, for your reward is great in heaven, for in the same way they persecuted the prophets who were before you" (Matt 5:12).

Jesus interprets his calling and his historical moment as a realization of the prophetic understanding of the "kingdom of heaven" as earthly and present, a return of the law of Moses and political sovereignty for Israel. The king who is to come will establish justice and liberate the oppressed in keeping with Yahweh's identity as defender of the poor (Isa 9:5-7; 11:1-9; Jer 23:3-8; Ezek 34:23-31). Happy are the poor now, because with Jesus liberation begins. It is more than a reversal of the way things are now between rich and poor.[49] It is an eradication of the bipolarity. The Beatitudes refer to the present as well as the future. The blessedness to which they refer is a present condition, discovered in the middle of Christ's restoration of this creation and this life. Here is where this solace begins and grows, though it is only fully actualized in the time to come.[50]

ADVICE YOU CAN'T FOLLOW: (Hyperbole)
Extreme and Impractical Admonitions

Admonitions in Proverbs

The genre of proverbs usually makes a declarative statement that the listener is called on to apply to whatever situation(s) in his or her life seems like an apt fit. "A soft answer turns away wrath, but a harsh word stirs up anger" (Prov 15:1). By contrast, an admonition offers explicit advice to the listener that he or she is to pursue a particular action. "Answer fools according to their folly, or they will be wise in their own eyes" (Prov 26:5). The opposite of an admonition, the prohibition seeks to dissuade its hearers from a particular course of action. "Do not say, 'I will repay evil'; wait for the LORD, and he will help you" (Prov 20:22; see also, 24:1, 17-18, 28-29). Admonitions and prohibitions are plentiful in Prov 24:23-34.

Some admonitions and prohibitions have a general application. It is always a good idea, for example, to avoid crooked speech (Prov 4:24), to honor the Lord with one's substance (Prov 3:9), to be faithful to one's spouse (Prov 5:15), and to plan ahead (Prov 24:27). It is never a good idea to envy the wicked (Prov 24:1), to be a witness against one's neighbor without cause (Prov 24:28), to turn gleeful cartwheels when your enemies fall (Prov 24:17), or to boast about tomorrow (Prov 27:1). With both positive and negative commands, the listener must decide which are most applicable to specific situations in his or her own life. The work of contextualization falls on the shoulders of the listener. Conventional wisdom counts on the listener fearing the Lord and approaching life with a listening heart. One who remains humble while gaining a measure of wisdom can most helpfully contextualize proverbial advice. It takes wisdom to use wisdom.[51]

Jesus' Version of Admonitions: Focal Instances

We have noted that Jesus' subversive versions of conventional wisdom are often extreme and impractical. This is nowhere more obvious than when we look at what New Testament scholar Robert Tannehill has helpfully called "focal instances." These sayings portray a specific scene and make a command relative to it. They are specific and extreme. They employ vivid metaphorical scenes and hyperbole. One interpreter has insightfully dubbed this strategy of hyperbole a "rhetoric of excess"; it is especially prominent in Matthew's Sermon on the Mount.[52]

Focal instances deal with the following subjects: temptations to sin (Matt 18:8a-9a = Mark 9:42-48), judging others (Matt 7:3-5 = Luke 6:41-42), inward motives and outward behavior (Matt 5:29-30), retaliation (Matt 5:39-42), private piety and public opinion (Matt 6:1-7), family ties (Matt 10:34-36 = Luke 12:52-53), and the call of God's kingdom (Matt 8:21-22 = Luke 9:57-62). They are not meant as general and literal regulations. Surely we aren't to actually cut off our own feet, tear out our own eyes, pull logs out of our eyes, stand still while someone slaps us twice, walk two miles with no covering, antagonize members of our own families, and skip our own fathers' funerals!

They function more like proverbs, prodding us to name situations in our daily lives in which they challenge our deeply entrenched attitudes and habitual behaviors. Their vivid pictoral scene combined with their "rhetoric of excess" dramatically contrasts the extreme teaching they advocate with conventional human behavior. They induce a new way of looking at a whole field of human behavior. We have to decide how and where they apply to our daily lives.[53]

QUESTIONS YOU CAN'T ANSWER: (Impossible Questions)

Rhetorical Questions in Proverbs

There are plenty of rhetorical questions in Proverbs. They beg for obvious answers and are useful didactic tools. Several deal with sexual temptation and fidelity. "Should your streams be scattered abroad, streams of water in the streets?" (5:16). "Can fire be carried in the bosom without burning one's clothes? Or can one walk on hot coals without scorching the feet?" (6:27-28). "Does not wisdom call, and does not understanding raise her voice?" (8:1).

Jesus' teachings include some rhetorical questions. They beg for obvious answers just as those in Proverbs do: "Are grapes gathered from thorns, or figs from thistles?" (Matt 7:16 = see also Luke 6:44).

Others questions ask whether it is preferable to give stones or bread to hungry children, whether one should bind the strong man before robbing him blind, and whether it is usual practice to place lamps under bushels (Matt 7:9; Matt 12:29 = Mark 3:27 = Luke 11:11-12; Matt 7:10; Luke 11:11-12; Matt 5:15 = Mark 4:21 = Luke 11:33).

Jesus' Version of Rhetorical Questions: Impossible Questions

In the subversive settings of Ecclesiastes, Job, and the synoptic sayings, a form called the "impossible question" surfaces. This is a subversive form in which the answers are not so clear. These questions point to the limits of human wisdom and knowledge and the inscrutability of God. For example, "How can the wise die just like fools?" (Eccl 2:16); "What do mortals get from all the toil and strain with which they toil under the sun?" (Eccl 2:22); "Where is the way to the dwelling of light, and where is the place of darkness?" (Job 38:19-20).

Several impossible questions appear in the synoptic teachings of Jesus. These include: "Can any of you by worrying add a single hour to your span of life?" (Matt 6:27 = Luke 12:25).[54] "What will it profit them to gain the whole world and forfeit their life?" (Matt 16:26 = Mark 8:36 = Luke 9:25); "Salt is good; but if salt has lost its saltiness, how can you season it?" (Matt 5:13 = Mark 9:50 = Luke 14:34).[55]

Jesus' distinctive voice is recognized in the way he coins sayings that conform to traditional wisdom forms like Beatitudes and proverbs, used not to resolve the conflicts of life but to heighten them. He uses them, not to preserve the status quo, but rather to push the hearer to question his own and society's assumptions and values. The synoptic sayings that seem most characteristic of his subversive voice take a wisdom insight and concentrate and intensify it. They do this most often by means of paradox and hyperbole. A number of these paradoxical and hyperbolic proverbs are in the material common to Matthew and Luke that many scholars call the Q document.

The Subversive Voice of Jesus' Parables

There are over forty parables attributed to Jesus in the Synoptic Gospels. Parables, as members of the *mashal* genre, at once concrete and evocative, are a venue tailor-made for a teacher who wanted to challenge conventional notions of wise and foolish, virtuous and sinful, chosen and outcast. While largely absent from the Hebrew Bible's Wisdom literature, the prophets do occasionally use proverbs. They seem to have been a prophetic modification of a wisdom form of utterance, the simile (2 Sam 12:1-3; Ezek 17:3-10; and perhaps also Isa 5:1-6). They are comparisons that have been elongated into brief narratives to serve prophetic concerns.[56]

Jesus' preference for teaching in parables was no random choice.[57] They are a genre uniquely qualified to convey the fourth wisdom virtue: the subversive voice. In this chapter we shall flesh out this statement with regard to several representative parables of Jesus.[58]

Throughout the long history of parables scholarship, they have been read in many ways. They have been read as allegories, moral example stories, or as stories that seek to make a broad ethical point about the kingdom of God. All these readings, in hastening toward ethical, theological payoffs, have tended to blunt the parables' subversive voice by ignoring two key features of Jesus' parables: their metaphorical quality and their social context. We must listen to the parables' literary and social features if we are to hear their subversive voice.

Most recent parable scholars agree that a helpful way to understand parables is to consider them as metaphors or similes or as narrative with metaphorical connections.[59] Metaphor and simile involve speaking of something less well-known to us in terms of something better known. The two are placed side by side, equated in metaphor, and said to be similar in some more specific way in a simile. Differences and similarities spark in the space between the familiar and the unfamiliar. Parables scholar Robert Funk, writing in the mid-1960s, described the subversive dynamic of metaphor as the juxtaposition of two things that affect the imagination and induce a vision of reality that cannot be conveyed by discursive speech.[60]

Jesus used parables as metaphorical answers to the question "What is the empire of God like?"[61]

Listening Strategy #4: Listening for Jesus' Subversive Voice through the Literary Features of the Parable

More than four decades ago, C. H. Dodd defined a parable as "a metaphor or simile drawn from nature or common life, arresting the hearer by its vividness or strangeness, and leaving the mind in sufficient doubt about its precise application to tease it into active thought."[62] Clearly, parables have subversive potential, for they are realistic and yet strange, metaphorical, paradoxical, challenging, and open-ended.

Realistic and Yet Strange

Jesus spoke a language of the familiar and concrete that places the point of contact between God and human beings in the everyday world of human experience. Often there is an element of the parable itself (the extraordinary harvest of Mark 4:8) or the order of payment (Matt 20:8) that shocks us into realizing that it is not quite our present, everyday reality the parable refers to.[63] Parables start off looking like commonplace stories set in familiar scenes from everyday life, but by the end of the story something uncommon has happened. A formal dinner party ends up packed with street people. A shepherd leaves ninety-nine sheep unprotected to go after one stray. A fool builds his house in the middle of a sandy arroyo. A gardener begs time to fertilize an absolutely dead tree. A boss congratulates a manager for marking down the boss's invoices. A Near Eastern father throws dignity to the winds and runs down the road to meet his undeserving son. The meaning of the parable begins to emerge at the point at which its realism begins to break down.[64]

All the parables, in one way or another, serve the message that the kingdom of God is powerful and active and that the world is in a process of transformation. The message of the kingdom is that it points beyond itself.[65]

Paradoxical and Challenging

The paradox in parables lies in its strange twist. It is often an equation of something we normally think of as odd or negative with something positive; something, in fact, that points to an aspect of God's presence and power in the world. A sign of corruption is put forth as a simile for the kingdom of God (leaven in Matt 13:33; Luke 13:20-21; *Gos. Thom.* 96:1). Someone looked down on and despised is the one who acts as the neighbor (Luke 10:30-35). A wily steward's dubious business practices are commended to those who would enter the kingdom of God (Luke 16:8*a*). Workers who work for one hour are paid the same as those who have worked all day (Matt 20:1-15).

The paradoxical twist is offered as a metaphor for an aspect of the kingdom of God. The metaphor's paradoxical quality draws us in, puzzled and thoughtful. We ask ourselves, If this is how the kingdom of God looks, which of my assumptions need to change? In this way parables shatter the preconceived world of rights and duties, sin and virtue. Thereby they open us to the advent of God's kingdom as a gift. How would daily life look different if we gave up our preconceptions and accepted the gift? Parables are not good advice, but good news, a vision of reality present but also yet to come.

John Dominic Crossan, in his treatment of parables, describes their paradoxes as seeming absurdities or juxtapositions of apparent opposites that conceal a deeper truth. He interprets this paradoxical language as an extension of the prohibition of images of God in biblical thought. God cannot be captured by a verbal image any more than by physical representations. Only when we stand before the limits of knowledge and language and the transcendence of God are we able to accept the inbreaking of God's kingdom as a gift. For Crossan, the most fundamental message of Jesus' parables is that we must be open to having our tidy vision of reality shattered so that God's alternative vision for human life can gain an entrance.[66]

Open-Ended

The parable is a question waiting for an answer, an invitation waiting for a response. Like a proverb, it fulfills its function as it is appropriated by an individual and then set in the context of that person's life, both alone and together with others in community. Like the proverb, the parable respects the free will of the listener and leaves it up to his or her wisdom to make applications.

Listening Strategy #5: Listening for Jesus' Subversive Voice through the Economic, Political, and Religious Threat Represented by His Parables

We have seen how the literary features of parables suit them to convey Jesus' subversive voice. The social analysis of the parables done recently by Bernard Brandon Scott and William R. Herzog helps us understand the threat that his subversive voice represented to the established economic, religious, and political status quo of his day.[67] Parables were part of Jesus' public teaching that provoked suspicion and, ultimately, his elimination. They must, then, have dealt with dangerous issues. By definition, dangerous issues would mean political and economic issues, since the preservation of power and the extraction of tribute from the peasant class were the dominant concerns of the ruling elites of the ancient world. Jesus' parables were threatening because they exposed the systems of oppression that controlled the lives of the poor and held them in bondage.[68]

Parables, in Herzog's view, did not focus on a vision of the glory of the reign of God as much as they did the gory details of how oppression served the interests of the ruling class. They were a form of social analysis as well as theological reflection. They were typified social scenes that exposed the contradictions between the actual situation of Jesus' hearers and the torah of God's justice.[69]

A clue to the parables' subversive purposes comes to us in the fact that they all shed light on the "kingdom of God." In the Synoptic Gospels Jesus describes his activity as the *basileia* of God. The term occurs over one hundred times in the Synoptic Gospels. We most commonly translate this term in English as "kingdom." When the word shows up in a nonbiblical text from the ancient world it is usually translated "empire." Jesus chose a very risky, political concept as the central metaphor for his ministry, for in his world there was only one empire, and that was Rome.[70]

Every time Jesus uses the term "the *basileia* of God" he is implying the injustice of the ruling elite. What ruling elites do in every age is set up social, political, and economic constructions of reality that justify their right to power, wealth, and privilege while simultaneously rationalizing the subsistence existence of the masses.[71] This dominant group controls education, both formally and informally, and codifies a "wisdom" that attributes the social status quo to a divinely ordained cosmology.

We remember that this was an ever-present danger for Hebrew Bible wisdom. When an educated, relatively prosperous group makes sense of their world, they are always tempted toward a rigid theory of retribution that attributes their own status to righteousness and the less auspicious situations of others to sin. Despite the sages' best efforts, a rigid theory of retribution was alive and well in Jesus' day. It served the social, economic purposes of both the Jewish religious elite and the Roman occupiers. What the religious elite presented as theological categories (clean or unclean; honorable or shameful; sinful or righteous) were, in reality, categories that had everything to do with maintaining the privileged status of those in economic, political, and religious power. Judging from the way he died, it would appear that Jesus' actions and teachings threatened the powerful in a powerful way.[72]

Jesus' actions and teachings threatened the powerful by exposing the exploitation of those the great hierarchy of the Roman Empire referred to as "the expendables," those society considered to have nothing to offer those above them, and who gradually fell through the cracks in the bottom of the system. These were the people who had no say in their lives, who did the jobs no one else wanted to do, like tax collecting, whose persons counted for nothing except as they could be used to fulfill the desires of others (for example, prostitutes).[73]

Stephen Patterson, in his analysis of the social context of Jesus' teachings, points out that the experience of being an expendable person in antiquity included three dimensions, each of which Jesus addressed directly in his teachings: the experience of being unclean (not clean), the experience of shame (not honor), and the experience of being regarded as sinful (not righteous).[74]

Unclean, Not Clean

Drawing on ancient Israel's connection between cleanliness and holiness (Lev 13:45-46; Deut 23:10-11, 13-14), being unclean, in Jesus' day, was viewed as a religious category. Jesus discerned the truth that it was often a condition that resulted from poverty, disease, and racial and gender prejudice.

He addresses his ministry to those who, by their very existence, are defined as unclean: lepers (Mark 14:3), Gentiles (Mark 7:24-30), and women classified as "sinners" (Luke 7:36-50). He insisted that the power to be clean lies in a pure heart (Matt 5:8), not in what goes into the mouth (Mark 7:15).[75]

Shame, Not Honor

Honor and shame were social and economic, not purely personal or religious categories. Honor and shame are the forces that give shape to communal life. To have honor is to have a place, a role, that is recognized by one's peers, which one competently performs.[76] Jesus challenges the honor of those wishing to stone the woman caught in adultery (John 7:53b–8:11). Just as nothing from outside can render one unclean, so one cannot be shamed from without. It does not lie within the legitimate power of one human being to shame another, to ostracize that person from divine and human company.[77] On repeated occasions, Jesus behaved "shamelessly," disregarding social, religious definitions of those with whom he should interact. Examples of Jesus' "shameful" dialogue partners include Bartimaeus, a blind beggar (Mark 10:46-52), and women—Martha and Mary (Luke 10:38-42) and the Syrophoenician woman (Mark 7:26)—who ought to have remained beneath a first-century rabbi's notice.[78]

Sin, Not Righteousness

"Sinner," in the ancient world is not just a moral category, it is also a social one. The assumption of Jesus' day was that expendables were on the bottom rung of the social ladder because they deserved to be. "Who sinned, this man or his parents, that he was born blind?" (see John 9:1-34, especially v. 2).

Those who had no other options than to do the jobs no one else wanted to do were linked with "sinners:" tax collectors, shepherds, dung collectors, tanners, peddlers, weavers, bath attendants, gamblers, and bandits.[79] Jesus quotes his opponents' condemnation of the company he keeps: "Look, a glutton and a drunkard, a friend of tax collectors and sinners!" (Luke 7:34*b*). Says Jesus of his own ministry: "I have come to call not the righteous, but sinners" (Mark 2:17). Jesus is not here thinking of "sinner" as a moral category but a social one. He invited into his company those society labeled as sinners, unclean, and shamed. Jesus, by his choice of companions at table and beyond it, honored those others considered "expendable." With his healing, exorcising, teaching, and presence, he proclaimed for them an empire, the empire of God, in which the means to life are free and accessible by God's own gracious hand.[80]

He is a subversive teacher, one who sought to help move people "from a dominated consciousness to a critically active consciousness." A dominated consciousness is characterized by fatalism, passivity, and silence. Those who live within it are overwhelmed by powerful and brutal forces, "overcome by an unrelenting hopelessness, and broken only by occasional and ineffectual appeals to magic or supernatural forces to alleviate their misery."[81]

Assumptions Subverted by Jesus' Parables

In the context of the Synoptic Gospels, the parables are an entrée into the theology of a given Gospel and a reflection of its major themes. It may be Mark's emphasis on crisis and secrecy, or Matthew's insistence that we be doers not just hearers, or Luke's emphasis on prayer and compassion for the poor. But they all contextualize parables according to their own purposes. Sometimes we gain an insight into that purpose through the lens of an evangelist's discernible redaction of the tradition. A couple of clear examples are Matthew's editing of Mark's parable of the Wicked Tenants (Matt 21:33-45 = Mark 12:1-11) and both Matthew and Luke's editing of the Great Feast from Q (Matt 22:1-11; Luke 14:15-24).

In the discussion that follows, I will briefly deal with two parables from Q (Leaven and Great Feast), one from Mark (Mustard Seed), one from Luke (the good Samaritan), and one from Matthew (Vineyard Laborers). Excellent treatments of the entire corpus of Jesus' parables abound for further exploration. I have chosen these particular parables because they clearly undermine several key assumptions of Jesus' social and religious context. Through them we hear him exercise the fourth wisdom virtue: the subversive voice.

It Will Not Be Under Your Control

The Leaven (Parable from Q)

Scriptures: Q 13:20; Matt 13:33; Luke 13:20; *Gos. Thom.* 96:1

> To what shall I compare the kingdom of God? It is like a leaven, which a woman took and hid in three measures of meal, until it was all leavened. (Q 13:20; Matt 13:33; Luke 13:20)

Scholarship on this simile in recent years has pointed out that "leaven" was a metaphor for "corruption" in the time of Jesus. Leaven has the connotation of evil in earlier Jewish literatures as well as elsewhere in Jesus' teaching (Matt 16:6; Mark 8:15; Luke 12:1a). By this view, the parable would represent Jesus' parody of the Jewish leaders' attitude toward the makeup of his followers: tax collectors and sinners, the scum of the earth in their view. The paradox lies in the juxtaposition of socially unacceptable people as agents of the kingdom of God.[82]

This brief parable subverts the understanding of the kingdom of God as imposed from above, obvious to all observers as mighty and impressive. It is nothing like the Roman Empire. And it is not the kingdom some Jews yearned for the Messiah to inaugurate, an earthly rule that would give the Romans the competition they deserved. It is more subtle, working from the inside out, hidden and growing in obscurity.

The fact that the leavening agent is a woman may have some significance, since women were not as highly regarded as men in Jesus' society. Here is a socially marginal person, wielding an agent that is usually thought of as insignificant and even negative. Jesus' parables take their images from the experiences of women as well as men. His healings and exorcisms make women whole. His announcement of "eschatological reversal" (Matt 19:30; 20:16; Mark 10:31; Luke 13:30) applies also to women and their impairment by patriarchal structures.[83]

The parable of the Leaven is like Mark's parable of the Mustard Seed (Matt 13:31-32; Mark 4:30-32; Luke 13:18-19; *Gos. Thom.* 65:1) in that both hold the promise that the end result will be far greater than what anyone observing Jesus and his band of disciples would have dreamed possible. Both parables have an extravagance about them. Mustard trees do not usually grow large enough to entice many birds to nest in them, and the three measures of flour that the woman leavens have been variously estimated as equaling a quantity of twenty-five to forty liters, capable of feeding over one hundred people![84]

It Will Take You Places You Hadn't Planned to Go

The Great Feast (Parable from Q)

Scriptures: Q 14:16-24; Matt 22:1-14; Luke 14:16-24; *Gos. Thom.* 64

The parable of the Feast, found in Q, makes its way into both Matthew and Luke (as well as *Gos. Thom.* 64). The Q version on which Matthew and Luke are based goes like this:

> "A man once gave a great banquet and invited many. At the time for the banquet he sent his servant to say to those who had been invited, 'Please come, for everything is now ready.' But they all began to make excuses. The first said to him, 'I've bought a farm, and I must go and see it. Please excuse me.' And another said, 'I've just bought five pair of oxen and I need to check them out. Please excuse me.' And another said, 'I've just married a woman and so I can't come.' The servant came and reported this to his master. Then the owner in anger said to his servant, 'Go out quickly to the streets of the town and bring in as many people as you find.' And the servant went out into the streets and brought together everybody he could find. That way the house was filled with guests."[85]

Matthew turns the feast into a wedding banquet for a king's son and adds the details about the wedding garment. Luke, with his special concern for the oppressed, refers to "the poor, the crippled, the blind, and the lame" (14:21).[86]

Subversive Messages

The background to the parable of the Feast is the notion of the great messianic banquet, a symbol of the salvation of the nations (Isa 25:6-10). During the intertestamental period, national pride and a concern for ritual purity began to narrow the guest list of the final banquet. According to *1 Enoch*, it would include only the Jews, excluding Gentiles (*1 En. 62*). The documents of the Essene community at Qumram depicted only the pure and the righteous eating at the messianic banquet. The Gentiles and the impure would be excluded, along with sinners, and the lame and the blind.[87]

The Pharisees sought to realize Israel's calling as a "nation of priests" by carefully observing the ritual purity of the "holy table." Jesus and his movement did not observe these purity regulations and even shared their meals with "sinners." Jesus' parables speak of the *basileia* of God in images not of a cultic meal but of a sumptuous, glorious banquet celebration.[88]

The parable of the Great Feast jolts the hearer into recognizing that the *basileia* includes everyone. No one is exempted. Everyone is invited, women as well as men, prostitutes as well as Pharisees. Only those who were "first" invited and then rejected the invitation will be excluded. Not the holiness of the elect but the wholeness of all is the central vision of Jesus.[89]

It Will Show Up Where You Will Least Expect It

The Good Samaritan (Parable from Luke)

Scripture: Luke 10:30-35

The lawyer "wanting to justify himself" asks Jesus, "Who is my neighbor?" Jesus responds with a story of somebody who, though from an ethnic group despised by the Jews, knew instinctively the answer to that question.

The unlucky traveler is unnamed and remains anonymous. A Jewish audience would naturally assume he is Jewish in the absence of any evidence to the contrary. After the robbers beat and strip him he is truly without identity.[90]

If, in hearing the parable, one identifies with the helpless man, the subversive message becomes: "You cannot rely on your national identity or religious pedigree. Your only choice now is to accept help from an unexpected quarter."

Half-dead means that, while not dead, he could be taken for dead. At this point in the story, he is joined by a priest and a Levite. The reader is not told why they pass by without helping, but might assume one of two motives: fear of robbers or concerns for ritual purity. According to Lev 21:1-2, a priest may not "defile himself for the dead among his relatives except for his nearest kin." However, the Talmud specifies that he may defile himself to bury a neglected corpse. So in this story, ritual purity turns out to be an insufficient excuse for the clergy to pass by on the other side of the road.[91]

From the perspective of a Gentile reader (Luke's audience), one could, with Luke, read this as an example story. But, given the longstanding enmity between Jews and Samaritans, a Jewish hearer would struggle mightily with seeing a Samaritan as a hero. The Jewish listener would have expected an Israelite to be the hero. In narratives of the time, the usual triad was priest, Levite, and Israelite, in which Israelite equals layman.[92] In fact, when the Samaritan appears, Jewish listeners would expect him to behave at least as badly as the priest and Levite and probably worse. The Samaritan's insertion into the story as its hero, the one who helps, shatters the hearer's expectation. If the story had shown an Israelite caring for a Samaritan, it would fit in with an existing genre of stories in which haves were encouraged to help have-nots. In these stories a rabbi helps a leper or a Roman who is suffering. But with a Samaritan as a hero, with whom can the listener identify?

Identifying with the Samaritan is problematic because of the great enmity between Jew and Samaritan. Identifying with the priest or Levite aborts the story. There is only one option if one wants to stay in the story: to identify with the half-dead man and suffer the compassion of a Samaritan.[93] Conventional hierarchies of priest, Levite, and Israelite, identification of insiders and outsiders, boundaries between religious categories are subverted.

This parable subverts our sense of who the hero ought to be. It subverts our understanding of religious observances like the ones the clergy were on their way to perform. We would expect such observances enhance the walk of faith, not impede its central responsibility: compassion for those who are hurting.

It Will Disrupt the Rules of Business as Usual

Day Laborers in the Vineyard (parable from Matthew)

Scripture: Matt 20:1-15

Herzog's Interpretation: Blaming the Victim: "The kingdom of heaven is most certainly not like . . . "

William Herzog believes it is a mistake to see in the landowner a God figure and to view the grumbling workers as the villains. For him the parable is an encounter between the expendables (day laborers) and a member of the landowning urban elite, the vineyard owner. Vineyards were used to create an exportable luxury product. Wealthier people would force peasant farmers to sell their small farms so the wealthy could increase the size of their vineyards. Day laborers were among the expendable class. Their lot was less secure than that of slaves, for most of their work came during harvest time. In between harvests, they begged and often starved to death. Once a person fell into the expendables class, they lived an average of only five more years.

Normally, the steward would pay those who came first before those who came last. It was a sign of honor for the length of time they had toiled in the hot sun. Traditional interpretations of the parable view the vineyard owner as gracious for starting with the last workers. In reality, Herzog insists, this was a way of dishonoring the first chosen and shaming them. The denarius was barely a subsistence rate for one person, let alone if one had any dependents. For the landowner to remind the workers that the land now "belongs to him" would be to rub salt in their wounds, to remind them that they were now landless, often due to wealthy people forcibly buying off their land. To accuse them of envy on top of the other indignities is to shame them further.

Herzog doubts that the original parable included the introductory phrase, "For the kingdom of heaven is like. . . . " He feels, rather, that Jesus is saying, "Here is a scene that shows us how things usually go—the poor, the expendables, are humiliated by the rich and powerful. Surely the kingdom of heaven isn't going to be more of the same, is it?"[94]

Divide and Conquer: A Lesson in Human Solidarity

One result of poverty, oppression, or powerlessness is an increase in violence, hostility, and resentment among the sufferers themselves. The day laborers in the vineyard become enraged when the owner pays everyone a day's wage regardless of the length of time worked (Matt 20:1-15). According to Pheme Perkins, this parable illustrates how "people become so corrupted that they can only relate to others in [selfish] terms. As a result even extraordinary acts of generosity by those [in power] can be ineffective. Justice requires something more than the redistribution of assets. It requires a conversion in the way people deal with others."[95] The workers must move beyond thinking of themselves as engaged in an individual struggle to compete with everyone else. She concludes, "Unless we overcome false perceptions, our justice will not reflect that of God."[96]

Another Perspective: "The Kingdom of Heaven is Like . . . "

What if, while acknowledging the usual victim status of day laborers and expendables, we saw this parable as honoring the labor of those who had come last? Since we are all in this together, let's not grumble among ourselves. Let's be glad that those hired last have something to show for it and pool our resources for the common good. Seen in this light, the parable would have threatened the economics of the Romans and the religious economy of the Jews in relation to the Gentiles. In Matthew's community the parable would have challenged the prejudice against Gentile converts to the new faith who had not first been Jews.

The Subversive Voice

Several of the world's great religions have their instigation in the subversive voice, the courage to speak out against unjust social systems. The prophet Muhammed incurred hostility and opposition by his insistence that Allah was not just the supreme God but the only god among the teeming competitors of sixth-century Mecca. His challenge to that city's polytheism threatened its economy as well as its moral laxity.[97]

Buddhism has it roots in the Buddha's challenge to the priestly caste of Hinduism (Brahmins) in sixth-century B.C.E. India. He objected to their fatalistic defeatism and insisted that women as well as men were capable of enlightenment.[98]

Confucius sought to subvert the brutality and social chaos of China in the sixth-century B.C.E. His teachings commend a life shaped by compassion and integrity geared toward familial and political harmony.[99]

In most religions, the original subversive edge of the founder's voice tends to dull, and the abuses this person protested have a way of reappearing after the founder's death. Religious traditions need the periodic subversion of current practices by individuals who seek to keep them true to the founder's roots.

CHAPTER NINE

TEACHING AND PREACHING WITH A SUBVERSIVE VOICE

The Purpose of Preaching and Teaching with a Subversive Voice: To Exchange Silent Compliance for Spoken Subversion of Unjust Aspects of Conventional Wisdom

We have discussed the role of the subversive sage—those responsible for the books of Job and Ecclesiastes—and Jesus the Sage as depicted in the synoptic sayings and parables. We have seen how this role involves undermining dominant wisdom systems insofar as they ignore and perpetuate the neglect and continual misery of those who don't fit their categories. Biblical scholar Walter Brueggemann, in his book *The Prophetic Imagination*, describes a similar though more direct role that Israel's prophets had in opposing what he calls "the royal consciousness." In terms that sound uncannily contemporary, Brueggemann describes that "royal consciousness" as "an imperial economics . . . designed to keep people satiated" so they do not get in touch with what I have called the listening heart. Brueggemann's version of the listening heart is a "passion . . . the capacity and readiness to care, to suffer, to die, and to feel." The "politics of royal consciousness is intended to block out the cries of the denied ones. Its religion is to be an opiate so that no one discerns misery alive in the heart of God."[1]

Cultural theologian Harold Recinos discerns the subversive voice speaking as the "Spirit of God questioning human designs on life" in the lives of "racially scorned and socially invisible Latinos." Says Recinos, "Latinos find in the various interpretations of Jesus located in the New Testament a prophet who was critical of the way mainline religion backed social structures and rules that worked against creating a sense of real human solidarity."[2] Recinos depicts a "hard-hitting," outspoken Jesus.

Brueggemann and Recinos's description of the role of opposition to the prevailing powers captures the intention of the subversive voice. The subversive sage takes a strategic, canny approach, co-opting the metaphors, stories, proverbs, and images of prevailing culture for redemptive ends. The subversive voice is out to undermine conventional, unjust, so-called wisdom. Its efforts have the quality of underground opposition rather than above-ground confrontation. While the subversive voice undermines unjust versions of wisdom, we are also calling it a pillar that supports the construction of a wise life and community.

The subversive voice undermines the values of our acquisitive, violent, individualistic culture. It subverts the shallowness of personal success wisdom and the absurdity of ranking a person's worth according to one's possessions, class, or ethnicity.

The subversive voice fulfills this function by building a life grounded in humility, respectful of the mystery and transcendence of God. The subversive voice upholds the wise life by expressing a respect for the ambiguity of life and the wisdom of others. The subversive voice is strengthened by a radical compassion that seeks out rather than blocks out others' sufferings, and the self-discipline to speak at the opportune time in the most persuasive way.

There are similarities between the constructive function of the prophets and the sages. To express the "prophetic imagination," Walter Brueggemann suggests that the contemporary pastor mine the memory of his or her people and equip them to use the tools of hope, metaphor, and symbol to contradict situations of hopelessness. Using the tools of hope, the prophet shows that the presumed world does not square with God's facts and points to a different reality, one that has its beginning and dynamic in the promising speech of God. The prophet brings suppressed hopes and yearnings to public expression, equipping people to imagine a world very different from the managed reality around them. The world of reality managed by "kings" who control information and hoard hope is false.[3]

Homiletician Christine Smith, in her book *Preaching as Weeping, Confession, and Resistance: Radical Responses to Radical Evil,* exercises a feminist prophetic imagination in focusing on the issues, social systems, pervasive values, and theological understandings that dominate and structure the world in which we preach. She labels the evils she seeks to subvert, confront, and overturn as handicappism, ageism, sexism, hetero-sexism, white racism (racism on the part of whites), and classism.

She believes that preaching is an act of public theological naming that articulates truths about our present human existence, sometimes shattering illusions and cracking open limited perspectives. That shattering occurs in order to transform and redeem reality, to bring a new reality into being.[4]

Womanist thought honors the role of black women and their literature in expressing the subversive voice. Ethicist and preacher Katie G. Cannon, one of the originators of womanist thought, affirms the faith and liberation ethics of African Americans to defy oppressive rules and standards of the controlling society.[5]

Says homiletics professor Teresa L. Fry Brown:

> Within the . . . black community there is a fundamental belief in the interconnectedness of creation and community. A person's life is nurtured, transformed, and sustained by the concern and power of a loving, just, and merciful God who is also present in the life of the entire community.[6]

Justo González and Catherine González in their book, *Liberation Preaching: The Pulpit and the Oppressed,* point out that Christian teachings have, through the centuries, been adapted to the views and interests of the powerful. A key example the Gonzálezes offer is the personalization of the definition of sin as sexual disorder to the neglect of social injustice. Another is the identification of humility with passivity and weakness and its elevation as the central Christian virtue. The benefits of this belief for those who hold social power, say the Gonzálezes, is obvious.[7]

The work of homiletician, poet, and hymn writer Thomas Troeger asserts that "politics begins in poetry, in the metaphors, myths, and symbols that command our loyalties and organize our social consciousness." "A group draws its reason for being, sustains its current life, and envisions and realizes its future" through "metaphors, symbols, and narratives. . . . These mythic-poetic realities constitute the 'landscape of the heart,' the nexus of meanings that filters our interpretation of the world and shapes our patterns of response and creativity."[8]

William F. Fore asserts that there are several dominant myths in television programming our preaching needs to contest through the power of metaphor, symbol, and narrative.

They include,

- The fittest survive
- Happiness consists of limitless material acquisition
- Consumption is inherently good
- Property, wealth, and power are more important than people
- Progress is an inherent good

Troeger suggests we substitute a communal poetic idiom for the current individualistic technical idiom.[9]

The purpose of the subversive voice, then, is to undermine the dominant myths of individualism, glamorized violence, and consumerism of our culture(s). Following the lead of the biblical sages, we do so by expressing our Christian worldview in proverbs, stories, and metaphors that undermine, challenge, and overturn dominant cultural wisdom. Proverbs exercises its subversive voice in its sprinkling of proverbs that point to human limits mixed with the optimistic wisdom whose primary message is "look what you can do and how well things will turn out if you do!" Qohelet utters his subversive voice in pointed, newly minted proverbs that contradict the claims of traditional wisdom. He offers poignant reflections on just those situations in life that conventional wisdom ignores. Job invites us into a divine-human encounter at the depths of human pain that contradicts our deepest-held notions of who God is and how God works. Jesus undermines the conventional wisdom of ritual purity and righteousness versus sinfulness in a series of subversive proverbs and parables that interrupt business as usual and cause listeners to question whether it should be allowed to continue.[10]

Preaching Out of a Subversive Voice: Characteristics of Our Teaching and Preaching

A Positive Motivation: "Because We 'Love the Justice of Jesus Christ' . . . "

Mechthild of Magdeburg (1207–1285), a Beguine mystic, once wrote, "If you love the justice of Jesus Christ more than you fear human judgment, then you will seek to do compassion."[11]

According to the second-century C.E. collection of rabbinic sayings, *Pirke Avot,*

> Suffering is the stuff of life,
> and through suffering
> one opens the heart to compassion,
> the shared pain of living beings.
> We withstand our trials by feeling the pain without abandoning the world.[12]

The Sage Desires to Point to Solutions, Not Just Highlight Problems

A Presbyterian pastor serving a church in a suburb near Orlando, Florida, remarked that

> I noticed a pattern with many of my colleagues in their preaching. They would preach with an introduction, introduce a problem, give illustrations of the problem several times over, and the end was always a hurried "but Jesus can fix it. Amen."
>
> I take a different approach. I say "As we all know, life is challenging, but thankfully, Scripture gives us some guidelines for help." Then I spend the bulk of the sermon looking at how to address the problem rather than elaborating on how bad the problem is.

The Sage Is Sensitive to the Particularities of the Cultural Context

Said the Japanese pastor from San Diego,

> The Japanese culture, looking at it from its Buddhistic and Confucian roots, does not have our concept of righteousness and evil and justice and injustice. The culture is based more on shame and honor. If a person can preserve his honor regardless of his guilt, there is a certain acceptance of that. A part of the way you preserve your honor is by not sticking your foot in your mouth and letting people know how much shame you deserve. That's changing some, but even with my generation growing up, we received a lots of messages of "don't do anything to bring shame on the family." So part of your reason for doing well was the

honor of the family. Part of the reason to keep it from being known that anything was wrong was to prevent shame or save face.

Japan has one of the highest suicide rates in the world. That is a function of the honor-and-shame culture and the fact that often there is no way to regain your honor. Once you are ashamed, suicide is the only honorable option left.

One thing that would bring shame is failure in relationships. In the Japanese culture there is no way to repair a broken relationship. That is an unofficial statement, of course, from my perspective and experience. So from our Christian perspective, when we talk about repentance and forgiveness, reconciliation and restoration, that is something very hard for Japanese people to accept. This is true between husband and wife, between business associates, and within a church. It's very hard to have a 70-30 vote in a Japanese church.

Honor is gained by achievement. There is a very high emphasis on education as a form of achievement. Wealth and professional standing are two others. Japanese society is a conformity-based society. There is an old Japanese saying that the nail that has its head sticking up will be driven back into the board. So you don't want to be the lone rebel or the prophetic voice.

The role of preacher as sage is more compatible with Japanese culture than the lone prophet speaking against the wind and against society. The teaching model of the rabbi, where people go to the rabbi and say, "Rabbi, what does the Torah say about this?" and the rabbi just sort of sitting there scratching his beard and he says, "Well, you know, as it says. . . . " That kind of teaching is more friendly to the Japanese culture.[13]

The Sage Names That Which Is Unhealthy in the Community

A Roman Catholic priest from a large suburban Dallas parish expressed his role as subversive sage in this way:

Being controlled by our people can lead to bad decisions. I see myself partly as a protector of spiritual truth. It is important to me to step in and name something that is not healthy in the community. I want to remind people of what is healthy. . . . We Catholics have a wonderful reserve of truth and so do others. It is wisdom or spirituality that will save the world, not a religion.

The Sage Challenges Injustices and Prejudices in One's Cultural Setting

A United Methodist pastor serving a church in rural north Texas said,

> There is a lot of racial prejudice in small Texas towns. A couple of year ago there was a young black boy who got mixed up with some older boys and was with a group of them when they killed a man and crippled his wife. I remember talking to people around town. "You know he was in on it," they would say. He was tried as an adult and is serving twenty years. I remember visiting him in prison. He looked at me with those big brown eyes and said, "I think I'm going home tomorrow."

The Sage's Speech Is Sometimes Direct

This same pastor told me,

> I was converted by Brother Johnson, a revival preacher, when I was thirteen. Brother Johnson was "tart." He said, "I don't care if you like what I say or not. I can preach and ride out of town." Brother Johnson came out from behind the pulpit and got right in our face.

A female African American Baptist pastor in Washington, D.C., said,

> I think we make a false distinction when we think that pastoral care is just about comforting and healing and that prophetic dealings are just about challenging and confronting. Pastoral care and counseling is about healing, but you can't heal without addressing issues of oppression and ways we interfere with others' healing and well-being. To love people you have to challenge them.

Speaking of the trials of an aspiring woman preacher in the Methodist movement in England in the 1770s, one commentator says,

> Madame Perrott preached the word of life to all who would hear, in private houses, both in town and country; and while thus engaged she was sometimes pelted with mud, and otherwise very roughly and cruelly treated.[14]

John Wesley came to recognize the preaching and teaching of women as an "extraordinary call" through which God was bringing renewed life to the Church of England.

To another woman preacher, Miss Martha Chapman, Wesley offered this stringent encouragement:

> If you speak only faintly and in-directly, none will be offended and none profited. But if you speak out, although some will probably be angry, yet others will soon find the power of God unto salvation.[15]

Wesley was firmly convinced that "whatever religion can be concealed is not Christianity."[16]

The Sage Is Sometimes Subtle

A United Methodist pastor of a large church in central Texas made these observations.

> I approach controversial issues indirectly. If I wanted to get across the point of a woman's right to equality, I might say something like, "Lydia bankrolled Paul's ministry." Hmm. Instead of, "You'd better wake up and realize that women. . . . " I often use the Ethiopian eunuch of an example of an outsider, yet a person Philip invites in as a brother. Hmm.

A Baptist pastor from Maryland offered this insight.

> One of my favorite passages in Proverbs is 8:22-31. I love the ending where it says Wisdom delights in all creation and in the human race. It is such an affirming text. It is not a passage that has been dwelt on much in Baptist life. We have the big controversy here about the pronouns for God. My own conviction is that we need to use more of the Bible's images. There are so many. I was telling the congregation just recently that in recent Baptist history, since 1900, "born again" is such an important phrase. And "born again" is a feminine image. Men don't give birth.

A Unitarian pastor from Dallas said this in response to my question, "Have you come up with any helpful strategies for dealing with hot-button moral issues?" She said,

> I feel strongly that confrontation is not the most efficient way to change people. Because once you've confronted them and they've gotten defensive, which is what most of us do when we are confronted, it takes energy to get them to a conciliatory place. I have never found that effective. I am more likely to be theologically controversial and let them make the political inferences.

The Sage's Wisdom Starts with Ourselves

An African American woman pastor serving at a black church in a middle-class suburb of Dallas told this story.

> I was working for the city of Dallas, earning good money. I had been made head of the Missionary Society and was making talks all over Dallas about raising youth in the right way. Then my teenage daughter became pregnant at age sixteen. This was a girl who had had lots of attention, private lessons—she was bright and beautiful. I thought I would die I was so hurt. I knew the ladies would whisper behind their hands: "Who is she to give us advice? She can't even control her own home!" I was thirty-six years old, not ready to be a grandmother. At church in Sunday school, they took her off the piano stool, even though they had no one else to play.
>
> As I was crying one night, God spoke directly to me. "What about your child?" God asked. So I went into her room and sat on the edge of her bed and hugged her and said, "We're going to get through this together." So I took that baby and raised her like my own until she was six. I carried her on my hip, this gorgeous little baby, to all my church activities. And you can't whisper about a beautiful baby reaching out for you. It melted their hearts. From that experience, I learned to confront the wrong where I see it, even in myself.

The Sage Shows Solidarity with Our People

An African American pastor, serving a large historic black church in Washington, D.C., said,

> You can be a prophet much more effectively if people see you as going the mile with them in their shoes, standing where they stand. If they feel you are with them, then they will allow you to critique their behavior. If they see you as fighting with them on their issues, they're much less likely to hear you out. Prophets did not have parishes, and if you want to lose your parish then try prophetic preaching without some pastoral dimension.

A Puerto Rican female pastor from an Episcopal church in Los Angeles shared these insights.

My church was the second black church west of the Mississippi and the first black church in California. The first black librarians came to this church in the 1940s and 1950s and the first black public-health nurse and one of the first black judges. There was a lot of pride here, class pride. Then when Hispanic people started coming, the black members felt they had been coming here for fifty years and these people are coming out of nowhere, they don't support the church financially the way that they should and they are going to take over. I realized that the primary issue was an issue of class communications, not race. Deep down, the black members feared a loss of their identity, feared displacement. There was a community history here that had to be respected and taken into account. I empathized with the black community as well as with the Hispanic group and, over time, they came to trust me. Being bilingual, I could be a bridge between the two communities. One of my recurrent themes is our identity as Christians, our identity as a church. No, we can't just say, "Why don't they go to that church down the street?" That's not what the church is.

The Sage Goes Beyond Our Comfort Zone

A United Methodist pastor of a church in north Texas aptly compared going outside our comfort zones with exercise by saying,

> I started working out again after years of not working out. My trainer said I should hurt the next day. "If you don't, it means you haven't stretched and pushed yourself enough."

A young black pastor from an inner-city United Methodist church in Dallas told me,

> Black churches have traditionally viewed celebration as the purpose of worship and have ended their sermons on a high note of celebration. Said one young black man who visited my church, "What is your church doing to help the community around it? I am not impressed by your celebration if I don't see your service."

Sages Take Risks

A sixtysomething Presbyterian pastor of a suburban church in central Pennsylvania had this to say.

This Sunday I'm preaching a sermon called "Love Is Risky." The text is the slaughter of the innocents. I am acutely aware of a number of family problems in the congregation, to say nothing of the bombings in the Middle East. I don't want to live in a country without an army, but in the sermon I say war is failure. That's not going to go over big, but that's what the New Testament says, as far as I'm concerned. And so it will not be received with great enthusiasm at my church. They would much rather have red, white, and blue Santa Clauses.

A white female United Methodist pastor serving a politically conservative, aging, one thousand-member church in a suburb of Dallas observed:

> I am no Jeremiah. I am less comfortable with the prophetic role, the convicting word. It is harder for me. I like to offer people the positive, hopeful message of 2 Isaiah, the pathways being made straight. If I preached on Central America and other cutting-edge social issues often I would be turned out of this church. With these issues I have to approach things very carefully. I'm preaching to a slice of George Bush's Texas.

Said one of the pastors I interviewed, who serves a conservative United Methodist church in a small town in central Texas:

> I give voice to people who would never have spoken without me. I take the heat for change to take place. I have paid for it several times over. It can be like walking through a minefield blindfolded.

In this regard, the following saying by the bold social reformer and evangelist Catherine Mumford Booth is comforting: "The waters are rising, but so am I. I am not going under, but over."[17]

The Sage Is Fearless

The Presbyterian pastor I mentioned above, who, in his sixties is persistently prophetic, said this:

> I've learned in twenty-four years of preaching to one congregation, "Don't be afraid to preach it, even if you know you're not going to get a lot of slaps on the back, even if your mouth is dry and you think you have overstepped the bounds."

A fortysomething Baptist pastor from a medium-sized church in a university town near Washington, D.C., told me:

> I think preachers need to be fearless in speaking what they believe to be the truth. Whether you are talking about what you think is sin or what you think is good news or whether you're talking about your own faults or you're talking about faults you perceive in others, you've got to stand up and tell the truth. There is great energy in that. There could be great hubris in that also, so the second thing is you've got to be correctable. If you're not, you become unbearable and insufferable and foolish.

> If you're not fearless, you end up playing it safe and saying nothing that touches anybody at all. I've listened to preaching like that all my life. I think sermons are like kites. The preacher may construct a beautiful kite, a well-constructed kite. But if you throw it in the air, does it take off? The preacher has something to do with that, and God has something to do with it, and the congregation has something to do with it. And fearlessness has something to do with it. You've got to throw it. At some point, you've just got to throw it. And if it falls flat, then there you are. But if the wind, if the Spirit takes it then, you've got something.

Sages Offer a Transformed Identity, Not Just an Informed Mind

A fortysomething white United Methodist pastor serving near St. Louis said,

> My congregation are typical suburbanites. They get their wisdom from the business world, from the public media, from general myths of American culture. . . . I want to offer up an alternative wisdom from our faith and the text that invites them to become questioners. I want them to see through an alternative lens rather than that of consumerism.

Sages Are Inspired by Our People's Moral Courage

This same pastor shared this,

> My people have showed me what discipleship in the world is like or could be like. In the late 1970s or early 1980s there was a farmer in the

172

rural church I was serving. He became convinced that he and the church had a responsibility to do something to help Indochinese refugees in this country. He "blamed it" on my preaching! As a result of his efforts, this rural community resettled twenty-two refugees, got them homes and jobs, taught them English. They were Laotians and they were welcomed in this rural, all-white Kansas town.

Sages Acknowledge the Continuum between the "Private" and the "Public" Realms

A male Presbyterian pastor serving a multicultural church in Los Angeles had this observation.

> I find that prophetic preaching often either just impresses those who happen to agree or angers those who happen to disagree. Preaching from a wisdom angle can achieve an *aha!* that is not under the control of the person who is speaking. But those listening get a sense that, "Yes, there is truth here that speaks to my life and experience and confirms, challenges, focuses it." I don't see myself changing anybody's mind about anything. At least that's not why I'm doing it. I think it happens, but rarely. I'm trying to give some different lenses. One of the things I have always tried to do in my preaching and in my ministry is to connect the personal and the public. We often create a chasm in our values, so I try to show it's more a continuum. I start out with the hypothesis that if something is true at one of those levels, it's true at the other. I try to help people take something they accept as true in their personal lives and apply that to the public scene. I try to show a story that is very intimate, very personal, and say, "OK, now here is another story that I think is about the same thing that is very public, very prophetic."

An African American Baptist clergywoman from Washington, D.C., said,

> In the black churches there is more preaching from the Old Testament, getting in touch with personalities. Job is used a lot. I've heard as many sermons from Proverbs, Job, and Ecclesiastes as I have from Matthew, Mark, Luke, and John. I like being able to focus on personalities, because I think early on in my preaching I did social-justice preaching because that was the tradition here. But even as I was preaching, it didn't feel like I was touching the people at their point of need. It was touching the global issues, but that didn't help anyone who was

struggling with how to get diapers, or wanted to go to school, or were living in an abusive situation. So I started focusing on the people in front of me. I brought in social-justice issues because the reason that some of these people are dealing with these things is because of some of the systemic types of things that can be addressed.

Sages Build on a Connection between Preaching and Teaching

This same clergywoman continued,

People expect us to preach on controversial issues, but we usually set it up in the Christian education medium. We did a Bible study and brought in a biblical scholar from a nearby seminary and really did a lot to lay the foundation so we could say, "This is what it means when we say our congregation is inclusive and that we do not meet people at a point of judgment but at a point of need. And we hold everyone accountable to holiness." So we use the Christian education department to undergird the preaching.

Sages Touch the Total Person: Mind, Heart, and Will

This woman also had a helpful insight into preaching to the total person.

I notice a difference when I preach to white congregations from when I preach to black congregations. When I preach to white congregations I sense that they want to know what they learned for that day, that they learned something new. And when I preach to black churches they want to be touched. They want to learn something, too, but they also want to be touched. There is a movement now in churches away from the old black style of touching people with emotion. It's a critique on the idea that you can come to church and get excited and emotionally filled and that's enough.

People need to learn things, to be educated. At the same time, if a sermon doesn't touch your heart, there is no action that goes with it. There's got to be both emotion and education. We talk a lot about trying to bring the intellect and the spirit together so people change their actions.

174

Preaching and Teaching about the Subversive Voice: Strategies for Interpreting Texts and Shaping Thematic Series

Interpreting Texts with a Subversive Voice: Listening for the Silences

Over the past thirty years, many voices in varieties of liberation theology have insisted on God's will for justice for all oppressed peoples as the common denominator of Scripture and practice.[18] The texts most commonly adduced have been those from the Prophets and the events of Israel's salvation history. Wisdom texts also affirm the insights of liberation, mujerista, womanist, and feminist biblical exegetes: the need to listen to the suppressed and marginalized voices in biblical texts as vehicles of God's justice.[19]

A Subversive Hermeneutic

To teach and preach with a subversive voice, two questions are particularly evocative.

1. Who is not being listened to in the text?
2. How does their perspective subvert (undermine, threaten, challenge) the status quo then and now?

Some strategies and questions to make our conversation with the text still more specific are:

- List all the characters and groups in the text.
- To whom are you listening or paying attention as you approach this text? Whom are you ignoring or discounting? (This question can apply to a narrative that deals with the interaction between individuals and groups of people. It also can apply to non-narrative texts, like legal codes or Epistles. There is always a story behind the story.)
- What does the focus of your attention say about what is important to you? About what you seek to protect? What does it say about what is too painful for you to see, hear, and acknowledge in life around you or within you?

175

- How, in your judgment, would various groups of people within your congregation answer the two sets of questions that immediately precede this one?
- To whom do people in the text seem to easily listen? Who seems to be the power-wielder?
- Rank your list of characters in order from more powerful (listened to more easily) to least powerful.
- What is the person or group who seems to wield the least power trying to say or do?
- How is this related to what you perceive to be the work of God or the gospel through this text?
- How would your life, your congregation's life, be different if we heeded the lesson of one we seldom listen to?

A Hermeneutic for Parables

Parables

With regard to parables, the following questions can be helpful:

- What is realistic about this parable?
- What is strange?
- What is paradoxical?
- What is challenging?
- What is open-ended?
- What is threatening to the religious, economic, and political system of the text's context, of our context?

What aspects of this parable seem to be:

- Out of control?
- Beneath our notice?
- Beckoning us to places we don't want to go?
- Liable to show up where we least expect it?
- Disruptive of business as usual?

Crucial Questions

- Strange Twist: What is the strange twist or barb of this parable? What seems to be not in keeping with life as you have observed it? What doesn't fit in with the way the world runs, the way people habitually act?

- Conflict: Is there conflict in the setting in which the parable appears? If so, what is it? What caused it? Remember that conflict can occur both in and behind a biblical text.
- Power: Who has power and who doesn't?
- Challenge: How does this parable challenge some of our ways of looking at the world? How might it challenge the ways we usually look at and handle certain situations?
- Comfort: In all of its strangeness, how might it be comforting, freeing, saving, good news in the daily situations we find ourselves in?
- Situations and People: Does it speak to something that is going on in the life of your congregation and community? How would the passage speak to the various situations people you know are going through? Think about variables like gender, race, economics, occupation, and generation. Think about specific people you know.
- A Personal Word: Does the text speak to something that is going on right now in your own life?

A Hermeneutic for Proverbs (Wisdom Sayings)

Does this saying confirm or subvert conventional wisdom? "A soft answer turns away wrath" (Prov 15:1) affirms the conventional value of wise speaking to maintain social harmony. "Blessed are you when people revile you and persecute you"(Matt 5:11) subverts the conventional value placed on a good reputation. "The highway of the upright avoids evil; those who guard their way preserve their lives" (Prov 16:7) affirms the conventional values of caution and moderation as ways of minimizing one's exposure to the chaotic aspects of life. "Those who try to make their life secure will lose it, but those who lose their life will keep it" (Luke 17:33) subverts those same values in favor of embracing the risk and sacrifice of the life of discipleship. We have to exercise discernment to decide whether conventional or subversive wisdom is most appropriate in a given situation.[20]

Can you envision a situation or situations that would benefit by the advice provided in this proverb? For example, a parent might learn that it is best to speak mildly to a teenager who is not at his or her best first thing in the morning.

Can you think of a situation that would not be helped by this proverb? That might call for a different piece of wisdom? It would not be an adequate response to our discovery of a vast inequity in books, supplies, and education between two elementary schools in adjoining towns in our community.

Thematic Series about the Subversive Voice

The Book of Job

The book of Job subverts several assumptions of the traditional wisdom of Proverbs. These assumptions lend themselves to a thematic series organized around several questions the book poses to us.

"What's in This for Me?"

Everyone serves God because, deep down, we hope for rewards.

"Does Job fear God for nothing?" (Satan's questioning of Job's motives for righteous living [Job 1:9]). This session or sermon could deal with human motives for obedience to God. Are they self-serving, to gain reward or to avoid punishment? Of course they are! To what extent is that inevitable? How can we purify our motives so that we enjoy our relationship with God and respond to God with praise and thanksgiving rather than with self-aggrandizing motives?

"Are You Playing the Blame Game?"

Everyone knows that when we suffer, it is because we have displeased God. "Is it for your piety that [God] reproves you?" (Eliphaz's challenge to Job [22:4]).

Because we are human, we like to explain things. When suffering strikes, we blame ourselves, God, someone else, the devil. We're willing to blame anyone or anything rather than admit that tragedy strikes the innocent. How can the person of faith direct his hurt and anger toward God, in relationship with God, rather than turn his or her face from God?

"Don't You Have It All Figured Out Yet?"

Traditional wisdom can figure out quite a bit about God and about how human beings should live to be in line with God's will.

The poetic interlude of chapter 28 raises this eloquent question, "Where then does wisdom come from? And where is the place of understanding?" (Job 28:20). The chapter ends with the affirmation, couched as God's words to humankind, "'Truly, the fear of the LORD, that is wisdom; and to depart from evil is understanding'" (Job 28:28).

We don't know all the answers about God and God's management of a complex and unwieldy universe. God is mysterious and transcendent. In a strange way, this is liberating news.

"Who Said It Would All Be Fair?"

God has promised us that we will be rewarded if we live wisely and punished if we don't.

Says who? God's response to Job out of the whirlwind to this assumption is, "Who is this that darkens counsel by words without knowledge?" (38:2). The notion of divine retribution says more about human beings than it does about God. Are we adventurous and faithful enough to live without our illusion and face life confidently, assured of God's presence in adversities of which God is not the cause?

"Who Are You?" ("You're Not Who I Expected!" [Job 38–42])

Meeting God in the whirlwind. In times of suffering it is tempting for us to complain and blame God more than to thank and praise God. It's quite a shock when God shows up in person, demands that we "gird up our loins," and hear things from God's side. We weren't expecting a show of Divine transcendence, power, and mystery. We weren't expecting a reminder that God has a lot more on the divine mind than us and our circle of suffering. Nor were we expecting the rigorous assurance that God is most present in times of suffering, that nothing can separate us from the presence of God in such times. We were hoping for an answer to the "why" question. Instead we receive the answer to a more modest, but even more important question: Is God present with us in times of suffering?

Qohelet

Many people think that Qohelet reinforces a sense of futility about life. What's the point? On a closer look, though, the book subverts such a sense of futility by its focuses on the pursuit of wisdom within a limited sphere and the enjoyment of work, relationships, food and drink.[21]

A thought-provoking teaching or preaching series would be to take up what are called the "impossible questions" of Qohelet. The impossible question is a subversive proverbial form that points to the limitations of human knowledge and the mystery of God. Such a series could be called "Right Between the Eyes" and could present these questions as the hard facts of life: that we all die, wise and fool alike, that we cannot see into what, if anything, lies beyond this life, and that life is fleeting. These "facts of life" subvert some of our priorities and preoccupations. We are obsessed with possessions and status that cannot follow us beyond this life and are quickly forgotten. We are buffeted by anxieties about the future that distract us from the real, though fleeting, joys of the present moment.

"How can the wise die just like fools?" (2:16)
"What do mortals get from all the toil and strain with which they toil under the sun?" (2:22) (What's the point?)
"Who knows whether the human spirit goes upward and the spirit of animals goes downward to the earth?" (3:21) (What's next?)
"The more words, the more vanity, so how is one the better?" (6:11) (Why should I bother?)
"Who knows what is good for mortals while they live the few days of their vain life, which they pass like a shadow?" (6:12) (How would I know?)
"Who can make straight what he has made crooked?" (7:13)
"That which is, is far off, and deep, very deep; who can find it out?" (7:24)
"What advantage have the wise over fools?" (6:8)

In preaching on Qohelet, I would want to subvert three of his assumptions: that God is distant and is the giver of justice and injustice alike, that there is probably nothing beyond the experiences of this life, and that there is not much we can do about the injustices that surround us except lose some sleep and feel bad for others. I would be careful to do justice to Qohelet's practicality, faith, and realistic joy. Feeling that we have to "rescue" Qohelet with New Testament texts short-circuits the depth and pathos of his good news.

Jesus the Subversive Sage

Series on Jesus' Subversive Sayings

An interesting series on Jesus' subversive sayings could be done in three sessions that correspond to the divisions in our earlier discussion.

Session One would be called "Opposites Attract" and would deal with Jesus' paradoxical sayings discussed above.

Session Two would be called "Blessed Are Who?" and would deal with Jesus' version of the Beatitude form from the Hebrew Scriptures.

Session Three would be called "Extreme Circumstances" and would explore Jesus' exaggerated scenarios or "focal instances." It would enter into their challenge, asking, "In what situations would this saying be a wise word?"[22]

Series on Jesus' Parables

A series of sermons or lessons on Jesus' parables could follow the headings I've outlined above in discussing the parables:

- It will never be under your control. (Leaven)
- It will seem beneath your notice. (Mustard Seed)
- It will take you places you hadn't planned to go. (Great Banquet)
- It will show up where you least expect it. (good Samaritan)
- It will disrupt the rules of business as usual. (Laborers in the Vineyard)

Meditations on the Subversive Voice

"A Different Drummer"[23]

Scriptures: Ps 1; Job 28:12-28; Matt 5:38-48
Almost everybody I've ever talked to about their call to ministry at one point in the story says, "Why me? Why would God choose me?"

God's answer is the same he gave to Solomon. " No one like you has been before you, and no one like you shall arise after you" (1 Kgs 3:12).

There is a lot that's unique about you—but today's sermon focuses on just one thing: your subversive voice. That is, your willingness to speak an unpopular, often unconventional word. The subversive voice is the fourth pillar of the wise character.

Jesus' words were seen as presumptuous. Many resented them. So today, when we speak our conscience, dare to subvert prevailing views, we will be criticized. It takes courage to raise your voice.

But if you fear the Lord and listen with your heart, you'll start saying, "Now wait a minute! What is wrong with this picture?" Not everyone will agree with your position or applaud you for your conscience. But at the end of your ministry, you will be able to say, "I let my voice be heard."

A pastor in north Texas was invited to participate in the funeral of a young man who had been killed in a one-car accident while driving just a little too fast on a rain-slick back road one night. The young man was just twenty-four years old. His young wife had grown up in my friend's church. The young man had been a member of the Baptist church in town. At the funeral, the Baptist preacher got up and said, "Friends, we don't know why, but it was John's time. God needed another flower in the heavenly bouquet, and who are we to question the Lord Almighty? John is in a better place and we thank God for that."

My friend got up to speak. "I know that some people find comfort in a notion of God needing people in heaven and taking them as members of the heavenly choir or flowers in a heavenly bouquet, but I have to tell you, friends, I don't find that vision of God very comforting. I believe John died in a tragic accident on a wet country road. I believe God welcomes him in love, but that God grieves with you and me today."

He was surprised by how many members of both churches thanked him that week with words like, "I was so glad to hear a minister say that. I've never believed God doled out tragedies like that. Thank you!"

A Bolivian pastor now serving a small Hispanic Methodist congregation in south Texas made this comment.

> My people's lives are filled with the reality of suffering, and they interpret suffering as God's punishment. I need to preach that it is not a punishment. Poor, marginal people in a Spanish setting believe that suffering is predetermined and deserved. "I am not good enough to please God," they say. "Suffering is our own fault." I must challenge this false belief.

Tony Freeman is the pastor of a Metropolitan Christian Church in San Diego. The MCC, as you may know, is a church that welcomes gays, lesbians, transgendered, and bisexuals to its worship and ministry. Pastor Freeman is clear that his congregation has a ministry to the community, not just itself. In a downscale section of town, the church serves soup, gives away clothes, prays with all who come there for help, tutors children at the homeless high school, and provides their school with supplies and clothes every year, and much more. On Gay Pride Sunday, his sermon title was "Whose Agenda?" and his theme was "Christ's Agenda, Not a Gay Agenda."

He heard that a United Methodist church nearby was holding a seminar to help gays and lesbians transform themselves and take up heterosexual lifestyles. He had lunch with the pastor and told him he planned to be there on the premises in his clerical collar when people arrived, as a peaceful witness. "I have to be there. My conscience won't let me stay away." So when participants arrived, he and five other local gay clergy were there, standing silently, prayerfully, in clergy garb, near the entrance.

In 1993 my dad ran for the state senate where I grew up. He was a Democrat running in a heavily Republican district against a familiar incumbent. My husband and I attended a kickoff dinner for the campaign. My husband had an interesting conversation with a young woman who turned out to be my dad's campaign director. Not knowing my husband was a family member, she confided in him, "The candidate is well meaning, but naïve. He refuses to do negative campaigning and he refuses to kowtow. He actually thinks it's all about the issues. He'll never win that way!" Sure enough, he didn't. I guess she was right.

Don't feel too bad, Dad. Jesus was not a very good politician either. Politicians placate those who have power over them, from whom they want favors. They settle scores with their detractors. Politicians strategize about their speech. They aren't afraid to speak harshly to underlings, to those who can't do anything for them. Somehow, Jesus got this whole principle backward.

Jesus never got angry at a personal affront. He didn't take things personally. He got angry when God was being disrespected—as in the case of the temple moneychangers. And even then, he didn't take it out on people in a one-on-one assault, but he engaged in a symbolic action by turning over the tables.

Jesus spoke his mind, often harshly, but not impulsively. His words strike me as quite strategic; the product of prior profound prayer and keen thought.

Sooner or later everyone called to preach or teach asks the question, "Why did God call me?" I believe our righteous anger and our spirit of lament is a big part of the reason God has called us into service. Every calling comes with a temptation. Ours is a lifelong temptation to become a politician rather than a minister of the gospel.

A young preaching student of mine called me the Saturday morning before Easter. "Dr. McKenzie, "he began, "I hate to bother you at home, but I did something really strange at the church where I'm interning, and I have to talk to somebody about it!"

I sat down and replied, "All right, David, what did you do?"

"I did something I've been fantasizing about for years! I was assigned to play Pontius Pilate in the reenactment of the passion. Everything was going along fine, I hadn't blown any of my lines, but when we go to the part where I was supposed to give Jesus over to be crucified, as the members of the Searchers Sunday school class, who were playing the part of the crowd, were chanting, 'Crucify him! Crucify him!' I heard myself yelling, 'No! Not this year! Everybody, be quiet! Settle down. Sit down. You heard me.'

"Martha, the director, sitting on the front row, glared at me and started chewing her bottom lip. The rabid crowd obediently sat down and arranged their itchy burlap robes over their knees, looking at one another as if I had completely lost it this time.

"The other intern, Rick, who was playing Jesus, who had been, up until now, a good friend of mine, was looking at me as if he intended to do me serious harm later, and he was asking me with his eyes, 'Where are we going with this?'

"'Now,' I said to the congregation, putting my arm around Jesus' shoulders, 'You obviously haven't been listening to this man closely enough or you would know that he is good and that his teachings bring life. I don't know what has kept you from listening, but I'm going to give you one more chance. I gestured to Jesus. 'Speak, good teacher, of the way of truth and this time we will listen.'

"I moved to sit down. Jesus grabbed my burlap sleeve tightly. 'No, you tell us, Pontius Pilate, what is truth? Tell us, which of my teachings is most memorable to you?' Then he sat down, arms folded across his chest, and smiled expectantly.

"Martha, the director, had her head in her hands. The seventh-grade Sunday school boys were leaning forward with their elbows on their knees, actually listening. The congregation as a whole had stopped rattling their phlegm and their candy wrappers.

"I thought to myself, 'Well, I've come this far . . .' so I delved into my memory bank and began to speak,

> You have heard it was said, an eye for an eye and a tooth for a tooth. But I say to you, "If anyone strikes you on the right cheek, turn the other also; and if anyone wants to sue you and take your coat, give your cloak as well; and if anyone forces you to go one mile, go also the second mile." You have heard it said, "Love your neighbor and hate your enemy," but I say to you "Love your enemies and pray for those who persecute you, so that you may be children of your Father in heaven." Those who have ears to hear, let them hear!

"After the service we were supposed to greet people at the back. I made a move to slip out, but I felt a small, viselike hand digging into my arm, and Martha's voice hissing, 'Oh, no you don't! You're going to stand here and face the music with me!' She turned as the first person came through the line.

"'Martha, terrific skit! You are so creative! It really made us listen up!'

"'Martha, really great. Where do you get your ideas?'

"'Martha, even my kids listened this year!'

"Finally the last person had gone through the line. Martha turned to me, her eyes narrowing: 'OK, David, lucky for you, you're off the hook this time. But promise me you'll never pull anything like this again!'"

"Oh, David," I said to him over the phone, "I hope you didn't make that promise. In fact, don't ever make that promise!"

Why would I give him that particular piece of advice? Because each of us, in all our uniqueness, has been called to a ministry of teaching and preaching upheld by the four pillars of wisdom: the bended knee, the listening heart, the cool spirit, and the subversive voice.

Because the words God spoke to Solomon centuries ago, God still speaks to each of us: "No one like you has been before you and no one like you shall arise after you" (1 Kgs 3:12).

NOTES

Introduction

1. Recounted by Bishop Leontine Kelly, telephone conversation with the author, December 2, 2003. The story is also recorded in Bishop Kelly's daughter's recent book. See Angella Current, *Breaking Barriers: An African American Family and the Methodist Story* (Nashville: Abingdon, 2001).

2. Only the most luxurious houses in that day had pillars, so seven is quite impressive, perhaps representative of the spiritual wealth that awaits us in her home. We are probably meant to picture the pillars in a circle around an interior courtyard. Robert Denton, "The Proverbs," in *The Interpreter's One-Volume Commentary on the Bible*, ed. Charles M. Laymon (Nashville: Abingdon, 1973), 309-10.

3. Dale C. Allison, *The Sermon on the Mount: Inspiring the Moral Imagination* (New York: Crossroad, 1999), 40.

4. In recent Gallup polls, 80 percent of respondents said they desired to grow spiritually; 54 percent said they were religious; 30 percent said they were spiritual but not religious; 6 percent said they were both. Cecile Holmes, "Gallup Sees Americans Rushing toward 'Religion a la Carte,'" *Baptist Standard*, February 23, 2000, http://www.baptiststandard.com/2000/2_23/pages/gallup.html. Originally published in the *Houston Chronicle*, n.d.

5. Richard B. Hays, "Wisdom According to Paul," in *Where Shall Wisdom Be Found? Wisdom in the Bible, the Church and the Contemporary World*, ed. Stephen C. Barton (Edinburgh: T &T Clark, 1999), 122-23.

6. There is a dearth of scriptural references to Wisdom books in the latest revision of the common lectionary for Sundays and major festivals. The three-year cycle contains only five passages from Proverbs, three from Job, and one from Ecclesiastes. See William P. Brown, *Character in Crisis: A Fresh Approach to the Wisdom Literature of the Old Testament* (Grand Rapids, Mich.: Eerdmans, 1996), 1.

1. The Role and Message of the Sage

1. T. Sarbin and V. Allen, "Role Theory," in *The Handbook of Social Psychology*, 3rd ed., ed. Gardner Lindzey and Elliot Aronson (New York: Random House,

1985), 1:551, 545, quoted in Carole R. Fontaine, "The Sage in Family and Tribe," in *The Sage in Israel and the Ancient Near East*, ed. John G. Gammie and Leo G. Perdue (Winona Lake, Ind.: Eisenbrauns, 1990), 156.

2. Sarbin and Allen, 497-98, quoted in "The Sage in Family and Tribe," 156.

3. William F. May's *Beleaguered Rulers: The Public Obligation of the Professional* (Louisville: Westminster John Knox, 2001) is an insightful exploration of the potential and the pitfalls of contemporary professional roles. It strengthens the case for the recovery of the wisdom-teacher as part of our role as leaders, whether clergy or lay.

4. Kathleen A. Farmer, "The Wisdom Books: Job, Proverbs and Ecclesiastes," in *The Hebrew Bible Today: An Introduction to Critical Issues*, ed. Steven L. McKenzie and M. Patrick Graham (Louisville: Westminster John Knox, 1998), 129. Among those described as wise in biblical narratives are Joseph (Gen 41:33, 39), the "wise woman of Tekoa" (2 Sam 14:2), and Solomon (1 Kgs 3:12).

5. The following psalms specifically mention "wisdom" or "wise": 37:30; 49:3; 51:6; 90:12; 104:24; 105:22; 111:10. A number of scholars have found wisdom terminology and themes beyond the traditional Wisdom books of the Hebrew Bible. Locations include Deuteronomy, Amos, Isaiah, the Song of Songs, Esther, the Joseph story (Gen 37–50) and the Succession story (2 Sam 9–20). For specifics, see R. B. Y. Scott, "The Study of the Wisdom Literature," *Interpretation* 24 (1970).

6. Farmer, "The Wisdom Books," 129.

7. James L. Crenshaw, "The Sage in Proverbs," in *The Sage in Israel and the Ancient Near East*, 206-8.

8. Roland E. Murphy, *The Tree of Life: An Exploration of Biblical Wisdom Literature* (New York: Doubleday, 1990), 4.

9. See for example 17:12; 25:14, 23.

10. Murphy, *The Tree of Life*, 5.

11. See Prov 16:10, 13; 20:2, 8, 26, 28. The prophets' focus was on the measurement of social praxis by the Lord's requirements that Israel be a just nation, as expressed in Mic 6:8. The prophets' approach is often direct and confrontative. The rigid separation of various genres and roles in the Hebrew Bible is reflective of contemporary culture and its perspectives. However, it remains accurate to say that, while there are wisdom influences in the prophetic literature and some concern for justice in the wisdom corpus, the roles and genres of prophet and sage had distinct focuses and strategies. J. David Pleins, *The Social Vision of the Hebrew Bible: A Theological Introduction* (Louisville: Westminster John Knox, 2001), 354. Donn Morgan, in his book, *The Making of Sages: Biblical Wisdom and Contemporary Culture* (Harrisburg, Penn.: Trinity Press International, 2002), 155-56, sets the role of sage in the context of contemporary culture.

12. Throughout Proverbs, several references to both father and mother reflect the communication of wisdom lore in the family (10:1; 15:20; 20:20; 23:22, 25; 30:11, 17). See Murphy, *The Tree of Life*, 3.

13. This is the theory advanced by Claudia V. Camp in her provocative book *Wisdom and the Feminine in the Book of Proverbs* (Sheffield: Almond, 1985).

14. Lawrence Boadt, *Reading the Old Testament: An Introduction* (New York: Paulist, 1984), 43.

15. Pheme Perkins, *Jesus as Teacher* (New York: Cambridge University Press, 1990), 7-8. For an extended discussion of the history of the sage in Israel, see Joseph Blenkinsopp's *Sage, Priest, Prophet: Religious and Intellectual Leadership in Ancient Israel* (Louisville: Westminster John Knox, 1995), 9-65.

16. Perkins, *Jesus as Teacher*, 11.

17. Ibid., 13.

18. Ibid.

19. Ibid., 14.

20. *Aspects of Wisdom in Judaism and Early Christianity*, ed. Robert L. Wilken (Notre Dame, Ind.: University of Notre Dame Press, 1975), xv-xvi.

21. Steven D. Fraade, "The Early Rabbinic Sage" in *The Sage in Israel and the Ancient Near East*, 431.

22. William McKane, *Proverbs: A New Approach* (Philadelphia: Westminster, 1970), 491.

23. Soozi Holbeche quoted in *The Way Ahead*, ed. Eddie Shapiro and Debbie Shapiro (Shaftesbury, Dorset; Rockport, Mass.: Element, 1992). This excerpt is printed in *Spiritual Literacy: Reading the Sacred in Everyday Life*, ed. Frederic Brussat and Mary Ann Brussat (New York: Scribner, 1996), 354-55.

24. John B. White, "The Sages' Strategy to Preserve *Shalom*" in *The Listening Heart: Essays in Wisdom and the Psalms in Honor of Roland E. Murphy*, ed. Kenneth G. Hoglund et al. (Sheffield: JSOT, 1987), 308.

25. For a complete list, see James Crenshaw, *Old Testament Wisdom: An Introduction* (Atlanta: John Knox, 1981), 81.

26. Lawrence E. Toombs, "The Theology and Ethics of the Book of Proverbs," *Consensus* 14, no. 2 (1988): 7-24, 12-13. See also W. O. E. Oesterly's discussion of the types of fools in *The Book of Proverbs*. WC, vol. 20 (London: Methuen & Co. Ltd., 1929), lxxxiv-lxxxvii.

27. Toombs, "The Theology and Ethics of the Book of Proverbs," 12-13.

28. William P. Brown, *Character in Crisis: A Fresh Approach to the Wisdom Literature of the Old Testament* (Grand Rapids, Mich.: Eerdmans, 1996), 22.

29. Dave Bland, *The Formation of Character in the Book of Proverbs* (manuscript), 14. The juxtaposition of seemingly contradictory proverbs is evidence of this strategy (Prov 26:4-5).

30. Ibid, 33.

31. Thomas P. McCreesh, O.P., "Wisdom as Wife: Proverbs 31:10-31," *Revue Biblique* (1985): 25-46.

32. An excellent, more recent resource is Dan Kindlon's book *Too Much of a Good Thing: Raising Children of Character in an Indulgent Age* (New York: Hyperion, 2001).

33. See Bernard T. Adeney's, *Strange Virtues: Ethics in a Multicultural World* (Downer's Grove, Ill.: InterVarsity, 1995).

34. Brown, *Character in Crisis*, 11-12.

35. *Summa Theologiae* I-II, q. 62, a.1, quoted in Brown, *Character in Crisis*, 12.

36. Toombs, "The Theology and Ethics of the Book of Proverbs," 11. Israelite wisdom was influenced by the understanding of the concept of *ma'at* in Egyptian wisdom writings. *Ma'at* was the cosmic and human order established by the gods at the creation of the world. To live according to *ma'at* was to enjoy a creative, dynamic, and successful life. In royal and cultic texts, *ma'at* is personified as a female goddess. In Israelite wisdom, Yahweh is clearly sovereign and Wisdom is the medium whereby God created the earth. She is a divine gift to human beings that enables them to discern how to live in alignment with divine intentions. She is a representation of Yahweh's will and his offer of salvation. By contrast, in Egyptian wisdom, *ma'at* is an impersonal principle to which the gods themselves are subject. See Camp, *Wisdom and the Feminine in the Book of Proverbs*, 31.

37. Roland E. Murphy, *The Tree of Life*, 115.

38. Roland E. Murphy, "Wisdom Theses," in *Wisdom and Knowledge*, ed. J. Armenti (Villanova, Pa.: Villanova University Press, 1976), 198.

39. See Ben Witherington III, *Jesus the Sage: The Pilgrimage of Wisdom* (Minneapolis: Fortress, 1994), chapter 4.

40. *In Search of Wisdom: Faith Formation in the Black Church*, ed. Anne E. Streaty Wimberly and Evelyn L. Parker (Nashville: Abingdon, 2002), 17.

41. Ibid, 51.

42. Wimberly and Parker, *In Search of Wisdom*, 34. See also Teresa L. Fry Brown, *God Don't Like Ugly: African American Women Handing on Spiritual Values* (Nashville: Abingdon, 2000), and Nicholas C. Cooper-Lewter and Henry H. Mitchell, *Soul Theology: The Heart of American Black Culture* (San Francisco: HarperSanFrancisco, 1986).

2. The First Pillar of Wisdom: The Bended Knee

1. The word for "fear" (*yireah*) has multiple meanings that intertwine in its usage in Proverbs: reverence, piety, and terror. See *A Reader's Hebrew-English Lexicon of the Old Testament* (Grand Rapids, Mich.: Zondervan, 1989).

2. Lawrence E. Toombs, "The Theology and Ethics of the Book of Proverbs," *Consensus* 14, no. 2 (1988): 7-24, 14.

3. Gerhard von Rad, *Wisdom in Israel* (Nashville: Abingdon, 1972), 67.

4. Ellen F. Davis, *Proverbs, Ecclesiastes, and the Song of Songs* (Louisville: Westminster John Knox, 2000), 28.

5. Charles F. Melchert, *Wise Teaching: Biblical Wisdom and Educational Ministry* (Harrisburg, Penn.: Trinity Press International, 1998), 37.

6. Paul Holmer, *Making Christian Sense* (Philadelphia: Westminster, 1984), 55. Holmer's understanding of "fear of the Lord" is discussed in Melchert, *Wise Teaching*, 38-39.

7. John Singleton, "At the Roots of Methodism: Wesley's Wisdom Lives in Sayings," United Methodist News Service. Online: http://www.umc.org/umns/ agency_meetings.asp?story={3FD503F6-5E34-46A8-9861-E8D79074F481} &mid=901.

8. Christian educator Charles Melchert points out that while contemporary psychologists and educators distinguish cognition and emotion, in an attempt at objectivity, the ancient Hebrews could not imagine an objective posture before God. Emotion and cognition intermingle in biblical wisdom's fear of the Lord. To fear the Lord is to experience blessedness (Prov 28:14), security (Prov 19:23) and humility (Prov 15:33; 22:4). Melchert, *Wise Teaching*, 38.

9. Toombs, "The Theology and Ethics of the Book of Proverbs," 15.

10. Ibid.

11. Ibid.

12. Davis, *Proverbs, Ecclesiastes, and the Song of Songs*, 29.

13. Benedicta Ward, trans. *The Sayings of the Desert Fathers: The Alphabetical Collection* (London: Mowbray's, 1975), 2.

14. Augustine, *Tractatus in Joannem*, xxv.16, quoted in Andrew Louth, *The Origins of the Christian Mystical Tradition: From Plato to Denys* (Oxford: Clarendon, 1981), 156.

15. R. E. Clements, "Wisdom in Old Testament Theology," in *Wisdom in Ancient Israel: Essays in Honour of J. A. Emerton*, ed. John Day, Robert P. Gordon, and H. G. M. Williamson (Cambridge: Cambridge University Press, 1995), 280-81.

16. Huston Smith, *The Illustrated World's Religions: A Guide to Our Wisdom Traditions* (San Francisco: HarperSanFrancisco, 1995), 146.

17. Smith, 155.

18. Lao-tzu, "Tao Te Ching," trans. J. Legge, in *Sacred Books of the East*, vol. 39 (1891). This translation can be found at http://www.sacred-texts.com/ tao/taote.htm.

19. William P. Brown, *Character in Crisis: A Fresh Approach to the Wisdom Literature of the Old Testament* (Grand Rapids, Mich.: Eerdmans, 1996), 28n 22.

20. Ibid., 26.

21. These excerpts from *The Sermons of John Donne* are found in Davis, *Proverbs, Ecclesiastes, and the Song of Songs*, 29.

22. Howard Thurman, *Deep Is the Hunger: Meditations for Apostles of Sensitiveness* (1951; repr., Richmond, Ind.: Friends United Press, 1973), 160-61.

23. Douglas R. A. Hare, *Matthew* (Louisville: John Knox, 1993), 106.

24. See also Prov 19:23 and 28:14.

25. Charles E. Carlston, "Proverbs, Maxims and the Historical Jesus," *Journal of Biblical Literature* 99 (March 1980): 92.

26. For a helpful discussion of images for Jesus, the Wisdom of God, see Craig R. Koester, *Symbolism in the Fourth Gospel: Meaning, Mystery, Community* (Minneapolis, Minn.: Augsburg Fortress, 1995). References in Proverbs to symbols for Wisdom abound (Light: 4:18; 6:23; 13:9); (Fountain of water: 13:14; 14:27; 16:22; 18:4); (Life: 3:16, 18, 22; 4:13, 22-23; 6:23; 8:35); (Way: 2:20; 4:11; 6:23; 8:20; 9:6; 10:29; 13:6; 16:9, 17; 22:6; 23:19). The epilogue to Proverbs describes Woman Wisdom who provides food and clothing for her household and whose "lamp does not go out at night" (Prov 31:18). There are also references to these symbols in Job and Ecclesiastes.

27. See Stephen C. Barton, "Gospel Wisdom," in *Where Shall Wisdom Be Found? Wisdom in the Bible, the Church and the Contemporary World*, ed. Stephen C. Barton (Edinburgh: T & T Clark, 1999), 93-110.

28. Leo G. Perdue, "The Wisdom Sayings of Jesus," *Forum* (1986): 2:3-35, especially p. 17.

29. The Greek word for Wisdom is *Sophia* and the Hebrew word is *Hokmah*. The Hebrew word for wisdom is feminine. See Raymond Brown, *The Gospel According to John*, vol. 1, AB (Garden City, N.Y.: Doubleday, 1966), cxxii. The idea of Jesus as Wisdom can be found in a variety of synoptic sources (1) Q: Matt 12:42/Luke 11:31; Matt 11:27; Luke 10:22; (2) L: Luke 21:15; 11:49; and (3) M: Matt 11:19, 28-30. Mark does not contain a great deal of Jesus' sayings and contains no Wisdom discourses. Its emphasis on an imminent apocalyptic crisis does not leave much need to develop the theme of Jesus as Wisdom.

30. James M. Robinson, "Jesus as Sophos and Sophia: Wisdom Tradition and the Gospels," in *Aspects of Wisdom in Judaism and Early Christianity*, ed. R. L. Wilken (Notre Dame, Ind.: University of Notre Dame Press, 1975), 10.

31. The apocryphal wisdom book *The Wisdom of Jesus Ben Sira* (6:23-31) speaks of Wisdom as a yoke, that, when taken on, brings rest. In Matt 11:28-30 Jesus applies those words to himself and the yoke of his teachings.

32. Ben Witherington III, *Jesus the Sage: The Pilgrimage of Wisdom* (Minneapolis: Fortress, 1994), 108. It is likely that Jewish wisdom and apocalyptic reflection from the first-century C.E. increased Christian reflection on Jesus as Wisdom. The books of 1 Enoch (first century C.E.) and 4 Ezra (also known as 2 Esdras—mid-second century C.E.) portray Sophia as the sender of prophets and spokespersons throughout Israel's history who has been so regularly rejected on earth that she finally returns to heaven (1 En 42:1-2; 4 Ezra 5:10), awaiting an auspicious time to return. Robinson, "Jesus as Sophos and Sophia," 12-13.

33. *Fourth Ezra*, also known as *2 Esdras* is a compilation of authorial efforts. The central portion (chaps. 3–14) was written by an unknown Palestinian Jew who probably wrote in Hebrew or Aramaic near the end of the first century C.E. The book was translated into Greek, and, in the middle of the next century, an unknown Christian editor added an introductory section, written in Greek, which now comprises chaps. 1–2. Nearly a century later another unknown Christian appended chaps. 15–16, also in Greek. *The New Oxford Annotated Bible, with the Apocryphal/Deuterocanonical Books*, ed. Bruce M. Metzger and

Roland E. Murphy (New York: Oxford University Press, 1991), introduction to *2 Esdras*, p. 300 of the *Apocrypha* section.

34. Robinson, "Jesus as Sophos and Sophia," 12-13.

35. Matthew's use of the Wisdom metaphor enables him to claim that opposition is not a sign of failure, but a legitimation of Jesus' teachings. Rejection authenticates Jesus' teachings (Matt 23:27f). See Celia M. Deutsch, *Lady Wisdom, Jesus, and the Sages: Metaphor and Social Context in Matthew's Gospel* (Valley Forge, Penn.: Trinity Press International, 1996), 147.

36. The thought of the first century Alexandrian Jewish philosopher Philo figures into the thinking of John's prologue. For Philo, Wisdom is the mother of the Logos. She is subordinate to God by virtue of her gender. Her name is female but her nature is male. By virtue of this nature she can teach and guide human beings in the ways of God. Philo characterizes Wisdom, in his later reflection, as the Mother of the Logos. The Logos is the Son of God. The Word of Logos comes to replace Wisdom's saving role as guide on the way that mediates salvation, as well as her role of representing God in the world of sense perception. See Sharon Ringe, *Wisdom's Friends: Community and Christology in the Fourth Gospel* (Louisville: Westminster John Knox, 1999), 44-45.

37. Elisabeth Schüssler Fiorenza, *Jesus: Miriam's Child, Sophia's Prophet: Critical Issues in Feminist Christology* (New York: Continuum, 1994), 147, 152. We see the attributes of Wisdom attributed to Christ without the use of her name elsewhere in the New Testament, notably in Phil 2:6-11; Col 1:15-20; and Heb 1:3. For further reading on the Logos/Sophia discussion, see Leo D. Lefebure, *Toward a Contemporary Wisdom Christology* (Lanham, Md.: University Press of America, 1988), 230-37.

38. Ibid., 155.

39. For a discussion of the nuances of patristic Christological reflection in relation to Wisdom, see Leo D. Lefebure, *Toward a Contemporary Wisdom Christology: A Study of Karl Rahner and Norman Pittenger* (Lanham, Md.: University Press of America, 1988), 234-36.

40. I am indebted to a conversation with my colleague, Bruce Marshall, professor of historical theology at Perkins School of Theology, on November 11, 2003, for this insight into the reception of Bugakov and Solov'ev's work.

41. Andrew Louth, "Wisdom and the Russians: The Sophiology of Fr Sergei Bulgakov," in *Where Shall Wisdom Be Found?*

42. Sergius Bulgakov, *The Wisdom of God: A Brief Summary of Sophiology* (New York: The Paisley Press; London: Williams & Norgate, 1937), 39.

43. Susan L. Bond, *Trouble with Jesus: Women, Christology and Preaching* (St. Louis: Chalice, 1999), 44. Bond is drawing on Gustaf Aulen's *Christus Victor* (New York: Macmillan, 1931), 20-23.

44. Louis Berkhof, *The History of Christian Doctrines* (London: Banner of Truth Trust, 1969), 172.

45. See Susan Bond's helpful discussion of Anselm's Christology in *Trouble with Jesus*, 54-57.

46. Pedro Negre Rigol, "Popular Christology—Alienation or Irony?" in *Faces of Jesus: Latin American Christologies*, ed. Jose Miguez Bonino (Maryknoll, N.Y.: Orbis, 1984), 67-68. Rigol charges that Latin American Protestant preachers have presented Christ as the bearer of an individualized, psychological salvation lacking in repercussions for public life. Catholic preachers have either presented the defeated, dolorous Christ of Good Friday, incapable of affecting the powers that be, or the monarchial, victorious Christ who vanquishes his enemies to rule the empire, in his case the Spanish Empire. Bonino argues that such a Christ endorses and fuels their rise to power.

47. Bond, *Trouble with Jesus*, 47.

48. Stephen Patterson (*The God of Jesus: The Historical Jesus and the Search for Meaning* [Harrisburg, Penn.: Trinity Press International, 1998], 64), uses this term, borrowed from Gerhard Lenski, to describe those who, in a system of patronage, fall through the cracks in the social pyramid to the bottom level. They are the beggars and the homeless, the persons who do jobs no one else wants to do like tax collecting. They are those whose persons who count for nothing, such as prostitutes. See Gerhard Lenski, *Power and Privilege: A Theory of Social Stratification* (New York: McGraw-Hill, 1966), 281-84.

49. Feminist and womanist theologians have criticized male liberationists for their overidentification of Jesus with a particular race and social condition, arguing that God's endorsement is not restricted to one race and economic stratum. See, for example, Kelly Brown Douglas's critique of the christological models of three black male theologians, in Bond, *Trouble with Jesus*, 82-83.

50. Bond, *Trouble with Jesus*, 83-84.

51. Ibid, 100.

52. Ibid, 103.

53. The metaphor of Woman Wisdom probably arose in the postexilic period when traditional male authority figures like king and priest were out of power and the shaky nation needed an alternative wisdom figure to guide and ground their young.

54. Claudia V. Camp, *Wisdom and the Feminine in the Book of Proverbs* (Decatur, Ga.: Almond, 1985). See especially chapter 4.

55. Elisabeth Schüssler Fiorenza, *Jesus: Miriam's Child, Sophia's Prophet* (New York: Continuum, 1994). See also Elizabeth A. Johnson, *Consider Jesus: Waves of Renewal in Christology* (New York: Crossroad, 1990).

56. Bond, *Trouble with Jesus*, 70. Bond is drawing on Johnson, *Consider Jesus*, 11.

57. Ibid.

58. Lefebure, *Toward a Contemporary Wisdom Christology*, 237.

59. One cannot reflect on Jesus' debt to Wisdom without recognizing that this is troubling to many people who regard it as an attempt to feminize Jesus. This

objection is helped by the realization that religious language is, by nature, metaphorical. We humans, with our limited minds, express our experience and understanding of God, by employing metaphors based on our human relationships and experiences. Clearly in the Bible, some of those are male and some are female. To be faithful to the scriptural witness and to the wisdom and needs of contemporary Christians, male and female, teachers and preachers of the faith need to acknowledge that Wisdom is one very important metaphor for the character and activity of the divine.

60. Witherington, *Jesus the Sage*, chapter 4. In this chapter, Witherington explores the likelihood that Jesus took the personification of Wisdom and suggested that he was its living embodiment, that he was both sage and the message of the sage—God's Wisdom (204). James D. G. Dunn arrives at a similar conclusion in his essay, "Jesus: Teacher of Wisdom or Wisdom Incarnate?" in *Where Shall Wisdom Be Found? Wisdom in the Bible, the Church and the Contemporary World*, ed. Stephen C. Barton. According to Dunn, "[Jesus] evidently saw in his ministry, in his own deeds and words, an expression of God's final will for his people Israel, something more than that which had been revealed through prophets and wise men of earlier generations, an authority which transcended the inspiration of patriarchs and fathers, a claim upon others which could be ignored only at the greatest peril." Dunn is convinced that the early Christian assessment that Jesus was the final embodiment of Divine Wisdom lies within the tradition of Jesus' deeds and words, their earliest memories and impact, rather than being superimposed upon a "thinner, less startling tradition" (91-92).

61. Leonardo Boff, *Jesus Christ Liberator: A Critical Christology for Our Time* (Maryknoll, N.Y.: Orbis, 1978), 113, 111.

3. Teaching and Preaching on Bended Knee

1. Rabbi Rami M. Shapiro, *Wisdom of the Jewish Sages: A Modern Reading of Pirke Avot* (New York: Bell Tower, 1995), II:17, 38.

2. Kathleen Norris, *Amazing Grace: A Vocabulary of Faith* (New York: Riverhead, 1998), 225.

3. Ibid., 226.

4. Ibid.

5. Ibid., 227.

6. Katie Sherrod, lecture at Brite Divinity School, Fort Worth, Tex., 24 June 1993, quoted in Joseph R. Jeter Jr., *Crisis Preaching: Personal and Public* (Nashville: Abingdon, 1998), 101.

7. Paul Scott Wilson, *The Practice of Preaching* (Nashville: Abingdon, 1995), 20-21.

8. Quoted in Jeter, *Crisis Preaching*, 23-24.

9. Charles F. Melchert, *Wise Teaching: Biblical Wisdom and Educational Ministry* (Harrisburg, Penn.: Trinity Press International, 1998), 39.

10. Shapiro, *Wisdom of the Jewish Sages*, V:10, 107.

11. See my *Preaching Proverbs: Wisdom for the Pulpit* (Louisville: Westminster John Knox, 1996), 32-35.

12. See my discussion in *Preaching Proverbs: Wisdom for the Pulpit,* 31.

13. This sermon was delivered at the New Mexico Annual Conference of The United Methodist Church held at Glorieta, New Mexico, May 30–June 1, 2002.

4. The Second Pillar of Wisdom: The Listening Heart

1. In 2 Kgs 3:9 Solomon is portrayed as asking the Lord for a "listening heart" that he may be able to judge the people of God and "distinguish right from wrong." Roland E. Murphy, *The Tree of Life: An Exploration of Biblical Wisdom Literature* (New York: Doubleday, 1990), 2.

2. W. O. E. Oesterley, *The Book of Proverbs.* WC, vol. 20 (London: Methuen & Co. Ltd., 1929), lxxvii-lxxx.

3. R. W. L. Moberly, "Solomon and Job: Divine Wisdom in Human Life," in *Where Shall Wisdom Be Found? Wisdom in the Bible, the Church, and the Contemporary World,* ed. Stephen C. Barton (Edinburgh: T & T Clark, 1999), 4.

4. Ibid., 4-5.

5. Ibid.

6. Gerhard von Rad, *Wisdom in Israel* (Nashville: Abingdon), 1972.

7. Frederic Brussat and Mary Ann Brussat, *Spiritual Literacy: Reading the Sacred in Everyday Life* (New York: Scribner, 1996), 52.

8. John Eaton, *The Contemplative Face of Old Testament Wisdom in the Context of World Religions* (London: SCM; Philadelphia: Trinity Press International, 1989), 41-42.

9. Macrina Wiederkehr, *A Tree Full of Angels: Seeing the Holy in the Ordinary* (San Francisco: HarperSanFrancisco: 1990), xii-xiii.

10. Ibid., xii.

11. Ibid., xiii.

12. Ibid.

13. Steve Wall and Harvey Arden, *WisdomKeepers: Meetings with Native American Spiritual Elders* (Hillsboro, Ore.: Beyond Words Publishing Inc., 1990), 100-101.

14. Kathleen Farmer, "The Wisdom Books: Job, Proverbs, Ecclesiastes," in *The Hebrew Bible Today: An Introduction to Critical Issues,* ed. Steven L. McKenzie and M. Patrick Graham (Louisville: Westminster John Knox, 1998), 129.

15. Joseph Blenkinsopp, *Sage, Priest, Prophet: Religious and Intellectual Leadership in Ancient Israel* (Louisville: Westminster John Knox, 1995), 34.

16. Prov 2:2; 3:21; 4:1, 23; 5:1, 7; 15:31; 23:26.

17. See also Prov 13:7, 25.

18. See also Prov 19:24; 23:13-14; 27:9.

19. See also Prov 16:32; 20:18-20; 21:6; 27:6, 17; 29:1; 30:32.

20. See also Prov 19:25; 21:13; 22:27.

21. For an excellent homiletics treatment of Job, characterized by both depth and accessibility, see John C. Holbert's *Preaching Job* (St. Louis: Chalice Press, 2002).

22. John Colllins, "Proverbial Wisdom and the Yahwist Vision," *Semeia* 17 (1980): 10.

23. Alice M. Sinnott, "Job: Cosmic Devastation and Social Turmoil," in *The Earth Story in Wisdom Traditions*, The Earth Bible, vol. 3, ed. Norman C. Habel and Shirley Wurst (Cleveland: Pilgrim, 2001), 90-91.

24. Gustavo Gutiérrez, *On Job: God-Talk and the Suffering of the Innocent* (Maryknoll, N.Y.: Orbis, 1987), 32. See Anthony Ceresko's discussion of Job's transformed perspective in his *Introduction to Old Testament Wisdom: A Spirituality for Liberation* (Maryknoll, N.Y.: Orbis, 1999), 83-84.

25. John Eaton, *The Contemplative Face of Old Testament Wisdom*, 42.

26. Holbert, *Preaching Job*, 146-47.

27. This is the perspective taken by Elsa Tamez in her recent book, *When the Horizons Close: Rereading Ecclesiastes* (Maryknoll, N.Y.: Orbis, 2000).

28. See Michael V. Fox, *Qohelet and His Contradictions* (Decatur, Ga.: Almond, 1989). Fox is convinced that Qohelet's use of the term *hebel* points to the absurdity that occurs when the expectations we have for God and life are belied by circumstances. Qohelet experiences life as a series of disappointments in the promises of conventional wisdom.

29. Rabbi Rami M. Shapiro, *Wisdom of the Jewish Sages: A Modern Reading of Pirke Avot* (New York: Bell Tower, 1995), 4 (I: 3, Antigonus of Sokho from Shimon the Righteous).

30. William Law in Eaton, *The Contemplative Face of Old Testament Wisdom*, 40.

31. Barbara Brown Taylor, *The Preaching Life* (Cambridge, Mass.: Cowley Publications, 1993), 50.

32. Thomas H. Troeger, *Creating Fresh Images for Preaching: New Rungs for Jacob's Ladder* (Valley Forge, Pa.: Judson, 1982), 12. In his more recent work, *Ten Strategies for Preaching in a Multimedia Culture*, Troeger is even more convinced of the necessity of metaphorical observation of life so that preachers can incorporate vivid sensory language and imagery into sermons for those who live in a media age of visual imagery.

33. Howard Thurman, *Deep Is the Hunger: Meditations for Apostles of Sensitiveness* (1951; repr. Richmond, Ind.: Friends United Press, 1973).

34. Charles F. Melchert, *Wise Teaching: Biblical Wisdom and Educational Ministry* (Harrisburg, Penn.: Trinity Press International, 1998), 58-59.

35. Huston Smith, *The Illustrated World's Religions: A Guide to Our Wisdom Traditions* (San Francisco: HarperSanFrancisco, 1995), 75.

36. Ibid., 162.

37. Ibid., 82.

38. John P. Meier, *A Marginal Jew: Rethinking the Historical Jesus*, vol. 2 (New York: Doubleday, 1991), 544.

39. For other examples of sayings attributed to Jesus that express sentiments common in his day, see Charles E. Carlston's "Proverbs, Maxims, and the Historical Jesus," *Journal of Biblical Literature* 99 no. 1 (1980): 100-101.

40. For a discussion comparing Jesus' parables to rabbinic parables, see Bernard Brandon Scott, *Hear Then the Parable: A Commentary on the Parables of Jesus* (Minneapolis: Fortress, 1989), 14-19.

41. For a list of the "strange twists" in Jesus' parables, see David Buttrick, *Speaking Parables: A Homiletic Guide* (Louisville: Westminster John Knox, 2000), 17.

42. See I. Howard Marshall, "Jesus—Example and Teacher of Prayer in the Synoptic Gospels," in *Into God's Presence: Prayer in the New Testament*, ed. Richard N. Longenecker (Grand Rapids, Mich.: Eerdmans, 2001), 113-31.

43. Moberly, "Solomon and Job," in *Where Shall Wisdom Be Found?"* 4-5.

44. Marshall, "Jesus—Example and Teacher of Prayer in the Synoptic Gospels," 118.

45. *The Upper Room Dictionary of Christian Spiritual Formation*, ed. Keith Beasley-Topliffe (Nashville: Upper Room Books, 2003), 51. An excellent biography is Elisabeth Elliot, *A Chance to Die: The Life and Legacy of Amy Carmichael* (Old Tappan, N.J.: Fleming H. Revell, 1987).

46. Rosemary Skinner Keller, "Georgia Harkness—Theologian of the People," in *Spirituality and Social Responsibility: Vocational Vision of Women in The United Methodist Tradition*, ed. Rosemary Skinner Keller (Nashville: Abingdon, 1993), 223.

47. Dorothee Sölle, *The Silent Cry: Mysticism and Resistance*, trans. Barbara Rumscheidt and Martin Rumscheidt (Minneapolis: Fortress, 2001), 290.

48. Ibid.

5. Teaching and Preaching with a Listening Heart

1. Marjorie Thompson, *Soul Feast: An Invitation to the Christian Spiritual Life* (Louisville: Westminster John Knox, 1995), 92-94.

2. Ibid., 17-30.

3. Dr. Ferris's gift for connecting to people is evident in his printed sermons. See, for example, *This Is the Day: Selected Sermons* (Dublin, N.H.: Yankee, 1980).

4. Henri J. M. Nouwen, *In the Name of Jesus: Reflections on Christian Leadership* (New York: Crossroad, 1989), 62.

5. Ibid.

6. The Third Pillar of Wisdom: The Cool Spirit

1. Quoted in Rabbi Rami M. Shapiro, *Wisdom of the Jewish Sages: A Modern Reading of* Pirke Abot (New York: Bell Tower, 1995), VI:1, 126.

2. Lawrence E. Toombs, "The Theology and Ethics of the Book of Proverbs," *Consensus* 14, 2:7-24 (1988): 19.

3. Ibid., 20.

4. William P. Brown, *Character in Crisis: A Fresh Approach to the Wisdom Literature of the Old Testament* (Grand Rapids, Mich.: Eerdmans, 1996), 34-35.

5. *The Westminster Collection of Christian Quotations*, comp. Martin H. Manser (Louisville: Westminster John Knox, 2001), 76.

6. Charles F. Melchert, *Wise Teaching: Biblical Wisdom and Educational Ministry* (Harrisburg, Penn.: Trinity Press International, 1998), 45.

7. Roland E. Murphy, *The Tree of Life: An Exploration of Biblical Wisdom Literature* (New York: Doubleday, 1990), 166.

8. Ibid, 25.

9. Wayne W. Dyer, *Wisdom of the Ages: A Modern Master Brings Eternal Truths into Everyday Life* (New York: HarperCollins, 1998), 251.

10. Joseph Blenkinsopp, *Sage, Priest, Prophet: Religious and Intellectual Leadership in Ancient Israel* (Louisville: Westminster John Knox, 1995), 34-35.

11. Melchert, *Wise Teaching*, 43.

12. John Singleton, "At the Roots of Methodism: Wesley's Wisdom Lives in Sayings," United Methodist News Service. Online: http://www.umc.org/umns/agency_meetings.asp?story={3FD503F6-5E34-46A8-9861-E8D79074F481}&mid=901.

13. Blenkinsopp, *Sage, Priest, Prophet*, 35-36.

14. Ibid., 34-35.

15. Melchert, *Wise Teaching*, 45.

16. What follows are a couple of examples from among many (Matt 7:24; 13:16; Mark 4:11-12, 24; 7:22; Luke 9:44). Many of the parables begin with Jesus' injunction to "Listen!"

17. For more background on the "expendables" in Jesus' time, see Stephen J. Patterson, *The God of Jesus: The Historical Jesus and the Search for Meaning* (Harrisburg, Penn.: Trinity Press International, 1998), 55-88.

18. Examples of Jesus' challenge to the religious elite, and, at times, to his own disciples, include Matt 11:7; 12:1-8; 15:1-12; Mark 8:11-12; 9:19; 10:35-45; 11:15-19; Luke 5:17-24; 5:33–6:5; 22:24-30; John 3:10. Examples of his comforting of the desperate, the marginal, and the poor include Matt 9:2, 27; Mark 5:34; Luke 7:36-50; John 19:26-27. Jesus could also be kind to the prestigious who evidenced faith (Matt 8:5ff) and curt with the desperate (Matt 15:24; John 4:17-18; 5:6). He did not hesitate to be blunt and challenging with his own disciples and even his own family (Matt 12:46-50; 20:22; Mark 3:31-35; 8:33; 10:38; Luke 8:19-21).

19. Huston Smith, *The Illustrated World's Religions: A Guide to Our Wisdom Traditions* (San Francisco: HarperSanFrancisco, 1995), 110.

20. Ibid., 22.

21. Smith, *The Illustrated World's Religions*, 74.

22. John Wesley *Letters*, V, 289. Letter to John Valton, November 12, 1771, in *Wesley Quotations: Excerpts from the Writings of John Wesley and other Family Members*, comp. Betty M. Jarboe (Metuchen, N.J.: The Scarecrow Press, Inc., 1990), 86.

23. John Wesley, *Letters*, VII, 101. Letter to John Valton, January 18, 1782, in *Wesley Quotations*, 86.

7. Teaching and Preaching with a Cool Spirit

1. A portion of this reflection was presented in sermon form to a North Texas Clergy Conference at Tanglewood Retreat Center, Lake Texoma, Texas, October 15, 2001.

2. This designation of the fool occurs in the following verses in Proverbs: 1:32; 7:7; 9:4, 6, 16; 14:15, 18; 19:24; 20:19; 22:3; 27:12.

3. For this threefold listing of what makes a person "mature" (focus on the cross, reliance on the Holy Spirit, motivation by love), I am indebted to Kevin Quast, *Reading the Corinthian Correspondence: An Introduction* (New York: Paulist, 1994), 37.

4. Dorothee Sölle, *The Silent Cry: Mysticism and Resistance* (Minneapolis: Fortress, 2001), 2.

8. The Fourth Pillar of Wisdom: The Subversive Voice

1. *Memoirs of the Spirit*, ed. Edwin S. Gaustad (Grand Rapids, Mich.: Eerdmans, 1999), 67-68. This story is taken from *The Autobiography of Peter Cartwright* (Nashville: Abingdon, 1984), 74-82.

2. For this reason, while some proverbs attribute poverty to laziness (6:6-11; 10:4; 12:11; 14:23; 19:15, 24; 20:4, 13; 21:5, 17; 23:20-21; 24:33-34), others assert that to dishonor the poor is to insult God (17:5; 22:22-23; 23:4-5, 10-11).

3. Leo G. Perdue, "Wisdom in the Book of Job," in *In Search of Wisdom: Essays in Memory of John G. Gammie* (Louisville: Westminster John Knox, 1993), 79-80.

4. Ada María Isasi-Díaz, "'Apuntes' for a Hispanic Women's Theology of Liberation," in *Voces: Voices from the Hispanic Church*, ed. Justo L. González (Nashville: Abingdon, 1992), 26.

5. Perdue, "Wisdom in the Book of Job," 80.

6. Ibid., 81.

7. Ibid., 85-86.

8. J. David Pleins, *The Social Visions of the Hebrew Bible: A Theological Introduction* (Louisville: Westminster John Knox, 2000), 500.

9. Ibid., 502-3.

10. Ibid., 505.

11. Ibid., 506.

12. Ibid., 506-7.

13. Ibid., 494.

14. Ibid., 497.

15. Ibid., 508.

16. Ibid., 499-500.

17. Eastern Orthodoxy acknowledges that while God reveals Godself, human language is ultimately incapable of describing God in its theology of negation, also called "apophatic" theology. Such an approach venerates the unknowable God through a series of negations that showed God as "ever beyond." See Gregory Mathewes-Green and Frederica Mathewes-Green, "Impact Pray-ers: Five Men Who Still Define Orthodox Spirituality," *Christian History* 16, no. 54 (1997): 28.

18. Qohelet uses the word *hebel* to describe the ephemerality of life (6:12; 7:15; 9:9), as something of little consequence (5:7; 6:4, 11), joy (2:1), human accomplishments (2:11; 4:4) and youth and the prime of life (11:10). See my chapter, "Biblical Proverbs that Subvert Order," in *Preaching Proverbs: Wisdom for the Pulpit* (Louisville: Westminster John Knox, 1996), 41-58.

19. Charles E. Carlston, "Proverbs, Maxims, and the Historical Jesus," *Journal of Biblical Literature*, vol. 99 (March 1980): 91. Recent scholarship has pointed out the similarities between Jesus and the itinerant Cynic philosophers. See, for example, Burton L. Mack, *The Lost Gospel: The Book of Q and Christian Origins* (New York: HarperColllins, 1993). Cynics were radical Stoics who rejected the cultural trappings of home and family. They lived wandering lives, at a subsistence level with regard to clothing, food, and shelter. Their themes of the foolishness of anxiety and dependence on social luxuries sound a common chord with some of Jesus' teachings (Matt 6:25-32; 10:7-11). However, the goal of their lifestyle and teachings was self-sufficiency, not radical reliance on the provision of God. See Pheme Perkins, *Jesus as Teacher* (New York: Cambridge University Press, 1990), 5-6.

20. See Kim E. Dewey, "Paroimiai (Proverbs) in the Gospel of John," *Semeia* (1980): 81-99.

21. The close kinship of proverbs and parables becomes clear when we observe that several of Jesus' parables bear an uncanny resemblance to sayings from Proverbs. The parable of the chief seats (Luke 14:7-11) is closely related to Prov 25:6f. The parable of the friend at midnight (Luke 11:5-8) is strangely similar to Prov 3:28. The parable of the two foundations (Matt 7:24-27; Luke 6:47-49) is very much in the spirit of Proverbs (see 10:25; 12:7).

22. Bernard Brandon Scott, *Hear Then the Parable: A Commentary on the Parables of Jesus* (Minneapolis: Fortress, 1989), 9, 13.

23. John P. Meier, *A Marginal Jew: Rethinking the Historical Jesus* (New York: Doubleday, 1991), vol. 1, 171. See also, vol. 2, 4-6.

24. Ibid., 177.

25. Leo G. Perdue, "The Wisdom Sayings of Jesus," *Forum* 2 (1986): 3-35. For a listing of the sayings that fit under each category, see 30-31.

26. James Williams has a helpful discussion of proverbs and aphorisms in his "Excursus: Aphorism and Proverb," in *Those Who Ponder Proverbs: Aphoristic Thinking and Biblical Literature* (Sheffield: Almond Press, 1981), 78f.

27. For Greco-Roman versions of these insights, see Charles E. Carlston, "Proverbs, Maxims, and the Historical Jesus," *Journal of Biblical Literature*, 99 (March 1980): 87-105. See also, Perdue, "The Wisdom Sayings of Jesus,", 7, for Perdue's list of folk sayings used by Jesus.

28. For preaching strategies built on this dynamic, see my *Preaching Proverbs: Wisdom for the Pulpit*, 79-100.

29. Carlston, "Proverbs, Maxims, and the Historical Jesus," 92.

30. Ibid., 93.

31. Ibid., 93-98.

32. Ibid., 97.

33. Ibid., 98.

34. Perdue, "The Wisdom Sayings of Jesus," 12.

35. Another equally common form is the comparative proverb, which makes analogies between two phenomena. For example, "A word fitly spoken is like apples of gold in a setting of silver" (Prov 25:11). Comparative proverbs abound in chaps. 25–29.

36. Jesus himself at times used this form, "The good person brings good things out of a good treasure, and the evil person brings evil things out of an evil treasure" (see Matt 12:35; Luke 6:45).

37. William Beardslee, "Uses of the Proverb in the Synoptic Gospels," *Interpretation* 24 (1970): 67.

38. Robert Tannehill calls these paradoxical proverbs "antithetical aphorisms." See Tannehill, *The Sword of His Mouth:* (Philadelphia: Fortress, 1975), 88f.

39. Beardslee, "Uses of the Proverb in the Synoptic Gospels," 67-68.

40. For an intriguing contextual interpretation of this important saying, see Madeleine Boucher, *The Mysterious Parable: A Literary Study* (Washington, D.C.: The Catholic Biblical Association of America, 1977), 64f.

41. See my treatment of Jesus' subversive sayings in *Preaching Proverbs*, 75-76.

42. Perdue, "The Wisdom Sayings of Jesus," 17.

43. Dale C. Allison, *The Sermon on the Mount: Inspiring the Moral Imagination* (New York: Crossroad, 1999), 41.

44. Perdue, "The Wisdom Sayings of Jesus," 18.

45. Allison, *The Sermon on the Mount*, 44.

46. J. Severino Croatto, "The Political Dimension of Christ the Liberator," in *Faces of Jesus: Latin American Christologies*, ed. José Míguez Bonino (Maryknoll, N.Y.: Orbis, 1984), 110-11.

47. Allison, *The Sermon on the Mount*, 43.

48. Ibid., 44.

49. Bonino, *Faces of Jesus*, 111.

50. David Hill, *The Gospel of Matthew* (Grand Rapids, Mich.: Eerdmans, 1972), 110.

51. Examples of straightforward admonitions and prohibitions in Jesus' teachings include Matt 15:26 = Mark 7:27; Matt 22:21 = Mark 12:17 = Luke 20:25; Luke 12:15; Matt 5:16; 7:6.

52. This designation is attributed to literary critic Frank Kermode. See James G. Williams, "Paraenesis, Excess, and Ethics: Matthew's Rhetoric in the Sermon on the Mount," *Semeia* 50 (1990):174ff.

53. Related to the focal instance is a form of saying called the "better than" saying. In Proverbs these sayings abound, contrasting foolish and wise behavior and their consequences in a clear-cut, conventional manner (16:8; 17:1, 12; 19:1; 27:5). Jesus' "better than" sayings juxtapose something unthinkable or impossible (a camel fitting through the eye of a needle, destroying our own hand, eye or foot), with something desirable—entering the kingdom of heaven, avoiding the fires of hell. Examples include Mark 10:25 = Matt 10:24; Luke 18:25; Matt 5:29-30; 18:8-9 = Mark 9:43-47. See Perdue, "The Wisdom Sayings of Jesus," 11-12.

54. Perdue, "The Wisdom Sayings of Jesus," 16.

55. Ibid., 14-15.

56. Ben Witherington III does not consider Judg 9:7-15 or 2 Kgs 14:9 to be parables, but fables. Fables are narrative fictions in which plants and/or animals discourse. Jesus does not offer any fables. Narrative *meshalim* as we find them in the Prophets, Jesus tradition, and early Judaism have human actors. They do not involve the pesonification of animals or plants. Witherington, *Jesus the Sage: The Pilgrimage of Wisdom* (Minneapolis: Fortress, 1994), 158. For an overview of parables in the Hebrew Bible and in apocalyptic literature, see John Drury, *The Parables in the Gospels: History and Allegory* (New York: Crossroad, 1985), chapters 1 and 2.

57. In this respect Jesus' narrative *meshalim* differ from those of the Hebrew Bible which convey a specific theme that is limited to their context. These *meshalim* also differ from rabbinic parables whose purpose is most often to expound a specific point in a scriptural text. While several narrative *meshalim* are inspired by passages of Scripture. The good Samaritan elucidates the question "Who is my neighbor?" in connection with the love commandment of Lev 19:18. "The parable of the Sower is connected to Deut 6:4-5 and Isa 6:8-10. The vineyard *meshalim* (Mark 12:1-12 and parallels; Matt 20:1-16; 21:28-32) have ties to

Isa 5. Behind the narrative *meshalim* in the Synoptic Gospels there is not, however, primarily an exegete of texts." Birger Gerhardsson, "If We Do Not Cut the
Parables Out of Their Frames," *New Testament Studies*, 37 (1991): 330.

58. There are five narrative *meshalim* in the Hebrew Bible (Judg 9:7-21; 2 Sam
12:1-4; 2 Kgs 14:9; Isa 5:1-6; and Ezek 17:3-10). The major difference between
them and Jesus' parables is that they occur in the context of a speech, an organized and coherent presentation that develops a specific theme. Narrative
meshalim in the Synoptic Gospels (parables) have an independence and an
intrinsic value themselves as objects of interpretation that none of the five narrative *meshalim* in the Hebrew Bible have. Birger Gerhardsson, "The Narrative
Meshalim in the Synoptic Gospels," *New Testament Studies*, 34 (1988): 348-49.

59. For an overview of recent parables scholarship see John R. Donahue, *The
Gospel in Parable: Metaphor, Narrative, and Theology in the Synoptic Gospels*
(Philadelphia: Fortress, 1988), chapter 1, "How Does a Parable Mean?" A more
detailed overview is found in William R. Herzog II, *Parables as Subversive Speech:
Jesus as Pedagogue of the Oppressed* (Louisville: Westminster John Knox, 1994),
chapter 1.

60. Beardslee, "Uses of the Proverb with the Synoptic Gospels," 69. In the
mid-1960s parables scholars Amos Wilder and Robert Funk examined parables
as poetic forms with keen appreciation for metaphor as a catalyst for theological
meaning. They were convinced that readers, in interpreting the parables, treated
poetry like prose, always searching for a single pedagogical meaning. They
thereby failed to do justice to the operations of the imagination in the
Scriptures—the poetry, the imagery, and the symbolism. See also John R.
Donahue, *The Gospel in Parable*, 8.

61. Stephen J. Patterson, *The God of Jesus: The Historical Jesus and the Search
for Meaning* (Harrisburg, Penn.: Trinity Press International, 1998), 121.

62. C. H. Dodd, *The Parables of the Kingdom* (New York: Charles Scribner's
Sons, 1961), 5.

63. For a list of the top-ten strange twists in Jesus' parables, see Buttrick,
Speaking Parables, 17.

64. Donahue, *The Gospel in Parable*, 15.

65. Ibid., 10.

66. Ibid., 15-16. Donahue is drawing on the thought of Crossan in his *Cliffs of
Fall: Paradox and Polyvalence in the Parables of Jesus* (New York: Seabury, 1980)
and his *In Parables: The Challenge of the Historical Jesus* (New York: Harper &
Row, 1973).

67. Herzog, *Parables as Subversive Speech* and Bernard Brandon Scott, *Hear
Then the Parable: A Commentary on the Parables of Jesus* (Minneapolis: Fortress,
1989).

68. Herzog, *Parables as Subversive Speech*, 27.

69. Ibid., 28.

70. Patterson, *The God of Jesus*, 60-61.

71. Herzog, *Parables as Subversive Speech*, 28.

72. Ibid. For an overview of the church's subsequent view of poverty and expendables in successive centuries, see George V. Pixley and Clodovis Boff, *The Bible, the Church and the Poor*, Theology and Liberation Series (Maryknoll, N.Y.: Orbis, 1989), especially part 3, chapter 9, "The Option for the Poor during a Thousand Years of Church History."

73. The term *expendable* comes from the analysis of anthropologist Gerhard Lenski in his classic work, *Power and Privilege: A Theory of Social Stratification* (New York: McGraw-Hill, 1966), 281-84.

74. Patterson, *The God of Jesus*, 68.

75. Ibid., 72.

76. Ibid., 74.

77. Ibid., 77.

78. Ibid., 77-78.

79. Ibid., 82.

80. Ibid., 82.

81. Herzog, *Parables as Subversive Speech*, 24. Herzog borrows this description of "conscientization" from Brazilian liberationist educator Paulo Freire.

82. Craig L. Blomberg, *Interpreting the Parables* (Downer's Grove, Ill.: Inter-Varsity Press, 1990), 286.

83. Elisabeth Schüssler Fiorenza, *In Memory of Her: A Feminist Theological Reconstruction of Christian Origins* (New York: Crossroad, 1994), 121.

84. Blomberg, *Interpreting the Parables*, 286.

85. Mack, *The Lost Gospel of Q: The Book of Q and Christian Origins* (New York: HarperCollins: 1993), 79. "I tell you, none of those invited shall taste my banquet." This last sentence is included by Ivan Havener in *Q: The Sayings of Jesus*. GNS 19. *With a Translation of Q* by Athanasius Polag (Collegeville, Minn.: Liturgical Press, 1990), logion 57, 141-42.

86. Buttrick, *Speaking Parables*, 158.

87. Ibid.

88. Schüssler Fiorenza, *In Memory of Her*, 119.

89. Ibid., 121.

90. Bernard Brandon Scott, *Hear Then the Parables: A Commentary on the Parables of Jesus* (Minneapolis: Fortress, 1989), 194.

91. Ibid, 197.

92. Ibid, 198.

93. Ibid, 198-99.

94. For his full discussion of this parable, see Herzog, *Parables as Subversive Speech*, 79-97.

95. Pheme Perkins, *Jesus as Teacher* (New York: Cambridge University Press, 1990), 89-90.

96. Ibid.

97. Huston Smith, *The Illustrated World's Religions: A Guide to Our Wisdom Traditions* (San Francisco: HarperSanFrancisco, 1995), 151.

98. Ibid., 68-69.

99. Ibid., 119-21.

9. Teaching and Preaching with a Subversive Voice

1. Walter Brueggemann, *The Prophetic Imagination* (Philadelphia: Fortress, 1978), 41.

2. Harold J. Recinos, *Who Comes in the Name of the Lord? Jesus at the Margins* (Nashville: Abingdon, 1997), 38. See Recinos's description of the "hard-hitting" Jesus, 50-51.

3. "Walter Brueggemann, Prophetic Energizing," in *The Company of Preachers: Wisdom on Preaching, Augustine to the Present*, ed. Richard Lischer (Grand Rapids, Mich.: Eerdmans, 2002), 159-60.

4. Christine M. Smith, *Preaching as Weeping, Confession, and Resistance: Radical Responses to Radical Evil* (Louisville: Westminster John Knox, 1992), 2.

5. Katie G. Cannon, *Black Womanist Ethics* (Atlanta: Scholars Press, 1988). See also her *Womanism and the Soul of the Black Community* (New York: Continuum, 1995). Cannon's work examines the life and work of Zora Neale Hurston as an expression of the moral wisdom of black women.

6. Teresa L. Fry Brown, *God Don't Like Ugly: African American Women Handing on Spiritual Values* (Nashville: Abingdon, 2000), 57. See also Teresa L. Fry Brown's *Weary Throats and New Songs: Black Women Proclaiming God's Word* (Nashville: Abingdon, 2003), a history of the legacy of black women preachers from the early 1800s to today.

7. Justo L. González and Catherine Gunsalus González, *Liberation Preaching: The Pulpit and the Oppressed* (Nashville: Abingdon, 1980), 23.

8. Thomas H. Troeger, "The Social Power of Myth as a Key to Preaching on Social Issues," in *Preaching as a Social Act: Theology and Practice*, ed. Arthur Van Seters (Nashville: Abingdon, 1988), 205.

9. Peter G. Horsfield, *Religious Television: The American Experience* (New York: Longman, 1984), 47-48. Quoted in ibid., 207.

10. See my *Preaching Proverbs: Wisdom for the Pulpit* (Louisville: Westminster John Knox, 1996), and my *Preaching Biblical Wisdom in a Self-Help Society* (Nashville: Abingdon, 2002). *Preaching Proverbs* looks at the proverbial genre's ability to both reinforce and subvert conventional wisdom in both biblical testaments and contemporary society. It suggests several models for preaching on proverbial texts with sample sermons. *Preaching Biblical Wisdom in a Self-Help Society* broadens its view to include the genres of reflection (Qohelet) and narrative (Job) in contemporary life as well as Scripture. It compares and contrasts the wisdom of contemporary self-help literature with biblical wisdom from Proverbs, Job, Ecclesiastes, and the Synoptic Gospels.

11. *The Westminster Collection of Christian Quotations,* comp. Martin H. Manser (Louisville: Westminster John Knox, 2001), 216.

12. Rabbi Rami M. Shapiro, *Wisdom of the Jewish Sages: A Modern Reading of Pirke Avot* (New York: Bell Tower, 1993), V:4, 101.

13. For more background, see David Yoo's article, "A Religious History of Japanese Americans in California," in *Religions in Asian America: Building Faith Communities,* ed. Pyong Gap Min and Jung Ha Kim (Walnut Creek, Calif.: AltaMira Press, 2002), 121-42.

14. Zechariah Taft, *Biographical Sketches of the Lives and Public Ministry of Various Holy Women,* 2 vols. (London: Published for the author, and sold in London by Mr. Kershaw, 1825–1828), 1:171. Very little is known about this Madame Perrott, other than the fact that she was one of the first Methodists on the Isle of Jersey. Paul Wesley Chilcote, *John Wesley and the Women Preachers of Early Methodism* (Metuchen, N.J. and London: The American Theological Library Association and The Scarecrow Press, Inc. 1991), 148.

15. February 25, 1774, Near London, Wesley, *Letters,* 6:74, here speaking specifically about the doctrine of Christian Perfection. Quoted in Chilcote, *John Wesley and the Women Preachers of Early Methodism,* 148.

16. John Singleton, "At the Roots of Methodism: Wesley's Wisdom Lives in Sayings," United Methodist News Service. Online: http://www.umc.org/umns/agency_meetings.asp?story={3FD503F6-5E34-46A8-9861-E8D79074F481}&mid=901.

17. Allan Satterlee, *Notable Quotables: A Compendium of Gems from Salvation Army Literature* (Atlanta: The Salvation Army), quoted in Norman H. Murdoch, "The Army Mother," *Christian History* 9, Issue 26, no. 2.

18. See the helpful anthology *The Bible and Liberation: Political and Social Hermeneutics,* ed. Norman K. Gottwald and Richard A. Horsley (Orbis, 1983). Among the contributors to this anthology are several well-known biblical scholars and theologians, offering various perspectives on a liberating hermeneutic that subverts traditional readings and meanings and posits constructive interpretations from the perspective of historically oppressed peoples. They include Renita Weems, Elsa Tamez, George Pixley, Juan Luis Segundo, Jose Miguez Bonino, Carols Mesters, Kwok Pui Lan, Elisabeth Schüssler Fiorenza, Walter Brueggemann, Norman Gottwald, Itumelong Josala, Richard Horsley, and Ched Myers.

19. A number of theologians and biblical scholars have recognized the liberative potential of wisdom texts for women, the exploited underclasses throughout history and the earth's ecosystems. Gustavo Gutierrez's work on Job views the book from the perspective of the exploited poor of postexilic Israel. Dianne Bergant has written *Israel's Wisdom Literature: A Liberation-Critical Reading.* Roman Catholic scholar Anthony R. Ceresko has written an *Introduction to Old Testament Wisdom: A Spirituality for Liberation.* Elisabeth Schüssler Fiorenza's *Jesus: Miriam's Child, Sophia's Prophet* surfaces gender liberative insights from

looking at Jesus' identity in the context of his ties to Woman Wisdom of the Hebrew Scriptures. The Earth Bible Series published by Pilgrim Press uses eco-justice principles inherent in Wisdom texts to critique conventional wisdom about human "dominion over" nature. Mexican theologian and biblical scholar Elsa Tamez in her book, *When the Horizons Close: Rereading Ecclesiastes*, explores Ecclesiastes' message for those whose hopes have been crushed by poverty.

20. My book, *Preaching Proverbs: Wisdom for the Pulpit*, includes several sample sermons on subversive wisdom sayings in both Old and New Testaments.

21. See my *Preaching Biblical Wisdom in a Self Help Society*, 145-68, for concrete suggestions on creating preaching series on themes and texts from Qohelet.

22. See my *Preaching Proverbs: Wisdom for the Pulpit*, chapter 9, for specific sermon models for preaching on Jesus' subversive sayings.

23. This sermon was delivered at the New Mexico Annual Conference session of The United Methodist Church held at Glorieta, New Mexico, May 30–June 2, 2002.